COMMONWEALTH IN FOCUS

130 YEARS OF PHOTOGRAPHIC HISTORY

Festival '82

Sponsored by the
Australia Council.

Arranged by The Royal Commonwealth Society, London

in association with

The International Cultural Corporation of Australia Limited
and the
Queensland Art Gallery.

Indemnified by the Commonwealth of Australia
through the Department of Home Affairs and Environment

Front Cover: W. L. H. Skeen & Company. Photographer at work during the Duke of Edinburgh's visit to Ceylon 1870.

CONTENTS

ISBN: 0 9594122 5 5

Opposite: W. L. H. Skeen & Company. Photographer at work during the Duke of Edinburgh's visit to Ceylon 1870.

Foreword

The Commonwealth is a significant force for peace and understanding in our time. In an uncertain world, the unique Commonwealth grows in importance.

However, it cannot survive, let alone achieve its full potential, without the support of the people in its member nations, support which can only stem from knowledge and appreciation of the Commonwealth.

The Secretary-General of the Commonwealth said in 1975 in India: 'The reality of a dynamic Commonwealth remains to be transmitted in its full strength to the mass of the people of our member states.'

These words remain true. This exhibition on the History of the Commonwealth in Photographs, will play a part in bringing the rich history of our international organisation to many of the people who comprise it.

It will be a worthy contribution to 'Festival 82,' appropriately linked to the Commonwealth Games in Brisbane.

This education process must continue, if only because the Commonwealth has changed more than most international organisations over the years. Indeed, it is now only the historical connection that would enable one to recognise that the present Commonwealth is a continuation of the organisation that was established half a century ago. The Statute of Westminster, enacted by the British Parliament in 1931, effectively established the Dominions as independent states with 'common allegiance' to the Crown and in 'free association' with each other as members of the British Commonwealth of Nations. The political reality, however, differed from the legal. To quote an often used metaphor, the Commonwealth, even thirty years after its formation, could be compared to a wheel, the hub of which was Britain and the spokes of which represented the other members.

However, the rapid decolonisation of the early 1960s led to a significant change in the character of the Commonwealth. The admission of India and Pakistan in 1947 had earlier marked the end of 'the Anglo-Saxon club,' and the readmission of India as a Republic in 1949 marked a fundamental change in the nature of the common allegiance to the Crown that the Statute of Westminster had proclaimed. From then on, all Commonwealth Members looked to the Crown as the Head of the Commonwealth, although many of them, including Australia, retain the Crown as Head of State.

The establishment of the Commonwealth Secretariat in 1965 relieved the British Government of its former administrative role. With the holding of the first Heads of Government Meeting (CHOGM) outside Britain in 1966, the modern character of the Commonwealth became established. The Commonwealth, through this fascinating transition, is now a thoroughly contemporary institution of over forty countries.

This exhibition looks at the peoples of the Commonwealth – their diversity and their links. It will illustrate the political, industrial and social developments of Commonwealth countries from their shared colonial backgrounds to the present time. They have similarities in law, education and other spheres; they have trade and economic links; they share a common language; and, most important of all, there are common underlying values which make it possible for citizens of Commonwealth countries to communicate more readily with each other, and for Commonwealth leaders to discuss issues in a family atmosphere rare in international gatherings.

Thus the Commonwealth is a combination of deep roots and new growth. It is this blend that gives the Commonwealth its unique features of informality, flexibility and dynamism and has resulted in a voluntary association based on the vital principles of partnership and equality across all barriers of distance, wealth and culture.

This evolution of the Commonwealth is a striking example of far-reaching adjustment achieved without sacrificing continuity. At a time when there is much negative and pessimistic thinking about global trends, it is timely to be reminded by the Commonwealth example that change need not mean disruption, and indeed rapid change is sometimes a condition for peace and stability.

The Commonwealth now contains almost all the elements which define and sometimes divide the world community. There are rich and poor countries, large and small, black and white, urban and rural, and many political systems. Commonwealth leaders have become aware of its potential as an association straddling these divides to promote the reconciliation of differences. They have worked towards the solution of world problems, using the Commonwealth's representative character in the search for global consensus.

As the Prime Minister of India, Mrs. Gandhi, said at the opening session of CHOGM 1981 in Melbourne, 'The Commonwealth is a useful international institution in the perplexed and trouble-torn world of today. It is a forum for mature deliberations. It helps to generate understanding and goodwill.'

The Commonwealth has played an important role in many of the great political, economic and social movements of the modern world. The process of decolonisation brought the Commonwealth itself into being, and the Commonwealth, collectively and through its individual members, has consistently acted as a catalyst in the progress to independence of colonial territories. Zimbabwe and Belize are recent examples.

The Commonwealth's basis in shared human values has caused it to speak out against racial discrimination in all its forms. The declaration of Commonwealth principles shows how closely the Commonwealth's general stand on human rights bears on the particular issue of apartheid.

The photographic exhibition will show the variety of the Commonwealth's interests and activities reflected in its flexible and informal approach. Commonwealth member countries co-operate in fields as varied as economic development, agriculture and food production, industry, law, education, health, youth and women's affairs, science and the professions. Many of these activities are organised by the Commonwealth Secretariat while others are run by specialised bodies set up by Commonwealth governments or interested non-government organisation. The Commonwealth does not seek to duplicate the efforts of major development organisations in the UN system but it can and does play a helpful catalytic role.

The Commonwealth's history and development, and activities and interests, are encapsulated in this comprehensive and diverse exhibition, and I am sure it will be a great success.

Malcolm Fraser

The Rt. Hon. Malcolm Fraser C.H., M.P.
Prime Minister of Australia.

Perspectives on the Commonwealth

First labelled approximately in its modern sense in Australia (by an Englishman), intimately associated with all its major ups and downs, recently re-energised and re-directed either by Australian initiatives or with substantial Australian assistance – it is highly appropriate that the Commonwealth of Nations (hereafter simply the Commonwealth) should be exhibited and understood in Australia.

In its contemporary sense the word 'Commonwealth' was first used, or at least anticipated, by Lord Rosebery in a speech in Adelaide in 1884 when he was on an extensive private visit to Australia, during which he spent a few days in Queensland, visited some of his cousins and interested himself considerably in the arguments for Australian Federation. Rosebery, in what one of his biographers rather solemnly calls his valedictory address to Australia, said to his audience:

'Does this fact of your being a nation – and I think you feel yourselves to be a nation – imply separation from the Empire? God forbid! There is no need for any nation, however great, leaving the Empire, because the Empire is a Commonwealth of Nations.'

It would be wrong to regard Rosebery, who later became Foreign Secretary and then Prime Minister in Britain, as being unusually prescient. He was in fact a Liberal Imperialist but he was also a cultured man reasonably acquainted with seventeenth century English history and the period of the Cromwellian Commonwealth. He had written a short monograph on Cromwell and it could be that the term 'Commonwealth' had pleasantly evocative connotations for him. It is true that a present day reader might smile at his attempt to square the circle of Empire with Commonwealth, but undoubtedly in associating Commonwealth with nationhood he was uncannily anticipating a central theme of Commonwealth history.

There is no one way to look at and characterise the Commonwealth because it is too big, complex and ever-changing to be encapsulated in any one vision or one exhibition. Therefore there are many possible ways of introducing the Commonwealth and many ways to supplement or contrast any particular introduction.

There are many excellent books on the Commonwealth (some of the most notable have been written by contemporary Australian scholars, such as Sir Keith Hancock and Professor J.D.B. Miller) to guide and instruct those who want to probe its richly diverse history; a selection is listed at the end of this essay.

This is, then, an essay drawing attention to certain trends and themes which seem to me important. It is not a treatise. It would not be helpful to try to say again, but in considerably briefer compass, all of what already has been so well said about Commonwealth history in the books of Hancock, Mansergh, McIntyre, Miller and others, books that are widely recognised as authoritative. Even so, I cannot avoid mentioning some of the familiar landmarks, stopping places or crossroads in the standard Commonwealth story.

The most authoritative single-volume exposition of the view that the Commonwealth, though the heir of the British Empire, is 'distinct and distinguishable' and 'in many respects inherently opposed' to it, was written by Nicholas Mansergh and published in 1969, with the title *The Commonwealth Experience.*

Mansergh's book is magnificent but is mostly devoted to discussion of political and diplomatic matters, to the comparative neglect of economic matters or what might compendiously be called the unofficial Commonwealth. Indeed, there is a richly varied book still waiting to be written which would trace the origins and main mutations of this diverse and still developing unofficial Commonwealth. Such a book would surely need to pay due account of migrations, money, markets, culture, literature, professions, exhibitions, festivals and fairs – and this is only to start a suggestive list. Arguably all non-governmental links are but gossamer which would be blown away if there was serious political conflict and confusion in the Commonwealth. This may be true but in fact recent trends have seen mounting optimism and activity and many new organisations formed in the unofficial Commonwealth. Ultimately the Commonwealth of governments and that of peoples must prosper or decline together for they are inescapably complementary.

Enough should have been said already at least, however, to suggest that any reasonably accurate explanatory account of the emergence and evolution of the Commonwealth into its complex and not widely understood present day condition cannot be a simple story. One should therefore be on guard against some currently fashionable oversimple versions, especially those emanating from Moscow.

According to the *Great Soviet Encyclopaedia* (which in its 1974 English translated edition puts the entry 'British Empire' next to 'the British Museum' – a conjunction which no doubt suits the humour of Soviet scholars) the term 'British Empire' first came into general official use in the mid-1870s. For contemporary Soviet scholars – as for some other commentators – the Commonwealth is regarded, oversimply and inaccurately in my view, as the mere reversionary of the British Empire, the evil end-product or prolongation of an evil past. Professor Lebedev, who wrote the Great Soviet Encyclopaedia article, concludes his 4000 word piece in the following demonological terms:

'The process of disintegration of the British Empire led to the appearance in its place of the so-called Commonwealth which comprises the majority of the liberated countries that made up the British Empire. The imperialist circles of Great Britain and of the "old dominions" seek to utilize the Commonwealth as a screen to conceal their neocolonialist policy, which is aimed at preserving their economic and political positions in the countries of the Commonwealth. The Commonwealth includes territories that are still under the rule of Great Britain – Australia and New Zealand – which attests to the retention by the Commonwealth of a number of features of the old British Empire. The African population of the British colony of Southern Rhodesia is waging a struggle for liberation from the rule of a racist regime supported by Great Britain. Great danger for the new independent states and colonial territories that belong to the Commonwealth is posed by the economic and political expansion of the USA, the chief bulwark of present-day colonialism. The peoples of the countries of the Commonwealth continue the struggle against all forms of colonialism and neocolonialism.'

Even the most assiduous readers of the Great Soviet Encyclopaedia in Australia and New Zealand would surely regard the judgement that their countries are still 'under the rule of Great Britain' rather wryly. Clearly this overall Soviet encyclopaedic view of the Commonwealth is hardly an up to date, still less a favourable account, especially in its doctrinaire determination to deny that there is any significant difference between Empire and Commonwealth. Even so, such a view is echoed by quite a lot of contemporary commentators who are apparently oblivious of or indifferent to the fact that the Commonwealth nowadays is mostly a post-imperial, post-independence voluntary association of member-states and peoples, future-oriented rather than fixated by their past, and made up of a growing group of governments and peoples who have shown themselves in some respects to be remarkably innovatory and forward looking.

The fact, however, that the Commonwealth is so fertile in generating and sustaining myths and giving rise to illusions does not mean that it is itself an illusion. On the contrary, it has the very actuality that the unusual and frankly improbable often acquire in human, and especially in international, affairs.

'If the Commonwealth did not already exist it would be impossible to invent' wrote a distinguished Australian academic long domiciled in Britain. In fact the author of this aphorism was enunciating a pregnant truth. The Commonwealth was not invented but evolved. That is why it is necessary to know something of its history to understand its present condition and potential. The dynamics of decolonization alone would have been sufficient to ensure, ever since 1945, that one could never step into quite the same Commonwealth twice. Changing (mostly meaning increasing) membership has been a major factor for general shifts in its characteristics, and has greatly affected the idioms and imagery with which the Commonwealth has been described over the last twenty-five years. But there have been and are many other reasons prompting a need for its continual appraisal.

The origins of the British Empire lie four centuries back, but for a view of those seeds in its modern development which eventually fructified into the contemporary Commonwealth we may start with the late 1830s as the young Victoria became Queen of England – and the art of photography began to be developed by pioneers in a number of countries.

The Queen was the apex of constitutional authority in every part of the Empire. She was the executive fount of each government, her assent was required for legislation to become fully legal and her refusal to give assent negated a bill. The very remoteness and aura of splendour surrounding the monarch probably invested the office and person with quasi-mystical, quasi-religious qualities in the minds of many subject peoples of the Empire throughout the world.

To some extent the Queen's representative in every part of the Empire basked in her aura, particularly her principal in India, the Viceroy – an office created in 1858 immediately after the Mutiny, which some Indians now describe as their first war for national liberation. He enjoyed the most coveted, magnificent and resplendent of all Imperial posts overseas. The Viceroy acted and lived like a monarch in India, except that his tenure of office was limited. His surroundings were stately and luxurious. Just as the Queen retired at certain times of the year to Osborne on the Isle of Wight or Balmoral in Scotland, so periodically, as Calcutta became intolerably hot and sticky at the height of summer, the Viceroy retired to his summer residence at Simla, the principal hill-station of the Raj.

In each colony of the Empire, however, though with markedly different degrees of grandeur and glamour, the Queen's representative was the Governor, who held his commission under the royal sign manual and signet and whose powers derived from letters patent issued under the great seal. Governors wrote their minutes and signed their names in red ink, and usually lived in what was by local standards an imposing residence, 'Government House', where the Union Jack flew every day from sunrise to sunset. He was addressed as 'His Excellency', and his appearance on a formal public occasion was the signal for the national anthem to be played.

The Governor exercised the royal prerogative of mercy and carried out 'royal' instructions. His functions were in practice carried out, however, under the direction not of the Queen but of the Secretary of State for the Colonies in London. He addressed his despatches to the Secretary of State, who sent him the instructions on which he was expected to act. He was required to consult his executive council in the colony on all matters related to the exercise of his powers and, although he might reject his council's advice, he had to report the circumstances of such a rejection.

The Secretary of State occupied a large and imposing room in the Colonial Office in London, though this was in fact a condemned building, being in an advanced state of dilapidation. It was from this small decaying edifice that metropolitan administration radiated outwards to a vast and complex Empire made up of a multiplicity of races and countries, differing in customs, law, religion and language. In 1870 the Colonial Office published a list which divided the colonies into various categories and formed the basis for all future official classifications of Britain's overseas possessions:

1 Crown Colonies in which the Crown had the entire control of legislation, while the administration was carried out by public officers under the control of the home government.
2 Colonies possessing Representative Institutions but not Responsible Government in which the Crown had no more than a veto on legislation but the government retained the control of public officers.
3 Colonies possessing Representative Institutions and Responsible Government in which the Crown had only a veto on legislation and the home government had no control over any public officers except the Governor.

One signal chapter in the complex history of the Empire transformed eventually into the Commonwealth tells of the growth of responsible self-government; it is a story which shows the piecemeal provision of new answers in a number of places to the problem which eighteenth century British government had so disastrously failed to solve; how much self-government could be conferred on or conceded to British settlers overseas. The first seminal sentences in this chapter were written, it is often and understandably claimed, by Lord Durham, who published his famous report on the political affairs of Canada in 1839, following his team's enquiry into the causes of rebellion in Upper and Lower Canada in 1836-37. From this came the union of Upper and Lower Canada in 1840 and, though not immediately, responsible government. In the 1860s negotiations between their representatives and those of the maritime provinces resulted in the British North America Act of 1867 and the creation of the Dominion of Canada, showing a way of political progress later to be followed in other parts of the Empire. A second and even more graduated way in which Canada was to become a pioneer in the emergence of the Commonwealth was by successively advocating and then demonstrating that the idea and practice of Dominion status was not just a variant of being a colony, but that it was compatible with the assertion of an independent autonomy and status in the matter of negotiating and concluding treaties with foreign powers, in the sending and receiving of envoys, in representation at international as well as imperial conferences. Indeed, gradually, cumulatively and eventually it was undeniable that Canada had become fully and formally an independent nation-state, and in many respects the precedent and pace-setter for others to follow. The full realisation of this lay in the future, but once the principle of responsible government in Canada had been accepted, its extension to New Zealand, Newfoundland, the Australian colonies, and Cape Colony followed rapidly, and developed further between 1900 and 1910.

Responsible government meant advances in self-government. This path also provided some amelioration of mounting military problems and expenses. The people of Britain disliked expenditure on armaments, and yet the Empire engaged in, and needed, considerable expenditure of this nature. The British Army had been split up into little garrisons and field forces all over the world, and only a small minority of its troops served at home. This wide dispersion, even when mitigated by the British Navy's mastery of the oceans, was bad for training and for operational efficiency and credibility, especially with the growth of rival military powers in Europe. Under the old colonial system Britain's regular troops had been frequently engaged in colonial wars with local opponents. The mother country had ultimate command and paid for the forces, and the colonists often plaintively complained that their local difficulties were aggravated by the decisions of the distant Colonial Office. With the spread of responsible self-government this imperial underpinning ceased. Self-defence, at least against local enemies, henceforth was regarded as a necessary task of a self-governing community. By about 1870 the regular garrisons were withdrawn from the free colonies, which henceforth had to take up the duty for themselves.

During the last quarter of the nineteenth century, however, as European inter-imperial rivalries quickened and became more intense, it became a commonplace for British publicists to employ analogies between the British and the Roman Empire, quite often in terms that were intended to show that the British had now surpassed in imperial achievement even this brilliant predecessor. It was Joseph Chamberlain, Secretary of State for the Colonies from 1895 to 1903, who coined the phrase 'Pax Britannica' as late as 1897, though the idea was present in the thoughts and speeches of many British leaders at least from the years of Palmerston's Foreign Secretaryships in the 1830s and 1840s. The maintenance of the Pax Britannica meant a willingness to wage small wars, and the record shows that this was frequently the case, particularly on the fringes of Empire.

The years when Joseph Chamberlain was Secretary of State for the Colonies, however, also mark the most significant generally sustained efforts to develop colonial economies before the First, indeed the Second, World War. The Imperial Penny Postage Act (1899), the Colonial Loans Act (1899), the Colonial Stock Act (1900), railway and harbour building in West Africa, Cyprus and Ceylon, the restructuring of the sugar industry in the British West Indies, postwar reconstruction in South Africa, the Great Pacific Cable (1903) – these are just some examples of imperial economic activity in these years.

Colonial Conferences had been held in the years of Queen Victoria's Jubilees, 1887 and 1897, and the Coronation of King Edward VII in 1902 also provided the occasion for such a gathering. It was then agreed to hold similar meetings at intervals of four years. The Conference of 1907 was therefore the first unconnected with some royal ceremonial, and it adopted general rules for holding and conducting 'Imperial Conferences', this title being adopted instead of that of Imperial Council suggested by some. These rules of 1907 also envisaged the possibility of subsidiary conferences on matters of special importance arising between meetings of the plenary conference. Within these terms were the Conference in 1909 on Naval and Military Defence, a Copyright Conference in 1910, and several minor gatherings.

The years between 1900 and 1914 saw the emergence of three Dominions – the Commonwealth of Australia formed by the federation of six colonies in 1901, New Zealand in 1907 and the Union of South Africa, embodying the two former Boer republics and the two British colonies, in 1910. Political pressures in the colonies of white settlement, as each gained Dominion status, and technological developments together sharpened the differentiation between Colonies and Dominions, a distinction which, while not always clear-cut (especially, of course, regarding India, always the great exception to any generalisation about the Empire) was nonetheless both significant and serviceable until 1947.

Rapid and more efficient communications certainly tended to produce more continuous and stronger control between the Colonial Office and the Crown Colonies and Protectorates. It also contributed to greater uniformity of practice and consistency of dealing.

In 1914 Sir Charles Lucas, the former – indeed the first – Head of the Dominions Department in the Colonial Office created in 1907, wrote with disarming frankness that successive grants of responsible self-government to the by now self-governing Dominions had been to a considerable extent necessitated by the difficulties of imperial control over vast distances, especially before steam power and telegraphy had become fully effective.

Indeed, between the time of the accession of Queen Victoria in 1837 and the outbreak of the First World War in 1914 the Colonial Office was transformed from being in the main a Crown Colony Office to become at once an administrative and diplomatic or semi-diplomatic office. This transformation was brought about principally because of the parallel but distinct extension of self-government to the former colonies of white settlement, and by the extension of more efficient communications.

When Lord Durham went on his mission to Canada in 1838, there was but one small railway in Canada, and none in any other of the Queen's 'dominions beyond the seas' – to employ a once familiar phrase. The same year saw the beginning of regular steam communication between Great Britain and America. It was only in 1837 that Cooke and Wheatstone took out their patent for an electric telegraph. The first submarine cable between Great Britain and North America was not laid until 1858, and some years passed before the communication was reliably and regularly established. No steamer ran from England to Australia till 1852. There was no direct telegraph line to Australia till 1872, and none to South Africa before 1879, the news of the disastrous defeat at Isandhlwana in January of that year being brought by ship to the nearest telegraph station, which was in the Cape Verde Islands.

If a telegraph helped enormously for the far flung parts of Empire to keep in touch with each other, it is also true to regard railways as in some cases acting as major propellants towards political unity. The railway was a crucial factor in forging links right across the continental width of Canada, The British North America Act of 1867, independent Canada's founding charter, is here especially revealing as it incorporated a declaration that the construction of a railway, called the Intercolonial Railway, to connect the Maritime Provinces with Quebec, was 'essential to the consolidation of the Union of British North America.' A little later the terms on which British Columbia agreed to join the Dominion were that the Canadian Government should undertake to secure the making of a railway 'to connect the seaboard of British Columbia with the railway system of Canada.'

The making of the Commonwealth of Australia undoubtedly was made more plausible and possible by the coming of the railway, just as it was hampered earlier by the want of railways to connect Western Australia with the eastern States, and the Northern Territory with the rest of the island-continent. Railways were equally important in influencing the pattern of political and economic development in South

Africa. They were a potent instrument of the British Raj throughout the South Asian subcontinent, and it was the extension of railways into the interior of Nigeria which facilitated the administrative union of Northern and Southern Nigeria by the British in 1914; while on the eastern side of Africa the Uganda Railway was seen as an important means of holding together the great East Africa Protectorate from the sea coast to the Victoria Nyanza. Rail tracks truly knitted many a Dominion or Colony together to empower politicians as well as railwaymen.

An Imperial Conference was held in 1911, but the implementation of some of its recommendations, and the holding of the meeting planned for 1915, were prevented by the outbreak of war in 1914. Britain's cause was supported throughout the Empire. Comradeship in arms could on occasion encourage effusions of solidarity and public displays of Empire-mindedness not usually forthcoming in times of nominal peace; Empire Day was first celebrated officially in England on 24 May 1916. Nevertheless there were influential voices questioning the future nature of the Empire relationship. The pedigree of the present day Commonwealth as a free association of Sovereign states has been described as the outcome of the development of self-government in the older British Dominions and, more immediately, of their demands during the First World War for greater say and influence in matters of foreign policy and defence directly affecting their interests. Some recognition was given to this quickening concern in the Dominions regarding matters of stature and substance in the resolution of the Imperial War Conference of 1917 which said that 'the constitutional relations of the component parts of the Empire . . . should be based upon a full recognition of the Dominions as autonomous nations of an Imperial Commonwealth.' Thus each of the Dominions (except Newfoundland) and India signed the Versailles Peace Treaty individually and entered the League of Nations as members in their own rights.

For the Commonwealth as a whole the period between the two World Wars is bisected by the passing of the Statute of Westminster in 1931. Before that date discussion and controversy principally revolved round constitutional and diplomatic issues concerning the precise status, domestically and internationally, of the Dominions. In the 1930s first economic and then security questions obtruded most prominently, during a decade that grew increasingly gloomy.

The Imperial Conference of 1917 had passed a resolution outlining an agenda for a postwar conference which would then determine new constitutional arrangements for the Empire-Commonwealth. This constitutional conference did not take place. The British assumed that the complete autonomy of the Dominions was established at the Versailles Peace Conference by their formal assumption of control over their foreign affairs in its treaty-making and by their separate signatures on the final documents. The proposal to set up some mechanism or at least agreed procedure for continuous joint consultation and action, also suggested in 1917, was not acted on now that the urgencies of world war were over. The practice of calling Imperial Conferences did not itself really amount to such a mechanism, for they were not continuous either in their composition or agenda, and were not even regular periodical meetings. Indeed, given the difficulties, including the time it would take for all participants to assemble, it is doubtful whether such a proposal in practical terms could have been implemented at this time.

Intra-imperial and inter-Dominion co-operation on non-political questions did continue and in some respects quickened in the years of postwar reconstruction, mostly through the agency of specially convened conferences. Four were held in 1920-21 alone: the Imperial Statistical, Entomological, Forestry and Customs Conferences, the general effects of which were to co-ordinate administration and to provide means for the collection and exchange of accurate information whilst encouraging professional contacts in these fields. Such conferences continued in the inter-war years.

In an endeavour to clarify the precise status of the Dominions, the Imperial Conference of 1926 set up a Committee under Lord Balfour which produced the famous but somewhat ambiguous definition of 'Autonomous communities . . . freely associated as members of the British Commonwealth of Nations,' which with some modifications was to be given legal definition in the Statute of Westminster of 1931.

The Empire/Commonwealth of the era between the two World Wars lasted until 1947 in terms of membership, but the war itself saw even more emphatically than the First World War unprecedented advances in the stature of the Dominions, Canada in particular gaining in importance as part of the North American war effort, but all undergoing great economic and political changes. The most striking effect however was in Asia. The winding down of Britain's military role 'East of Suez' (Kipling's phrase from 'Mandalay' which was much re-used and misused in Britain in the 1960s) was foreshadowed and substantially implicit in the British evacuation from India.

It has been plausibly said that half the structure of the Empire was mere scaffolding for the possession of India. After 1947 many a British colony had lost its *raison d'etre,* having previously been placed within that dualistic Imperial system that oscillated between Britain and India. The British attitude to the world, shaped so long by assumptions of naval superiority in the world's oceans (and certainly in the Indian and Atlantic Oceans) and the availability of a great manpower reservoir of trained forces in India for policing duties around the Empire, slowly and painfully shifted. The Commonwealth was fast becoming not a facet or even a hyphenated portion of the British Empire but a replacement for it.

Thus there was a positive side to the loss of the brightest jewel in the imperial diadem. India, though determined to be a republic was also willing to do so whilst being within the Commonwealth, if the other members agreed. Thus in the years 1947-1949 in what is by now in broad outline a well-known story, India became a republic and Jawaharlal Nehru became for many the personification of the post-1947 Commonwealth. The British monarch became by general governmental assent (including that of a somewhat dubious King George VI) Head of the Commonwealth. It now became not just the white Dominions and Britain, but with India, Pakistan and Ceylon as members, it had a substantial South Asian component, and, with the departure of Eire in 1949, a membership of eight. Above all, perhaps, India's independence had shown that the erstwhile British Commonwealth was no longer a rather exclusive white man's club but was potentially open to other races. India had become independent without adopting the status of a Dominion, and the term indeed became decreasingly used by existing Commonwealth members.

The constitutional changes of 1947-9 were widely regarded as important displays of the Commonwealth's appeal, practicality, and constructive qualities. There were some considerable outpourings of praise for this now greater Commonwealth which had, by Britain's enlightened disimperialism, thrown diplomatic bridges across the continents, and especially into Asia, while helping to show, in Jawaharlal Nehru's happy phrases, that membership could mean 'independence plus' and could bring 'a touch of healing' to an embattled world.

Then from 1948 to early 1957 no new members joined. There

were no more formal acts of British decolonization until Ghana and Malaya achieved independence in 1957. Both these international baptisms were celebrated – was it entirelv accidentally? – at a time when each of the new States had very substantial sterling balances to its credit. The intervening years 1948-57 had not been notable for new thoughts or even new activities in intra-Commonwealth matters. Generally, the collectivity had been reactive rather than active. This epoch was well summed up in Professor J.D.B. Miller's neat phrase coined in 1958 – that the Commonwealth is a 'concert of convenience.'

Commonwealth relationships were put under considerable strain by the Suez crisis of 1956. Widespread criticism of Eden's actions came from African and Asian countries and a more sympathetic attitude from Australia and New Zealand, but Canada played the major role in finding diplomatic solutions to the military situation and in establishing the United Nations Emergency Force.

In the 1960s there was considerable expansion of the membership, despite the departure of South Africa in 1961, an episode emphasising the incompatibility of apartheid with the Commonwealth idea. Numbers reached 21 at the 1965 Conference, at which the Commonwealth Secretariat and the Commonwealth Foundation were set up. At this time, as she sought full membership of the E.E.C. (though not achieving it until 1973) Britain abdicated her historic headship of the Commonwealth and what went with it – her hitherto implicitly permanent ex officio chairmanship of the club and all its collective activities.

However, those who feared in 1965 that the Commonwealth was becoming humdrum, bureaucratic, and because much less Britaincentred therefore more indefinite, misread or misunderstood the significance and potential of a Commonwealth endowed with a Secretariat such as was to be shaped and activated first by Arnold Smith, ex-diplomat from Canada, and then by Shridath Ramphal who had been Foreign Minister of Guyana. Furthermore, the very lively, varied and vitalising Commonwealth Arts Festival of 1965 surely gave the lie to those who thought of the Commonwealth as being in a condition of grey self-crippling decline. In 1982 the Commonwealth is very much alive.

As well as personifying the Commonwealth and heading and directing the Commonwealth Secretariat the Secretary-General has to interpret and articulate the Commonwealth consensus on major issues, wherever possible in practical terms. He cannot afford to be actively partisan as between various members, but it is within his discretion to nudge members ahead. Recently, in April 1982 for example, the Secretary-General sent out a message to all members of the Commonwealth reminding them of certain relevant general principles relating to the Falkland Islands. Soon after the Argentinian invasion he was visiting the Caribbean and whilst there made his own views emphatically clear, whilst also not disguising that they were his personal views.

More generally it is the task of the Commonwealth Secretariat to help shape and then to implement recommendations for action emanating from Commonwealth Heads of Government Meetings (CHOGMs) and other Commonwealth Ministerial Meetings. Serving and servicing the Commonwealth is thus the intrinsic purpose of the Secretariat.

The Commonwealth Foundation was set up in 1966 to foster links in the non-governmental dimensions of the Commonwealth, and in particular to assist professional associations to function efficiently and co-operatively. The word professional is interpreted very widely and at present about twenty associations receive help. Some get seed money in the hope that they will become self-sustaining in due course. What is striking is that many of these organisations are entirely new (like the Commonwealth Journalists Association, founded in 1978) or substantially remodelled (like the Commonwealth Trade Union Conference) thus confuting the always wrongheaded notion that the Commonwealth is a mere reversionary of Empire, when it has time and time again shown itself to be innovatory, practical and creative.

Consultation and co-operation are two venerably serviceable terms in the lexicon of Commonwealth relationships, in what might be described as 'Commonwealth-ese.' There has been considerable growth of both consultation and co-operation within the Commonwealth since 1965, and not by any means only in its intergovernmental dimensions. Informed evidence for this – and more Commonwealthese – can be seen in the rather long but certainly full reports prepared by the Secretary-General just before each Commonwealth Heads of Government Meeting and in the full communiques issued publicly at the end of each CHOGM.

The established routines of the Commonwealth's official business are manysided, but at the highest level comes the Commonwealth Heads of Government Meetings (CHOGMs), held every two years, with the next one due to be held in New Delhi in 1983. Ministers of Finance meet every year, and ministers of education, health and law every three years; other ministers meet as often as they deem necessary. There are also meetings of officials and specialists in many fields. The very fact that many but not all these activities are regular attests to the practiced adaptable ever-evolving quality of contemporary Commonwealth co-operation and consultation – on North-South issues, for example.

The Commonwealth today consists of forty six member countries; a few of them are among the world's most populous, but half of the members have populations of less than a million people each, and a quarter have less than 200,000. Clearly the opportunities and capacities of particular members vary considerably. Clearly also the inputs of each vary with situations and personalities. In recent years the Australian input into the Commonwealth has been considerable and imaginative. It has consisted, for example, in doing much by skilful diplomacy to facilitate the transition from Rhodesia to Zimbabwe, to monitor Uganda's elections, to launch and help sustain the Commonwealth Heads of Government Regional Meetings (CHOGRMs) for the Asian and Pacific members (the next, third in sequence, will be held in Suva, Fiji, later this year) in efforts to assist the mini-states, especially those of the S)uth Pacific, and, above all, in conducting a dramatically well organised and constructive CHOGM in Melbourne in October 1981, held in the famous Exhibition Hall there, scene of so many memorable moments in Australia's history.

The essence of the British Empire was its exclusiveness, the predominance of a single metropolitan centre and the compulsory membership of its subordinate parts; the essence of the contemporary Commonwealth of Nations is that it is a voluntary association of formally equal members acknowledging no common superior or single centre – despite the continuance of some considerable – though functional – London-centricity.

The British Empire sought to be a self-sustaining, self-insulated, even at times a self-sufficient system; the Commonwealth today – despite its many and multiplying organisations and arrangements – inescapably is commingled with the wider world. The Commonwealth, at its best, is a unique post-imperial working comity of governments and peoples.

The Commonwealth, in this respect like the Empire that preceded it, is the product of evolution and development, not of a single deliberate design. The process of change is continuous and has not ended. As the old relationships of central authority and outer dependence between the United Kingdom and the Dominions were gradually superseded, new forms of co-operation have taken and are continuing to take its place. The Crown from being the prime expression of central domination has become the cardinal ingenious symbol of voluntary association and common enterprise.

In speaking eloquently and frequently about the contemporary Commonwealth, its present Secretary-General has often expressed the need to view it in global terms, that humanity has but 'One World to share.' Here he is recoining and reemphasizing an idea with an ancient pedigree and yet of great contemporary pertinence; that it is important to see the Commonwealth of Nations as part of the Commonwealth of mankind.

PETER LYON

Select Reading List

BELL, James B. *Literary glimpses of the Commonwealth* (Toronto, 1977).

CHADWICK, John *The unofficial Commonwealth: the story of the Commonwealth Foundation 1965-1980* (London, 1982).

GARNER, Lord *The Commonwealth Office 1925-1968* (London, 1978).

HALL, H.D. *Commonwealth: A History of the British Commonwealth of Nations* (London, 1971).

HAMILTON, W.B. et al. (eds), *A Decade of the Commonwealth, 1955-1964* (Durham, NC, 1965).

HANCOCK, Sir Keith *Survey of British Commonwealth Affairs: Problems of Nationality 1918-1936: Problems of Economic Policy 1918-1939.* 3v (London, 1937-1942).

INGRAM, Derek *The Imperfect Commonwealth* (London, 1977).

McINTYRE, W. David *The Commonwealth of Nations: origins and impact 1869-1971* (Oxford, 1977).

MANSERGH, Nicholas *The Commonwealth Experience* (London, 1969).

MANSERGH, Nicholas *Survey of British Commonwealth Affairs: Problems of External Policy 1931-1939: Problems of wartime co-operation and post-war change 1939-1952. 2v* (London, 1952-1958)).

MILLER, J.D.B. *The Commonwealth in the World,* 3rd edn (London, 1965).

MILLER, J.D.B. *Survey of Commonwealth Affairs: Problems of Expansion and Attrition, 1953-1969* (London, 1974).

MORRIS, James *The Pax Britannica Trilogy: Heaven's Command: Pax Britannica: Farewell the Trumpets* (London, 1968-1978).

RAMPHAL, Shridath, *One World to Share: Selected Speeches of the Commonwealth Secretary-General* (London, 1979).

REESE, Trevor R. *The History of the Royal Commonwealth Society 1868-1968* (London, 1968).

SMITH, Arnold C. *Stitches in Time* (London, 1981).

TETT, Norman and CHADWICK, John *Professional Organizations in the Commonwealth.* 2nd ed. (London, 1976)

The role of the Photographer

This exhibition, sponsored by the International Cultural Corporation of Australia and first shown during the 1982 Commonwealth Games in Brisbane, aims to illustrate the history of the Commonwealth from the early years of photography to the present day. A collection of such prints can only hope to provide a selective and subjective record of 130 years of history within the great diversity of countries and topics concerned, and the exhibition is arranged in ten thematic sections which trace in a narrative and broadly chronological sequence the evolution of the present day Commonwealth from the nineteenth century British Empire. Particularly in the early years, the presence of a photographer at a specific time and place, and the survival of his photographs, has governed the emphasis given. The availability of material is in turn determined by the changing nature of photographic techniques and the role of the photographer. Thus certain events which would merit inclusion in terms of their historical importance are excluded from the exhibition for lack of a visual record: The cutting of the first sod of the Ceylon Railway in 1858 was considered by contemporaries worth recording by the camera, but Mr. Parting's efforts were a complete failure, succeeding only in capturing the back view of a lady 'with a most portentous breadth of crinoline culminating in a bonnet of delightful minuteness.' And even where technical limitations did not intervene, certain events were not photographed either because the remoteness of their location precluded the presence of a photographer, or simply because they were not at the time considered of any great significance. The mass of surviving material would however, be sufficient to fill several exhibitions, and it is hoped that the photographs included give a reasonable picture in broad outline of the major events of Commonwealth history while also illustrating the impressive work of both major and minor nineteenth century photographers. With the advent of the twentieth century and the development of miniature cameras, fast films and other equipment, the role of the photographer changes,as does the sort of picture taken. The ease of modern photography has meant that almost any event can be captured on film without the formalities of rigid posing and elaborate setting up which characterize much nineteenth century work. What this has meant in terms of photographic standards is arguable, but the change is reflected in the later sections of the exhibition, where the vastly increased output of photographs available has made it possible to adopt a slightly different approach, although here again significant examples have been given rather than attempting an impossible comprehensiveness.

Grateful acknowledgement is made of the permission of the Earl of Snowdon and the Inchcape Group to display at the time of this exhibition, a selection of his coloured photographs of countries of the Commonwealth. We are also indebted to Commonwealth Governments, the Commonwealth Institute, and other co-operating bodies, for the coloured slides used to illustrate aspects of the present-day life of members of the Commonwealth.

The four photographers whose work is featured in this introductory section, and whose photographs also appear in the course of the exhibition, have been selected to illustrate something both of diversity of geographical location and the photographers' differing purpose, market, and approach to their subjects. Frederick Dally *(The Colonial Hotel on the Cariboo Road at Soda Creek, British Columbia. 1867-70.)* arrived in British Columbia in 1862 and opened a studio on Vancouver Island in 1866. For the early professional photographer operating in a small settlement the market for work was limited and the rapidly expanding population on the mainland provided a welcome additional outlet both in terms of new customers and new subjects for photography. Between 1867 and 1870 Dally travelled the length of the Fraser River Waggon Road to the Cariboo mines photographing mining scenes and settlements; in 1868 he opened a studio in the heart of the mining area at Barkerville, but this was destroyed in the fire of the same year. The importance of Dally's work lies in its documentary record of frontier life in a young community and his photographs form part of a body of work produced by photographers who travelled to the goldfields in Canada, Australia and South Africa to take advantage of their abundant, if in some cases short-lived, prosperity. When Samuel Bourne *(Mundapum with facade of stone horses at Trichinopoly. c1868)* left his job as an employee in a Nottingham bank to earn his living as a photographer in India in 1863, he was going to a land which could boast not only an indigenous civilisation stretching back thousands of years, but also a settled British presence with a sophisticated taste in photography which formed an enthusiastic market for his work. During his period in India (1863-70) Bourne not only made three long photographic journeys in Kashmir and the Himalayas, but also travelled throughout India photographing the architecture (Indian and European), landscape and peoples of the sub-continent. In 1866, he was able with his partner Charles Shepherd, to issue a catalogue listing 1500 views for sale. The firm of G.R. Lambert & Co. *(The Boat Quay, Singapore River, looking towards Fort Canning. c1890)* was founded in 1875 by the Dresdener of that name, of whom little is known apart from the fact that he ran the firm only until 1885. The work of a firm like Lambert's encompassed the general concerns of the majority of commercial photographers based in the rapidly expanding commercial centres of the later nineteenth century: architecture, townscapes, racial types and characteristic occupations and the industrial scenes of a great port. Employees of the firm also ventured further afield and recorded life and scenery throughout the Malayan Peninsula. The final figure, A. Hugh Fisher, represents a departure from commercial work and shows an interesting application of photography as an educational tool in the service of the Colonial Office Visual Instruction Committee. Further photographs by Fisher and a note on his work for this body can be found at G3 and 4. The photographs on display here, taken between 1907 and 1910, show: *The caravanserai at Jamrud; Professor Waite with a moa skeleton in the Christchurch Museum, New Zealand; Daly's Farm, Alberta; View from Battery Path, Hong Kong; S.S. 'Wodonga' at Bowen Jetty, Queensland; E.S. Higgins and Havildars of the Somaliland Coast Police.*

Face to face

Of the many subjects tackled by the photographers of the nineteenth century in all parts of the world, some of the finest work falls into the category of what may be broadly termed 'ethnographical'. For the commercial operator, portraits illustrating the exotic and picturesque customs and costumes of little known peoples found a ready European market, and prominently placed in the advertisements of a great many photographers are references to series of prints forming a comprehensive collection of 'native types' available to the tourist or other purchaser. As new territories came under European control and administration, and were opened up for settlement, it became standard practice for the enterprising photographer to document both the landscape and peoples of these acquisitions: thus the Lisk-Carew Brothers made tours from their Freetown base to photograph the trades, costumes and institutions of the Sierra Leone hinterland, while on the other side of the world G.R. Lambert and Co sent out employees from Singapore to document both the Malayan peninsula and the newly opened plantation lands of Borneo.

For the photographer specialising in this type of portraiture, the normal difficulties attendant on nineteenth century photography – the bulky equipment, delicacy of chemical manipulation and the inconvenient length of exposure necessary – were exacerbated by the natural suspicions of peoples unused to the camera and its threatening cannon-like lens. In China John Thomson was set upon and stoned while attempting to take photographs, and almost all the operators who travelled to localities little visited by Europeans remarked on the unwillingness of their subjects to pose and the consequent unnaturalness of the resulting picture. Samuel Bourne, after finally cajoling a group of Kashmiri nautch girls into sitting for him, found that they 'squatted themselves down on the carpet which had been provided for them and absolutely refused to move an inch for any purpose of posing'. Also in India, Captain Cookesley discovered when visiting the Lushai in 1871-72, that his subjects were fascinated by the camera and would remain perfectly still while the plate was being prepared, but would stroll out of the picture while the exposure was being made. Joseph Thomson encountered similar difficulties during his explorations in East Africa, although by 1893 the inhabitants of the Lagos mainland, according to the Governor Gilbert Carter, quickly appreciated the photographer's purpose: 'I was much struck at the way they composed themselves to submit to this ordeal, and seemed to understand precisely what was required of them: I noticed the younger ones especially arranging their clothes, and even the old lady gave an additional touch to a kind of turban which she wore upon her head'.

While for the commercial photographer the recording of racial types was biased towards the picturesque and marketable, and this sometimes resulted in culturally inexact groupings of artefacts and peoples for the sake of effect, the amateur work of many colonial officials produced a more precise and comprehensive rendering of the tribes and races among whom they worked and in many cases studied over a number of years. Maurice Vidal Portman for instance, during the course of his career in the Andaman Islands, produced an extensive series of photographs of racial types (placed against a chequered background for comparison with other races, and complete with anthropometrical measurements) and the methods of manufacture of various artefacts and implements. This use of photography by administrators became more common after 1880 when dry plate photography came into general use and substantially reduced both the difficulties of photography and the amount of equipment needed: thus Charles Hose during his period in Sarawak was able to make a detailed photographic survey of the types, customs, architecture, clothes and pastimes of the Dyak peoples he encountered.

European colonial expansion inevitably focussed attention on peoples hitherto unencountered or little-studied, and it is not coincidental that the spread of European populations was contemporaneous with the growth of interest in the scientific study of ethnology which resulted in the formation in 1843 of the Ethnological Society of London. With the rise of this new science and the increasing importance to it of accurate representations of the races of the world, the want of illustrated material was keenly felt, and many photographers attempted to supply the lack, whether by genre studies and tableaux, individual portraits or rigorously scientific documentations. Although the Colonial Office had sent out a circular in 1869 asking for portraits of the indigenous inhabitants of the colonies and collections were bought or commissioned from several photographers, there was little central organisation and the idea does not appear to have been followed up in any systematic manner. While commercial and amateur photographers produced a large amount of such material, it was only in India that an attempt was made to make a detailed ethnographical record of the country, which by an alliance between official sponsorship and amateur enthusiasm resulted in the publication of *The people of India* (1868-75), a massive undertaking whose eight volumes contain 479 pasted-in photographs.

While the motives, both scientific and artistic, behind this widespread recording varied both in approach and thoroughness, much of the work thus produced was informed by a strong sense of the need to capture the image of cultures rapidly changing and sometimes disintegrating before the impact of an alien civilisation and technology. Such considerations were implicit in Charles Woolley's portraits of the last Tasmanian Aborigines, simply posed as they are to most fully illustrate for posterity the facial characteristics of his subjects. This purpose is underlined by the photographic work of the Royal Engineers during the North American Boundary Commission of 1858-62: Charles Wilson, Secretary to the Commission and possibly involved with some of the photography which resulted in the fine series of Indian portraits, was well aware of the destructive aspects of European settlement, and would have appreciated the value of a photographic record when he wrote that 'Whiskey and civilization are doing their work quickly and surely amongst them; in twenty years time they will be a matter of history'.

Wigwam, an Ojibway half-breed, Lake Superior. 1858. (B2/4)

B1 H. TOOSE. **Aborigines beside the photographer's cart, Australia. 1860s-70s.**

B2 THE AMERICAS

1 ROYAL ENGINEERS PHOTOGRAPHER. **Schweilp or Colvile woman and child. 1860-61.** 'When a child is born, it is first laid on a heap of very soft moss or weed, which grows on the stones in the shallows of the Columbia River . . . In putting an infant up in the cradle, the head rests on the backboard and each leg is wrapped up separately, with moss, rags, etc . . . The flatness of the back of a full-grown Indian's head, and the peculiar shape of his legs, are probably in some measure due to the native mode of cradling.'
C.W. Wilson, *Report on the Indian tribes inhabiting the country in the vicinity of the 49th Parallel of north latitude (Transactions of the Ethnological Society of London,* n.s. vol. 4, 1865, p. 295).

2 ROYAL ENGINEERS PHOTOGRAPHER. **Cristine McDonald, daughter of Hudson's Bay Company chief trader at Colvile. 1860-61.** Cristine McDonald was the daughter of Angus McDonald, for many years in charge of the Hudson's Bay Company depot at Fort Colvile, and of a Nez Percé Indian mother. She was herself married to another Scottish H.B.C. employee, James Mackenzie.

3 HUMPHREY LLOYD HIME. **Letitia Bird, a Cree half-breed. 1858.** This and the following portrait, photographed at Red River between September and October 1858, are two of a selection of thirty prints taken during the Assiniboine and Saskatchewan Exploring Expedition which were offered for public sale in a portfolio entitled *Photographs taken at Lord Selkirk's settlement on the Red River of the North to illustrate a narrative of the Canadian exploring expeditions in Rupert's Land* (J. Hogarth, London, 1860). Hime's Indian portraits were the most accomplished of all the photographs he produced in the course of the expedition.

□ 4 HUMPHREY LLOYD HIME. **Wigwam, an Ojibway half-breed, Lake Superior. 1858.**

5 NORTON BROTHERS. **East Indian immigrants, British Guiana. c1880.** East Indian immigration as indentured labour to the West Indies began in 1838, and after a period of suspension two years later, was reintroduced in 1844. The majority of these workers came to British Guiana and Trinidad. Between 1838 and 1917, when immigration ceased, approximately 239,000 East Indians came to British Guiana, the majority remaining after their period of indenture was ended.

□ 6 PHOTOGRAPHER UNKNOWN. **Yucatecans and Caribs, British Honduras. c1872.** Two of a series of portraits sent to the Colonial Office in 1872, the European clothing of these groups was evidently intended to indicate the civilising and progressive effects of British rule.

7 PHOTOGRAPHER UNKNOWN. **Carib family, St. Vincent. c1900.** A portrait group purporting to show the last family of true Carib blood in St. Vincent.

B3 AFRICA

8 LISK-CAREW BROTHERS. **Bundu Devils, Mende country, Sierra Leone. c1910.** The Bundu Devils, a powerful female secret society, investigated cases of misbehaviour as well as appearing at various ceremonial occasions. These women remained completely concealed by their costumes while in public and never spoke, communication being afforded by gesticulations with the bundles of twigs held in each hand. The *digbas,* or acolytes, stand beside the devils, holding the mats behind the privacy of which the costumes might be removed.

9 LISK-CAREW BROTHERS. **Weaver of country cloth, Mende country, Sierra Leone. c1910.** An example of the series of portraits of types and crafts produced by Alphonso and Arthur Lisk-Carew in the early years of the century.

□ 10 GRAY BROTHERS. **African chiefs at Kimberley. 1874.** 'As I know that it is commonly believed in the Cape Colony, and perhaps also in England, that the Native inhabitants of the territories referred to are mere savages, and not worthy of much consideration, I transmit herewith some Photographic representations which I have caused to be taken of the Camps, the Chiefs and Councillors, the Chiefs separately, and the Messenger of the Montsioa . . . And I may add that a large and very valuable trade is carried on by British subjects in the Native country.' (Extract from a despatch, enclosing photographs, from Lieutenant Governor Southey to the Governor of the Cape Sir Henry Barkly, dated Kimberley, May 15 1874.)

11 PHOTOGRAPHER UNKNOWN. **Oil Rivers chief and retinue, probably Frederick Sunday Jaja of Opobo. c1912.** Frederick Sunday Jaja (1873-1915) was the son of the important trader King Jaja of Opobo. Educated in England, he was a member of the deputation sent by his father to the Foreign Office in 1887 complaining of the British infringement of King Jaja's trading rights. After the ousting of King Jaja from Opobo by Harry Johnston in 1887, he joined his father in exile in the West Indies in 1888. He acceded to the Opobo kingship in 1893.

12 WILLIAM D. YOUNG. **Masai moran, East Africa. c1900.** A group of young warriors photographed by Young during the construction of the Uganda Railway.

B4 AFRICA & THE MEDITERRANEAN

13 A.G.S. HAWES. **The Yao chief Kapeni, Nyasaland. 1886.** During his period as consul in Nyasaland Hawes took a series of portraits of Yao, Makololo and Angoni chiefs met with on his tour with J.T. Last from Blantyre to Angoniland in 1886.

14 PHOTOGRAPHER UNKNOWN. **King Overami of Benin and wives in exile in Calabar. c1912.** The once considerable importance of the kingdom of Benin had suffered greatly as a result of the suppression of the slave trade and in 1892 King Overami was persuaded to sign a treaty placing his country under British protection and opening it up to European trade. This treaty was later repudiated and, after the murder of the acting consul general in 1897 and the subsequent British military expedition against, and occupation of Benin, Overami was exiled to Calabar where he remained until his death in 1914.

15 W.S. TURTON. **The Balé of Ogbomosho and his wives. 1893.** A photograph taken in February 1893 during the Lagos Interior Expedition. The Governor of Lagos, Sir Gilbert Carter, wrote of the Balé as 'a very intelligent kindly man, who evidently appreciated my visit to his town and sympathised with the object I had in view.' During the visit the Balé presented Carter with a gift of 20 bags of cowries, a horse, a cow, 18 sheep, 100 loads of yams, four pots of palm oil and over 2000 eggs. Carter reciprocated with the present of a drum.

Above: **Yucatecans and Caribs, British Honduras. c1872.** (B2/6)
Below left: **African chiefs at Kimberley. 1874.** (B3/10)
Below right: **Swahili girl at Zanzibar. c1900.** (B4/17)

□ 16 JOHN THOMSON. **A Cyprian maid. 1878.** A portrait reproduced in woodburytype in Thomson's *Through Cyprus with the camera in the autumn of 1878* (1879): 'It may be added that they dress modestly, and many of them follow the Turkish fashion in keeping the greater portion of their face covered. Their complexions are generally fair, though bronzed by exposure, their features regular, and the colour of their hair varies from light brown to black. Some of them, notably those living in the mountainous districts of the island, are not unworthy descendants of the Cypriote maids of classic fame . . .'

□ 17 A.C. GOMES & SON. **Swahili girl at Zanzibar. c1900.**

B5 AUSTRALIA

18 J.W. LINDT. **Aboriginal group, Grafton, New South Wales. c1872.** This group forms one of a fine series of portraits issued by Lindt in portfolios containing twelve prints, 'the choice subjects of a very large collection which he has during three years residence on the Clarence laboured assiduously to obtain . . . As a souvenir from Australia to friends in Europe Mr Lindt's album will be acceptable to many.' (*Sydney Morning Herald*, November 24 1874.) Taken in the studio with scenic backdrops and an extensive use of props, the portraits bear out Lindt's statement of 1883 that 'in thus attempting to adhere closely to the truth, I have frequently succeeded in stealing a march upon Nature in her most pleasing and attractive moods.'

19 J.W. LINDT. **Umbertha, Qingella Tribe, Gilbert River, North Queensland. c1893.** This portrait comes from an album of fifty photographs of Queensland Aborigines compiled by Lindt in 1893. These unadorned portraits, together with the scrupulous identification of names, tribes and location, highlight the scientific aspect of Lindt's ethnographical photography.

20 J.W. LINDT. **Koiari Chiefs at Sadara Makara, New Guinea. 1885.** In 1885 Lindt accompanied Sir Peter Scratchley's tour of Britain's new possessions in South East New Guinea as official photographer. The expedition is described in Lindt's *Picturesque New Guinea* (1887), a volume illustrated with 50 collotypes from Lindt's photographs: 'By this time the people in the village above us had discerned our approach, and were waiting to welcome us . . . The name of this Koiari village is Sadara Makara. It looked as if newly built, and contained about twenty huts of the usual description, four of these being perched on the tree-tops, full forty feet above the ground. It chanced that the great chief of the tribe was just then in the village, and being a particular friend of Hunter, we were introduced to him, I myself being emphasized as an artist who had come to take pictures of the village to be sent to far off lands beyond the sea.'

□ 21 CHARLES WOOLLEY. **Truganini, the last Tasmanian Aborigine. 1866.** Truganini was one of the earliest converts to G.A. Robinson's misguided attempts to bring all the Blacks in from the bush in the latter phases of the hostilities between the European settlers and the original inhabitants of Tasmania. In 1847 the remnants of the tribes were moved from the settlement on Flinders Island to the former convict station at Oyster Cove near Hobart. James Bonwick, who met Truganini there, was much impressed with her lively personality: 'When I saw her, thirty years after her wonderful career with Mr Robinson, I understood the stories told of her vivacity and intelligence . . . Her mind was of no ordinary kind. Fertile in expedient, sagacious in council, courageous in difficulty, she had the wisdom and fascination of the serpent, the intrepidity and nobility of the royal ruler of the desert . . .' (James Bonwick, *The last of the Tasmanians,* 1870). Truganini died in 1876.

22 CHARLES WOOLLEY. **William Lanné, the last male Tasmanian Aborigine. 1866.** William Lanné, also known as King Billy, worked on whaling ships out of Hobart Town until his death in 1869. The previous year he had met the Duke of Edinburgh on the latter's visit to Hobart: 'Clad in a blue suit, with a gold-lace band round his cap, he walked proudly with the Prince on the Hobart Town regatta ground, conscious that they alone were in possession of royal blood.' (James Bonwick, *The last of the Tasmanians,* 1870.)

B6 THE PACIFIC

23 AUCKLAND STUDIO OF THE AMERICAN PHOTOGRAPHIC CO. (STOCK ACQUIRED BY BURTON BROTHERS). **Maori portrait. (?)1870s.**

□ 24 JOSIAH MARTIN. **Tawhiao Matutaera Te Wherowhero. 1880s.** The King Movement had attempted to instil a sense of national identity amongst the Maori population in the face of the European colonisation of New Zealand. Tawhiao (King Potatau II) was the second Maori king, succeeding his father (who had refused to sign the Treaty of Waitangi in 1840) in 1860. Although he took no active part in the Maori wars, he retained his claim to the kingship until his death in 1894 and refused the pensions offered by the government.

25 PHOTOGRAPHER(S) UNKNOWN. **Four Maori portraits. 1880s.** Commercial photographers in 19th century New Zealand were much concerned to capture on film the more exotic examples of Maori tattooing *(moko)* and often resorted to retouching to bring out the swirling patterns of the incised lines more clearly. By the end of the century the practice of *moko* had largely died out, although in recent years there has been a resurgence of female tattooing using Japanese methods rather than the original, extremely painful carving of the lines.

□ 26 J. DAVIS or A.J. TATTERSALL. **Uo, Chief at Mulinu'u, Samoa. c1890.** Uo was a close friend of Robert Louis Stevenson during the writer's residence in Samoa.

27 PHOTOGRAPHER UNKNOWN. **Espiritu Santo chief, New Hebrides. 1880s.**

B7 CEYLON & FAR EAST

□ 28 FELIX BEATO. **A Shan beauty, Burma. c1890.** Situated on the plateau of hills in eastern Burma between the Irrawaddy and the Mekong, the tribes of the Shan Hills ostensibly acknowledged a titular allegiance to the Burmese throne. In fact the Shan States formed a number of largely autonomous kingdoms within Burma and even after the British military campaign of 1885-86, which dethroned King Thebaw and placed Burma under the authority of British India, it was several years before the Shans were pacified.

29 G.R. LAMBERT & CO. **A Rajang River Dyak house, Borneo. 1880s.** Meticulously posed by the photographer, the Dyak group is arranged to display not only the members of the family, but also as many artefacts and utensils as possible. At the left is a *slabit* for carrying back loads and a frame for stretching yarn, and beside these a drum, fish trap and rice basket. The mother and father sit at the left of the group, while in the centre stands a girl in festive attire, her dress almost hidden by festoons of beads.

30 CHARLES T. SCOWEN. **Rambukpota, a Cinghalese chief and wife. c1875-80.**

A Cyprian maid. 1878. (B4/16)

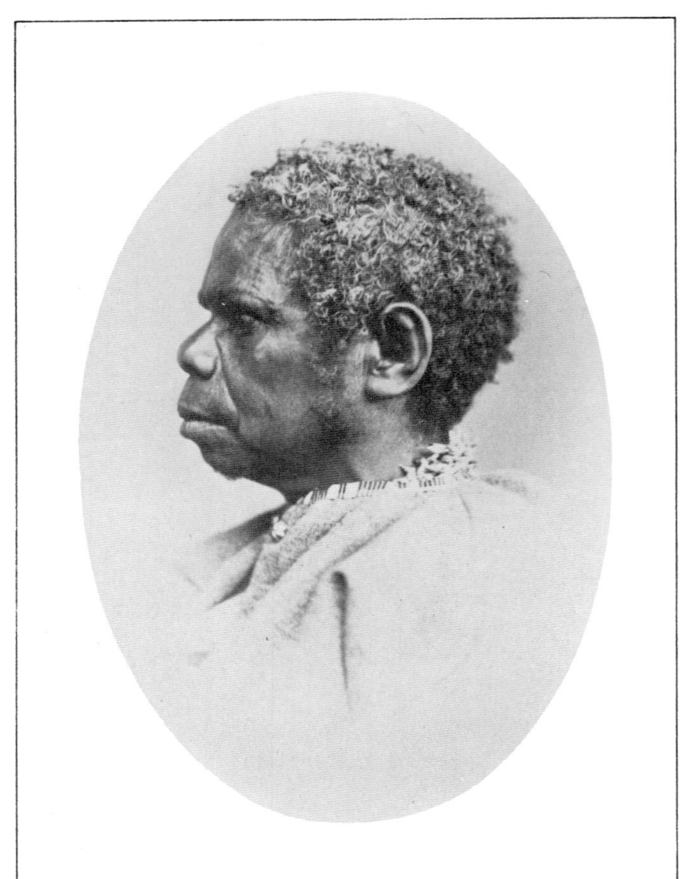

31 CHARLES T. SCOWEN. **Cinghalese headman. c1875-80.**

32 CHARLES T. SCOWEN. **A Mudaliyar, Ceylon. c1875-80.** During the period of Dutch rule in Ceylon the Mudaliyar class commanded the lascarins as well as forming an important link in the administration of, and collection of revenue from the cinnamon plantations. Their position as a landed aristocracy was consolidated under British rule, despite sporadic attempts to lessen their influence.

□33 CHARLES T. SCOWEN. **Malay girl, Ceylon. c1875-80.** The Malay population in Ceylon was first imported by the Dutch from Java for military purposes. With the advent of British rule they continued in this function, making up a significant proportion of the Ceylon Rifles and the police force.

□34 CHARLES HOSE. **Youthful Sea Dyaks (Ibans) in gala dress, Sarawak. 1890s.** '. . . The Iban especially delights in winding many yards of brilliantly coloured cloth around his waist, in brilliant coats, gorgeous turbans, feathers and other ornaments. By means of these he manages to make himself appear a very dressy person in comparison with the sober Kayan . . .' (Charles Hose, *Natural man, a record from Borneo, 1926).* The 'corset' worn by the woman consists of rings of rattan sheathed in small rings of beaten brass.

□35 PHOTOGRAPHER UNKNOWN. **Two merchants in Mandarin uniform, Hong Kong. 1890s.**

B8 INDIA

36 WILLIAM JOHNSON. **A Mussulman of Bombay. c1856.** This portrait of a Muslim inhabitant of Bombay is one of a large series of 'genre' studies produced by Johnson in the 1850s, possibly in collaboration with William Henderson, with whom he was briefly in partnership in the middle years of the decade.

37 WILLIAM JOHNSON. **Ghur-Baree (householding) Gosavees, Bombay. c1856.** William Johnson and William Henderson were joint publishers of *The Indian amateurs photographic album* (1856-58), each issue containing three prints by various Bombay photographers, they themselves contributing to a series entitled *Costumes and characters of Western India.* A few years later, declaring that 'photographic delineations of the numerous Peoples and Tribes frequenting . . . Bombay . . . have long been desiderata both among students of geography and ethnography, and the lovers of art, notwithstanding partial attempts to supply them made by local amateurs,' Johnson published *The oriental races and tribes, residents and visitors of Bombay* (2 vols., London, 1863 and 1866). By a fairly crude use of montage he placed many of the figures against Bombay backgrounds (using his own landscape photographs) or against hastily sketched-in foliage. His original enthusiasm appears to have waned, or possibly the books were not well received, since the projected third volume never appeared.

Previous left hand page:
Above left: **Truganini, the last Tasmanian Aborigine. 1866.** (B5/21)
Above right: **Tawhiao Mautuaera Te Wherowhero. 1880s.** (B6/24)
Below: **Uo, Chief at Mulinu'u. Samoa. c1890.** (B6/26)

Previous right hand page:
Above left: **A Shan beauty, Burma. c1890.** (B7/28)
Above right: **Malay girl, Ceylon. c1875-80.** (B7/33)
Below left: **Youthful Sea Dyaks (Ibans) in gala dress, Sarawak. 1890s.** (B7/34)
Below right: **Two merchants in Mandarin uniform, Hong Kong. 1890s.** (B7/35)

□38 SHEPHERD AND ROBERTSON. **The Maharajah of Bhurtpore in Durbar. 1862.** 'This photograph is an excellent illustration of a native independent chieftain of the highest class, in his durbar or court. The young prince sits in the centre of his guddee or royal seat, which is of velvet richly embroidered with gold . . . Behind him are four servants, two of whom, outside, hold merchauls of peacocks' feathers, and the chouree of yak's tail hair; another, possibly the prince's pan and spice box . . . In two rows on each side of the Rajah, the nobles and sirdars of the state are seated, who may be relatives, or officers in various parts of the state services.' (John Forbes Watson and John Kaye, *The People of India, vol. 7, 1874).* Jaswunt Singh, aged about eleven when this photograph was taken, ruled through a council of regency presided over by the political agent. He was invested with the administration of Bhurtpore in 1869 and in the same year entertained the Duke of Edinburgh.

39 BENJAMIN SIMPSON. **Tibetan musician. c1871.** An early and enthusiastic member of the Photographic Society of Bengal, Simpson's major interest was in the portraiture of the racial types of India, in which he showed a remarkable ability in blending a sympathetic approach to his subjects with his scientific interest in ethnology and the contribution to it which photography could make. 80 of his portraits of North Bengal types were exhibited at the International Exhibition of 1862 for which he won a gold medal. This portrait of an itinerant musician was probably taken while he was stationed at Darjeeling and was exhibited at the Bengal Photographic Society Exhibition of 1872 under the title of 'A wandering minstrel.'

□40 A.T.W. PENN. **Toda family, Nilgiri Hills, Madras. c1880.** An aboriginal cattle rearing tribe of the hills south west of Madras, the Todas were the subject of much ethnological enquiry and speculation in the nineteenth century, and were photographed both as a tourist curiosity and for scientific reasons. Early monographs, such as Henry Harkness' *A description of a singular aboriginal race inhabiting the Neilgherry Hills . . .* (1832), presented a romantic picture of the tribes, but later studies employed photography in a quasi-scientific approach to their ethnological singularities. Two works which utilised photography in this way were W.E. Marshall, *A phrenologist amongst the Todas* (1873) and J.M. Breeks, *An account of the primitive tribes and monuments of the Nilagiris* (1873).

41 M.V. PORTMAN. **Ilech, a young Andaman Islands child. 1890s.** Maurice Vidal Portman was first appointed to the Andamans in 1879 and in addition to writing lengthy studies of the languages and history of the group, offered in 1889 'to make for the British Museum a series of photographs of the Andamanese aborigines, in their different occupations and modes of life.' Portman's was a scientific rather than artistic project and many of his subjects were posed against a two inch square grid which acted as a scale for ethnological comparison with other races. In addition detailed measurements were made and notes taken from each sitter. Although Portman's methods have little modern scientific validity, his work remains the single most important attempt in the ethnological field to use photography as a scientific tool.

Above: **The Maharajah of Bhurtpore in Durbar. 1862.** (B8/38)
Below: **Toda family, Nilgiri Hills, Madras. c1880.** (B8/40)

Exploration & Empire

Ernest Lacan, writing in reference to the Paris International Exhibition of 1855, had extolled the way in which photography had 'sailed the oceans, conquered mountains, crossed continents' in order to bring back to Europe images of distant places previously only known through paintings, engravings and lithographs; and by 1863 Samuel Bourne, writing in *The British Journal of Photography*, was able to declare that 'there is now scarcely a nook or corner, a glen, a valley, or mountain, much less a country, on the face of the globe which the penetrating eye of the camera has not searched, or where the fumes of poor Archer's collodion have not risen through the hot or freezing atmosphere.' This ubiquity had been hard won however, and for early photographers the struggle had often been disproportionate to the results.

Almost as soon as Daguerre had made the public announcement of the details of his process in 1839, photographers had been commissioned to travel throughout Europe and North Africa in search of pictures for publication as copperplate engravings in N.P. Lerebours' *Excursions Daguerriennes* (1841-43), and in succeeding years photography was used in a number of travel books, perhaps the most notable being Francis Frith's documentation of the landscape and monumental architecture of Egypt, Sinai and Palestine where he toured between 1856 and 1859. Frith used the wet collodion process, which necessitated coating the glass plate, exposing, and developing the resulting photograph before the film dried, and his descriptions of the difficulties he encountered as he half-suffocated in his sand-filled dark tent while attempting to coat plates with chemicals that boiled in the heat, make his and other photographers' achievements all the more remarkable, and highlight the skill and determination needed by the operator in almost impossible circumstances. James Augustus Grant, who accompanied Speke on his African expedition to the source of the Nile in 1860-63, did not possess Frith's dedication to photography, and after successfully taking a few photographs at Zanzibar at the start of the expedition, soon abandoned his claustrophobic dark tent in favour of a sketching pad. John Kirk, a more accomplished photographer, experimented with a number of processes while attached to Livingstone's 1858 Zambesi expedition, including waxed paper (a variation of Fox Talbot's paper negative-positive process), Hill Norton's dry collodion and ordinary wet collodion, and took many successful photographs. Charles Livingstone, the explorer's brother and official photographer to the expedition, was on the other hand almost entirely unsuccessful, producing once 'something having a faint likeness to a picture', but hampered by his lack of knowledge of either chemistry or manipulation as well as by the harsh conditions.

The very sporadic successes in early expedition photography were doubly frustrating when considered in the light of the hopes for the craft's potential which had been expressed by the *Art Union Journal* in 1846. Commending the portability of the Talbotype (or calotype), which obviated the need for a great deal of bulky equipment and whose light paper negatives could be coated in advance, the journal suggested a number of more or less practical applications for 'an instrument of new power placed at the disposal of Ingenuity and Art.' Urging that the camera should 'be henceforth an indispensable accompaniment to all exploring expeditions', it argued that 'by taking sun pictures of striking natural objects the explorer will be able to define his route with such accuracy as greatly to abbreviate the toils and diminish the dangers of those who may follow in his track.' In the exploration of Australia in particular, this type of photography, by recording landmarks in the vicinity of water, would swiftly open up the continent to travellers. Equally ambitious roles for photography were advocated in the exploration of the African waterways where spots 'fearfully infected by miasmata and malaria' could be pinpointed and avoided.

The ambitiousness of such schemes was rarely in practice fulfilled, but more practical attempts to utilise photography as a documentary tool in the extension of British influence overseas were made: the Government of India had the foresight to engage the services of the professional photographer John Burke to record the Second Afghan War, but it was the Corps of Royal Engineers who most fully realised the practical benefits that photography could supply in their professional activities. Sappers had first been trained in photography in order to take pictures of the Crimean War, but a series of mishaps bedevilled these attempts and a School of Photography was not formally constituted at Chatham until 1856. The applications of photography to such activities as bridge and railway building, public works and armaments testing were self evident, but Engineer officers were also instructed to photographs scenes while on active service 'interesting as illustrative of History, Ethnology, Natural History, Antiquities, etc.' Some of the Corps' most interesting work thus forms a vivid record of life and settlements in Canada in the 1850s, 1860s and 1870s during the periods of the British North American Boundary Commissions. Although during military campaigns the main function of the photographers was to provide copies of maps and other official documents for the use of staff officers, the photographs of most lasting value have proved to be the semi-official portraits, landscapes and camp scenes which record service life in the field on a more human level. While, in the words of Captain Henry Schaw, there was little likelihood in the present knowledge of the art 'that any good results should be obtained under the unfavourable conditions of hurry, dust, smoke, etc., inseparable from active military operations', the 10th Company of the Royal Engineers succeeded in producing important photographic documentations of both the Abyssinian Campaign of 1867-68 and the Suakin Campaign of 1885.

By the 1880s the processes involved in photography had become sufficiently straightforward, and photography itself so natural an activity that few travellers failed to record their journeys: the work of William Ellerton Fry with the Pioneer Column into Mashonaland in 1890 and Ernest Gedge with the Imperial British East Africa Company caravan to Uganda in 1888-90 lack something of the compositional and technical skills of their predecessors, but still provide a unique and personal glimpse of important historical events as they happened. Whether adapted as woodcuts for publication in contemporary newspapers, or reproduced in the personal accounts and memoirs of the participants in these events, photography had swiftly become an indispensable witness of the growth of Britain's empire in the nineteenth century.

C1 PHOTOGRAPHER UNKNOWN. **Raising the British flag at Kerepunu, South East New Guinea. November 1884.**

C2 TRADERS & MISSIONARIES IN NYASALAND

1 A.G.S. HAWES. **The Manse at the Livingstonia Mission, Nyasaland. 1886.** Livingstone's appeal at Cambridge University in 1857 for missionaries to open up Central Africa for 'commerce and Christianity' inspired an abortive attempt in 1861 by the Universities' Mission to set up a station on the Zambesi. This was withdrawn to Zanzibar in 1863, but was followed in 1875 by the Free Church of Scotland Livingstonia Mission which set up its headquarters on Cape Maclear at the southern end of Lake Nyasa. The first head of the Livingstonia Mission, Dr Stewart, returned to the mission college at Lovedale in the Cape in 1877 and his place was taken by his deputy Dr Robert Laws who ran the mission until a few years before his death in 1934. In 1881 the mission felt secure enough to extend its operations into a more populous district and the headquarters were removed to Bandawe on the western shores of the Lake. Livingstonia was left under the control of an African headman and a teacher to continue the work of the school which had been set up.

2 A.G.S. HAWES. **The Church at Blantyre, Nyasaland. 1886.** Swiftly following in the footsteps of the Free Church, the Church of Scotland in 1876 also moved into Nyasaland. Establishing their mission in the Shiré highlands south of Lake Nyasa, they named their headquarters Blantyre after Livingstone's birthplace. Initial staffing difficulties, and an ill-organised and overweening authoritarianism which illegally assumed powers of civil jurisdiction led to the replacement of almost all the original members of the mission. The mud and thatch church at Blantyre was built in 1881. After the mission's initial setbacks, Alexander Hetherwick (who was to dominate the Blantyre mission as Laws did at Livingstonia) arrived in 1883 and was to remain in service until 1928.

□3 A.G.S. HAWES. **Group at H.M. Consulate, Blantyre. January 1886.** The problems of transport, administration and trade severely taxed the limited manpower of the Livingstonia Mission and in 1878 a limited company was set up in Glasgow to oversee the commercial development of the mission's area of activity. Originally entitled the Livingstonia Central Africa Lakes Company, it soon changed this name to the African Lakes Company and in 1879 began operations in Africa. The company also supplied the trading needs of the other missions working in Nyasaland. Standing at either end of the group are the two managers, Frederick Moir (1852-1939) and John Moir (1851-1940). Frederick Moir's wife Jane is seated in the centre of the group. Second from the left stands Alexander Hetherwick (1860-1939).

4 A.G.S. HAWES. **The headquarters of the African Lakes Company, 'Mandala,' Blantyre. 1886.** On their first arrival at Blantyre the Moirs used a mission bungalow as the headquarters of the African Lakes Company, but in 1881 they acquired land away from the mission and in 1882 John McIlwaine, a ship's carpenter who had joined the company, erected the first brick building in the territory. Situated on the south eastern outskirts of Blantyre, the house was named 'Mandala,' the Yao word for a flash of light, in reference to John Moir's spectacles. Behind the house was a store and a defensive stockade which served as a refuge for the European population on a number of occasions: in 1884 after the murder of Chief Chipatula by George Fenwick, again in 1884 when the Angoni chief Chikusi raided from Angoni Land, and finally in 1915 during the Chilembwe Rising.

5 A.G.S. HAWES. **African Lakes Company station at Matope, Upper Shiré, Nyasaland. 1886.** Situated on the bank of the Shiré due west of Zomba, Matope was the limit of navigation on the upper part of the river. The Company, inefficiently run by the Moir brothers, gained a bad reputation for poor administration and profiteering. The British South Africa Company obtained a controlling interest in 1889 and until a British Protectorate was announced in 1891, the African Lakes Company incompetently administered the territory on its behalf. In 1893 the African Lakes Company transferred all its assets to the British South Africa Company and went into liquidation. Its trading functions (as the African Lakes Trading Corporation) continued under the management of the vastly more efficient Monteith Fotheringham.

C3 EXPLORING CENTRAL AFRICA

6 A.G.S. HAWES. **The Royal Geographical Society Expedition at the summit of Mount Kiladzulu, Nyasaland. 1886.** In 1885 the R.G.S. organised an expedition 'to fix the position of the confluence of the Rivers Lugenda and Ruvuma, and to study their resources for the advancement of commercial enterprise.' Under the leadership of Thomas Joseph Last (1847-1933) the expedition started inland on October 28 1885 and after fulfilling the main purpose of the expedition, arrived in Blantyre in mid January 1886. Delayed for several months by fever and the onset of the wet season Last, accompanied by Consul Hawes, made a trip from Blantyre to Angoni Land between May and June during which a series of photographs was taken. Kiladzulu (or Chiradzulu) lies mid-way between Blantyre and Zomba. Last stands beside the theodolite at the right of the photograph.

7 A.G.S. HAWES. **Encampment at Katunga's, Lower Shiré, Nyasaland. 1886.** As well as the expedition to Angoni Land with Hawes, Last made a number of smaller excursions between January and May 1886, including one to the Makololo people on the Lower Shiré. Katunga's village was at the foot of the Murchison Cataracts.

□8 A.G.S. HAWES. **T.J. Last giving lessons in breadmaking at H.M. Consulate, Blantyre. 1886.** This and the following photograph were presumably taken between January and May 1886 when Last accepted Consul Hawes' offer of accommodation in Blantyre until the end of the wet season.

9 A.G.S. HAWES. **Lessons in the laundry, H.M. Consulate, Blantyre. 1886.**

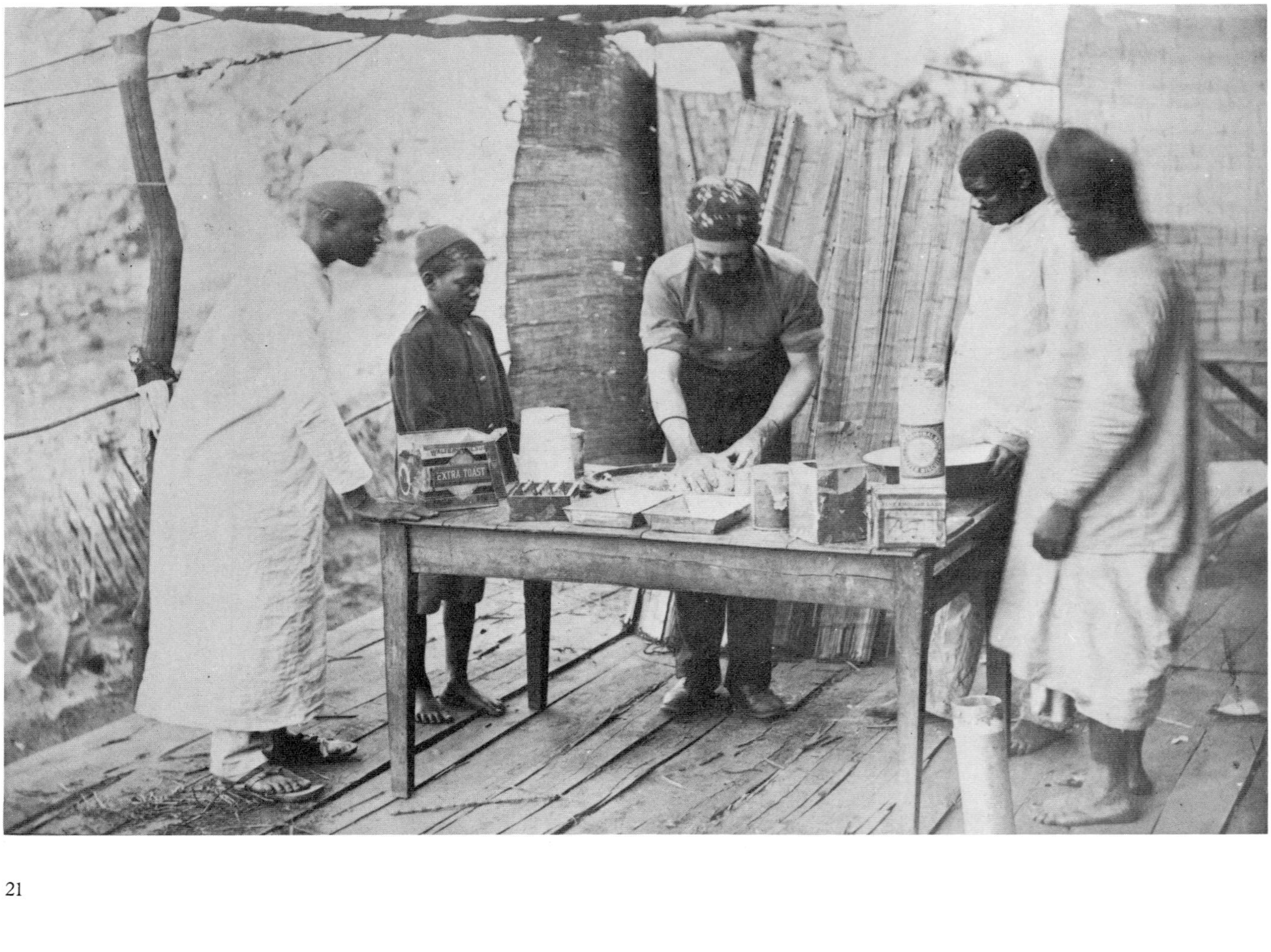

C4 IBEACo.

10 ERNEST GEDGE. **Frederick Jackson at Turquell, East Africa. January 1890.** In 1888 the East African Association was granted a Royal Charter, becoming the Imperial British East Africa Company and empowered to make treaties and set up an administration on behalf of the British Government. Pressure from the government to open up the interior forced the company to send a caravan to Buganda, at this period torn by civil and religious strife and a target for German colonial expansion. Frederick Jackson (1860-1929), who had first come to East Africa in 1884 and whose knowledge of the country was unrivalled, was chosen to lead the expedition. Throughout the company's period of operation it was constantly torn by the demands of its shareholders seeking dividends and the expensive and unprofitable liabilities implied by its charter. When the company's flag was replaced by the Union flag in Uganda in 1893 and in East Africa in 1895, it had given little satisfaction to its investors but had opened up East Africa for British rule. In later life Sir Frederick Jackson was a Commissioner in the Uganda and East Africa Protectorates and finally, from 1911-17, Governor of Uganda.

11 (ERNEST GEDGE). **Ernest Gedge at Turquell, East Africa. 1890.** Before joining IBEACo in 1888, Gedge (1862-1935) had spent some nine years as a tea planter in Assam. When the caravan reached Buganda in April 1890 and after Jackson's departure in May, Gedge stayed behind to look after company interests. From August to December 1890 he was in German territory to the south of Lake Victoria (where he met Emin Pasha and took the last known portrait of the German administrator) and in January 1891 left Buganda for England. Much of his later life was spent in travel to a wide variety of places, in the main prospecting and carrying out mineral surveys for a number of companies.

□ 12 ERNEST GEDGE. **Treaty making in Kikuyu. August 11 1889.** The IBEACo treaty with Kamiri was signed in the expedition's camp at the edge of the Kikuyu Forest: '...Before exchanging treaties with Kaniri (sic), the local chief, and presenting him with a Company's flag, we submitted, at his request, to the ceremony of making blood-brotherhood with him and two of his councillors. Many people scoff at such a ceremony and consider it disgusting. After all, what is it? Simply swallowing a small bit of well-cooked meat or liver of a goat, killed for the occasion, with a tiny speck of each other's blood on it. Personally I had no qualms in such matters, feeling that it was only done in a good cause, at the expense of a little self-sacrifice.' (Frederick Jackson, *Early days in East Africa*, 1930). With Jackson are James Martin and Dr Archibald Mackinnon (1864-1937), a medical officer with IBEACo from 1888-91 and later employed by the Uganda and Zanzibar governments.

13 ERNEST GEDGE. **The expedition headman at Machakos. August 2 1889.**

Previous left hand page:
Above: **Group at H.M. Consulate, Blantyre. January 1886.** (C2/3)
Below: **T.J. Last giving lessons in breadmaking at H.M. Consulate, Blantyre. 1886.** (C3/8)

Previous right hand page:
Above: **Treaty making in Kikuyu. August 11 1889.** (C4/12)
Below: **James Martin and Kavirondos at Mumia's. November/December 1889.** (C4/14)

□ 14 ERNEST GEDGE. **James Martin and Kavirondos at Mumia's. November/December 1889.** The Kwa Sundu chief Mumia stands in his village with a group of wives and tribesmen. Mumia (c1849-1949) in the course of his long life witnessed the growth of British power in East Africa from its beginnings to its decline. Meetings with him are described by the explorer Joseph Thomson (in 1883), Bishop Hannington (in 1885) and by Lugard (in 1890). Almost all the Europeans who met him described his pleasing manner and helpfulness to travellers. Also seen in the group is James Martin (1857-1924), a semi-literate sail maker of Maltese origins who joined IBEACo in 1889 and was later a District Commissioner in the newly formed Uganda Protectorate.

C5 FOUNDING OF RHODESIA

□ 15 W.E. FRY. **The Administrator and his Civil Staff, Mashonaland. 1890.** Shortly after Lobengula's concession of mineral rights in Matabeleland, a Royal Charter was granted to Rhodes' British South Africa Company in 1889, and the next year saw the realisation of his dream of expanding northwards and colonizing Mashonaland. There had been some talk between Rhodes and his lieutenant Frank Johnson of extending company rule by military action against Lobengula, but at Selous' suggestion an armed wagon trek to Mashonaland, skirting Matabeleland, was agreed upon. Seen in this photograph are Archibald Colquhoun (1898-1914), the first Administrator of Mashonaland from 1890-91; Christopher Harrison, his secretary; the celebrated hunter and explorer Frederick Courteney Selous (1851-1917), who acted as Intelligence Officer; and Dr Leander Starr Jameson (1853-1917), who succeeded Colquhoun as Administrator from 1891-96. Jameson also administered the Matabeleland territory of the defeated Lobengula for the last two years of this period and before his trial and imprisonment after the Jameson Raid of 1895.

16 W.E. FRY. **Police Officers of the Pioneer Column. 1890.** The Pioneer Column which trekked into Mashonaland was recruited by Frank Johnson on Rhodes' behalf and was to comprise a representative cross-section of trades and professions to set up the new community. For military protection while on the trek the company increased its police strength to about 500 men, the Pioneers and police under the command of Lieutenant Colonel Edward Pennefather (1850-1928), seated here third from right.

□ 17 W.E. FRY. **An incident on the road to Mashonaland. 1890.** The route of the Pioneer Column, from Macloutsie to Tuli and on to Charter and the present site of Salisbury, lay through land just passable for wagons with a team of roadmakers moving in advance of the main body. Accidents, as John Willoughby describes, were not uncommon: 'Many of the oxen...began to knock up. As it was most necessary to give them a rest, they had to be replaced with untrained slaughter oxen, and these gave us no end of trouble. Some declined to be inspanned at any price and were constantly breaking away and careering wildly through the bush; others either refused to pull at all or pulled in the wrong direction, while others again would lie down, out of sheer perversity, and stubbornly refuse to get up, although they might be half choking themselves with the yokes.'

Above: **The Administrator and his Civil Staff, Mashonaland. 1890.** (C5/15)
Below: **An incident on the road to Mashonaland. 1890.** (C5/17)

18 W.E. FRY. **Chief Chibi and his followers, Tokwi River. 1890.** Chibi (second from the right with blanket) was the title of the paramount chiefs of the Mari, a branch of the Karanga known as the Banyai in the nineteenth century. The Chibi (or Chivi) in 1890 was Madhlangwe (d. 1907). Chibi's kraal, which the main body of the Pioneers reached in early August, was situated about 12 miles south east of Providential Pass near the River Tokwi. The column found to its surprise that it was expected at Chibi's, but this was explained by the presence of Matabele warriors who said that they had come to make sure the column was having no difficulties securing supplies. This unexpected goodwill left the Pioneers doubly suspicious, but no attack in fact materialized. Behind Chibi stands Robert Beale (1859-1907), a member of 'B' Troop who later served in the Matabele War of 1893 and the Rebellion of 1896.

19 W.E. FRY. **The Camp, Fort Salisbury. September 1890.** The main body of the Pioneer Column arrived at Fort Salisbury on September 12 and on the following day the seven pounders fired a salute and the Union flag was raised over the site of the future capital of Southern Rhodesia. The Pioneers were then demobilised with their titles to the 15 mining claims promised to each, their rifles, 100 rounds of ammunition and three months' rations. This small band of settlers then began the task of consolidating Rhodes' dream.

C6 EXPLORERS

(A) HORSBURGH. **David Livingstone. c1857.** Ordained as an L.M.S. missionary in 1840, Livingstone (1813-73) made several smaller journeys of exploration before embarking on the expeditions which were to make him famous in the 1850s. In 1849 he crossed the Kalahari and found Lake Ngami; the Zambesi was discovered in 1851 and the Victoria Falls in 1855. Livingstone severed his connection with the L.M.S. in 1857 and returned to Africa as British Consul. In 1858-64 he explored much of what is now Malawi, and in his final expedition, lasting from 1866-73, he travelled from Mikindani around the southern shores of Lake Nyasa, discovering Lake Mweru and Lake Bangweolo in 1869.

□ (B) J.E. BRUTON. **Stanley and his followers at Cape Town. November 1877.** After his famous meeting with Livingstone at Ujiji in 1871, Henry Morton Stanley (1841-1904) returned to Africa to follow up Livingstone's explorations. In one of the greatest feats of African exploration, he crossed the continent from east to west in the years 1874-77, tracing the River Congo to its mouth and opening up the interior for European exploitation. This photograph shows Stanley and his followers on their way back to Zanzibar via the Cape at the end of the journey.

(C) J.A. GRANT. **Bombay at Zanzibar. 1860.** Without the Africans who acted as interpreters, porters and guides, the European exploration of the African interior would have been infinitely more difficult. Bombay (c1820-1885), an African of Yao origin who had been sold into slavery and taken to India in his youth, was one of the most experienced of this band and was employed in turn by Burton (1857-59), Speke (1860-63), Stanley (1871-72) and Cameron (1873-76).

(D) THOMAS MITCHELL or GEORGE WHITE. **H.M.S. 'Alert' stopped by ice off Cape Prospect. 1875.** The British re-entered the race to find a route to the North Pole with the Royal Navy's British Arctic Expedition of 1875-76, an attempt to find a route to the Pole via Smith Sound. Under the command of (Sir) George Strong Nares, who had been transferred from his command of the *Challenger* voyage, the *Alert* was able to navigate the channel between Greenland and Ellesmere Island and winter at the edge of the Arctic Ocean. No further seaborne progress was made, but sleigh parties from the ship in the spring of 1876 reached the furthest position north so far attained, and verified beyond doubt that the Arctic Ocean was permanently ice-covered.

□ (E) A.W. PAUL. **Group at Giagong, Macaulay mission to Sikkim. 1884.** This photograph is one of a number pasted into Colman Macaulay's *Report of a mission to Sikkim and the Tibetan frontier* (1885), and shows Macaulay and other members of his party with a group of Tibetans at Giagong. In 1884 Macaulay received permission to mount an expedition to the Tibetan border to open discussions on trade with Tibet seen by merchants as a ready market for Indian tea and English broadcloth and as a source for gold and wool. The results of the journey were encouraging but Macaulay's hopes of following up the mission with an expedition to Lhasa were destroyed by subsequent political events.

(F) H.E. HULL. **Mary Kingsley, 1890s.** Mary Kingsley (1862-1900) made two journeys of exploration in western and central Africa in 1893 and 1894, and her subsequent writings had great influence. Sympathetic to the position of European traders in Africa, she argued against the extension of formal colonial administrations and supported the retention of indigenous methods of government.

(G) R. HALL. **John McDouall Stuart. 1863.** Stuart (1815-1866) emigrated to South Australia in 1839 and after two unsuccessful attempts crossed Australia from coast to coast in 1862.

(H) PHOTOGRAPHER UNKNOWN. **Joseph Elzéar Bernier. c1900.** In his nine Arctic voyages the sailor and explorer J.E. Bernier (1852-1934) annexed several islands for Canada and was considered to know the northern archipelago better than any man alive.

C7 THE 2ND AFGHAN WAR

28 BOURNE & SHEPHERD. **Lord Lytton, Viceroy of India. 1877.** Having declined the governorship of Madras the previous year, the choice of Edward Robert Bulwer Lytton (1831-1891), a minor poet and skilled diplomat in the courts of Europe, as Viceroy of India was a surprising one. In a period of office (1876-80) harshly criticised at the time, he did in fact make some notable contributions to Indian administration. He was however, also largely responsible for Britain's second major intervention in Afghanistan, pushing an aggressive forward policy by presenting the Afghan government with a series of ultimatums and the Home government with a series of diplomatic *faits accomplis.* The original outbreak of hostilities was over the refusal of the Afghans to accept a British mission at Kabul to counterbalance the Russian presence, but by the time of his recall in 1880 Lytton, in a remarkable change of viewpoint, was arguing that Britain should quit the area as her presence would be unduly provocative to Russia.

Above: **Stanley and his followers at Cape town. November 1877.** (C6/B)
Below: **Group at Giagong, Macaulay mission to Sikkim. 1884.** (C6/E)

29 PHOTOGRAPHER UNKNOWN. **Lieutenant General Sir F.S. Roberts. c1882.** Frederick Sleigh Roberts (1832-1914), 1st Earl Roberts of Kandahar, Pretoria and Waterford, had spent almost all his military career in India when he was selected to command the central column of the advance into Afghanistan in 1878: gazetted into the Bengal Artillery in 1851, he won the V.C. in the Mutiny and had extensive experience of the North West Frontier. As an advocate of the forward policy towards Afghanistan, he was a natural choice for the command of the Kurram Valley Field Force and on the first advance into Afghanistan inflicted a notable defeat on the Afghans at Peiwar Kotal in December 1878. His popular fame was the result of the march to Kandahar and the subsequent battle later in the campaign. After his successes in the Afghan War he was appointed to a succession of senior appointments, including Commander-in-Chief of India (1885-93), South Africa (1899-1900) and of the British Army (1900-04).

30 JOHN BURKE. **Lieutenant General Roberts and staff inspecting captured Afghan artillery at Sherpur, Kabul. October 1879.** British self-congratulation at the successful conclusion of Roberts' first advance into Afghanistan and the subsequent installation of a British Agent at Kabul was destroyed in the early hours of September 5 1879 when news reached Simla that Sir Louis Cavagnari, his staff and guards had been killed by Afghans two days before. A fresh campaign was immediately organised and, after repeating the tactics of Peiwar Kotal at Charasia on October 6 1879, Roberts and the Kurram Valley Field Force took Kabul and held a victory parade through the city on October 13.

31 JOHN BURKE. **View from Fort Onslow showing east end of Bemaru defences, Kabul. 1879.** Soldiers pose for the photographer on the fortified positions above the Sherpur Cantonments. The Bemaru Ridge, running along the northern side of the Cantonments, was the scene of a mishandled engagement in November 1841 during the First Afghan War.

32 JOHN BURKE. **5th Punjab Infantry, Sherpur Cantonments, Kabul. December 1879.** With Kabul occupied and the Field Force's defensive position secure in the cantonments north of the city, Roberts set about restoring order and installing a suitably compliant government, while other British forces attempted to subdue Afghanistan's eastern borders. But by early December it was clear that the war was far from over as the cry for a holy war went out to the Afghan tribes and forces converged on Kabul. At 5.30 on the morning of December 23 1879 the whole Afghan force attacked Robert's position in a battle which lasted until midday. Roberts had been warned of the attack however, and the Afghans retreated leaving 1000 dead on the battlefield against negligible British losses. Kabul was reoccupied on Christmas Day. The war itself was not to end until May 1881, after a disaster at Maiwand (July 1880) and the revenge at Kandahar (September 1880). On May 4 1881 the last British troops left Afghanistan to the rule of Amir Abdur Rahman: little alteration of Afghanistan's strategic position in relation to India had been effected, and all that had been gained at immense cost in money and manpower was the insignificant territorial acquisition of part of Baluchistan.

C8 EGYPT & THE SUDAN

☐ 33 L. FIORILLO. **Court martial in Alexandria after the bombardment. July 1882.** The army rebellion of 1881 led by Arabi Pasha against the Anglo-French Condominium administering Egypt quickly gathered force, and, in the face of widespread violence against Europeans in Alexandria, a British fleet under the command of Vice Admiral Sir Frederick Beauchamp Seymour commenced a ten hour bombardment of the city on July 11 1882. After the destruction of the waterfront fortifications and the retreat of Arabi Pasha's army, marines landed in the city to restore order, with instructions that looters were to be flogged and incendiaries caught in the act were to be shot. The photographer L. Fiorillo afterwards issued a volume of photographs entitled *Album souvenir d'Alexandrie: Ruines,* a grim record of the havoc wreaked by the bombardment.

34 PHOTOGRAPHER UNKNOWN. **British troops at the Sphinx after the Battle of Tel el Kebir. 1882.** The bombardment and subsequent liberation of Alexandria had not defeated Arabi Pasha's army, which still controlled Cairo and a large part of Egypt, and General Wolseley was despatched to Egypt for the final confrontation. After an audacious and risky night march, Wolseley's force made a surprise dawn attack at Tel el Kebir on September 13, defeating Arabi's army at a cost of 399 British casualties. Two days later Cairo was taken and Arabi captured. After his trial in December 1882 he was banished to Ceylon, but pardoned in 1901.

36 ROYAL ENGINEERS PHOTOGRAPHER. **The camp at Tambuk, Suakin Campaign. 1885.** After the death of Gordon at Khartoum in 1885 and the recall of General Wolseley's rescue expedition, the Red Sea port of Suakin remained Britain's one stronghold in the Sudan against Mahdist forces. Lieutenant General Graham V.C., who had garrisoned the town in 1884, returned in 1885 to crush Osman Digna, a noted Mahdist leader, and to build a railway from Suakin to Berber. Graham's campaign was successful, but its gains were not followed up and the railway was abandoned. Tambuk, five miles west of Otao and on the projected line of the railway, was occupied by the Scots Guards and a company of Royal Engineers on April 19 1885. Mahdist forces under the Khalifa (the Mahdi had died shortly after the taking of Khartoum) subsequently remained in effective control of the Sudan until the campaign of 1896-98.

☐ 37 ROYAL ENGINEERS PHOTOGRAPHER. **Native officers of the 9th Bengal Cavalry, Suakin Campaign. 1885.** '...A more magnificent regiment no one could wish to see. Their loose-fitting dress, made of Kharkee, with blue puttees instead of long boots, and with blue-and-grey turbans as a headdress, the appearance of these fine, swarthy-looking warriors was enough to strike terror into any foe. They were very grand-looking men and splendid horsemen... Their arms are a sword and a carbine, which they wear on a cross-belt over either shoulder... They all wear steel-chain shoulder bands, which serve as an excellent protection against a sword-cut.' *(Suakin, 1885... by an officer who was there* (E.G. Parry), London, 1885). As well as the Indian contingents, a sizeable force from Australia also served during the campaign.

Above: **Court Martial in Alexandria after the bombardment. July 1882.** (C8/33)
Below: **Native officers of the 9th Bengal Cavalry, Suakin Campaign. 1885.** (C8/37)

38 FRANCIS GREGSON. **Slatin Pasha and Colonel Wingate, Sudan Campaign. 1898.** For a decade after the inconclusive Suakin Campaign no major attempt was made to re-impose British mastery in the Sudan. The Dongola Campaign of 1896 heralded a reassertion of imperial authority in the area as Kitchener's forces moved south, aided by an efficient Egyptian army and the newly constructed Sudan Military Railway. By 1898 the position was sufficiently consolidated for the Sirdar to attempt the final destruction of Mahdism. Rudolf Slatin, who had returned to the Sudan at Gordon's invitation in 1879, was Governor of Darfur until his capture by the Mahdi in 1883. He escaped from imprisonment in Omdurman in February 1895 largely through Wingate's efforts and served during the campaign on Wingate's intelligence staff. Sir Francis Reginald Wingate (1861-1953) was governor General of the Sudan from 1899-1916 and High Commissioner in Egypt from 1917-19.

39 FRANCIS GREGSON. **The Mahdist leader Mahmoud after capture at the Battle of Atbara. April 8 1898.** Escorted by soldiers of the 10th Sudanese Battalion, the wounded Mahmoud is led to Wingate for questioning. One of the Khalifa's ablest generals, Mahmoud and his army were encamped in a fortified zariba at Atbara when attacked by Kitchener's force at dawn on April 8. In an action lasting 40 minutes the Anglo-Egyptian army sustained losses of 80 men to 3000 Mahdist fatalities. The killing power of European weaponry allied to an efficiently organized army against numerically superior forces was to be demonstrated again at Omdurman on September 2.

40 FRANCIS GREGSON. **Raising the British flag over Gordon's Palace at Khartoum. September 4 1898.** The success of Kitchener's reconquest of the Sudan was sealed at the Battle of Omdurman when possibly 10,000 Mahdist soldiers perished before the withering superiority of the Anglo-Egyptian armoury. On September 3 Kitchener entered Omdurman, and on the following day Gordon's admonishing ghost was laid and imperial pride restored in the ceremony held among the ruins of Gordon's Palace. It remained for the correspondent G.W. Steevens to voice a note of doubt over this imperial adventure: 'The poor Sudan! The wretched dry Sudan! Count up all the gains you will, yet what a hideous irony it remains, this fight of half a generation for such an emptiness.'

C9 MISSIONARIES

A LOMBARDI & CO. **James Hannington, first Bishop of Eastern Equatorial Africa. 1884.** James Hannington (1847-1885) first went to Africa as a missionary in 1882, but was invalided home in the following year. In 1884 he was consecrated first Bishop of Eastern Equatorial Africa. He attempted to reach Uganda by the Masai route and after some difficulty arrived at Busaga. By this time Mutesa had been replaced by Mwanga as Kabaka of Buganda, and on the king's orders Hannington and most of his porters were murdered near Jinja.

B PHOTOGRAPHER UNKNOWN. **Bishop Samuel Ajayi Crowther. 1860s.** Sold as a slave and rescued by a British slavery patrol, Crowther (1808-1891) was taken to Freetown where he was educated by the C.M.S. and baptized in 1825. After further study he was ordained in England in 1845 and returned to Yorubaland as a missionary. As part of a missionary plan to create a West African diocese with an indigenous pastorate, Crowther was consecrated as the first African Bishop of the Anglican Church in 1864. The policy subsequently came under attack and in 1890 Crowther was forced to resign. As well as his missionary activities, Crowther also made valuable scholarly contributions to the study of the Yoruba language.

C ELLIOTT & FRY. **John Smith Moffatt. 1860s.** A son of the missionary Robert Smith Moffatt, John Smith Moffatt (1835-1918) was born at Kuruman and ordained and accepted by the L.M.S. in 1857. His first missionary activities were on a freelance basis (assisted by his brother-in-law David Livingstone) and in 1859 he helped to found the first mission to the Ndebele in Matabeleland. In 1864 he rejoined the L.M.S. and worked for them mainly at Kuruman until 1879, when he resigned to become a colonial administrator.

D PHOTOGRAPHER UNKNOWN. **Revd. A.N. Wood at work translating, Usagara, East Africa. 1890s.** Revd. Arthur North Wood (c1862-1908) was a C.M.S. missionary in East Africa from 1886-1908 and during his period of service there translated a number of texts into Kimegi.

□ E C.W. HATTERSLEY. **C.M.S. School for boys, Mengo, Uganda. 1906.** The Church Missionary Society High School for Boys at Mengo was founded by Charles Hattersley in 1905.

F PHOTOGRAPHER UNKNOWN. **The Bishop Patteson Memorial Chapel, Norfolk Island. 1884.** The consecration of John Coleridge Patteson as first Missionary Bishop of Melanesia in 1861 led to the establishment of a training school and headquarters on Norfolk Island in 1866 and in October of the same year Revd. J. Palmer arrived with 16 Melanesian pupils. By 1899 there were 200 Melanesian students on the island. This photograph shows mission staff and pupils grouped outside the St. Barnabas Memorial Chapel, built between 1875 and 1880 in commemoration of Bishop Patteson, who had been killed by Solomon Islanders in 1871.

□ G DR HENRY WELCHMAN or REVD. ARTHUR BRITTAIN. **Feather money brought to Mr Forrest's house at Nelua, Santa Cruz. 1892.** Bishop H.H. Montgomery visited A.E.C. Forrest, a lay worker with the Melanesian Mission, while making a tour of the Pacific mission stations on behalf of Bishop Selwyn. The tour lasted from August to November 1892 and is described in Montgomery's *The Light of Melanesia* (1896). Photographs were taken by various members of the party using equipment loaned by the Hobart photographer W. Beattie (who later sold the pictures commercially). The coils of feather money seen in this picture were brought to the mission as the price of a girl purchased as a teacher's wife. Montgomery was assured by Forrest that the money had only come into use in Santa Cruz during the previous 30 years.

Above: **C.M.S. School for boys, Mengo, Uganda. 1906.** (C9/E)
Below: **Feather money brought to Mr. Forrest's house at Nelua, Santa Cruz. 1892.** (C9/G)

C10 CANADIAN BOUNDARY COMMISSIONS

41 ROYAL ENGINEERS PHOTOGRAPHER. **Officers' Quarters, Pilgrim's Rest Barracks, Esquimalt, Vancouver Island. 1859-60.** The decision to make British Columbia (generally known at this time as New Caledonia) a Crown Colony was hastened by the influx of prospectors heading for the newly opened gold fields on the Fraser River. In order to set up an administration and lay the foundations of the new colony a 'Columbia Detachment' of volunteers was formed from the men of the Royal Engineers and in September 1858 this force set sail for Canada. The equipment taken, which included a printing press, telegraph apparatus, mining tools and several miles of iron for the construction of a railway, indicates the soldiers' more than military function. The main body arrived a few months after the proclamation of the colony in November 1858 and were stationed there until 1863. The majority of the detachment remained as settlers in British Columbia after the breaking up of the original garrison.

□ 42 ROYAL ENGINEERS PHOTOGRAPHER. **Sappers cutting the 49th Parallel on the right bank of the Moyie River, British Columbia. 1860-61.** Shortly before the arrival of the Columbia Detachment, another body of Royal Engineers had commenced work in British Columbia. By the terms of the Oregon Treaty of 1846 it was agreed that the boundary between the United States and Canada should follow the 49th Parallel of north latitude from the Lake of the Woods to the Pacific, but this had never in fact been properly surveyed. With a rapidly expanding population this became a matter of urgency and a joint British and American commission (working independently but in conjunction) was set up to mark out the boundary at its western end. In the four seasons' work from 1858-62 the Engineers surveyed over 400 miles of virgin land, often, as here, cutting twenty foot tracks through dense forest.

43 ROYAL ENGINEERS PHOTOGRAPHER. **Sinyakwateen depot camp on the left bank of the Pend D'Oreille River. 1860-61.** The Pend D'Oreille River ran adjacent to the boundary line just east of Fort Shepherd, a Hudson's Bay Company trading post built in 1856-57 to replace Fort Colvile which was found to be in American territory.

44 ROYAL ENGINEERS PHOTOGRAPHER. **Surveyor East's party at N.W. Angle, Lake of the Woods, Ontario. 1872.** The survey of 1858-62, while completing the most urgent section of the boundary, left uncertain the portion of the Canadian border east of the Rockies along the southern limits of Alberta, Saskatchewan and Manitoba to the Lake of the Woods. Manitoba entered the Dominion of Canada in 1870 and it became particularly necessary to determine the Province's extent. From 1872-76 therefore, a boundary commission under the command of a Royal Artillery officer Captain Donald R. Cameron, worked its way along the southern border of Canada, operating in much the same way as its predecessor.

45 ROYAL ENGINEERS PHOTOGRAPHER. **Red River Transportation Company steamer 'Dakota' at Dufferin, Red River. c1872.** The sternwheeler *Dakota* was used to transport the British Commission up the Red River on the last leg of their journey to North Fort Pembina at the start of survey operations.

□ 46 ROYAL ENGINEERS PHOTOGRAPHER. **Cook house, Turtle Mountain Depot. c1873.** 'This district of Turtle Mountain will be invaluable to settlers in the future, furnishing, as it does, an ample supply of wood for building and fuel purposes, and wintering ground for stock, while the adjacent plains will serve as grazing ground during the summer. During the operations of the Boundary Commission a depot was kept up here for storing supplies, and a large storehouse constructed of poplar logs, in which the caretakers lived during the winter months.' (Captain Samuel Anderson, *The North American Boundary*... R.G.S. Journal, Vol. 46, 1876).

C11 CONSOLIDATION IN WEST AFRICA

□ 47 ROYAL ENGINEERS PHOTOGRAPHER. **Steam engine for the Ashanti Expedition. 1873.** Hostilities in the early years of the 19th century between the British on the Gold Coast and the expanding power of the Ashanti Confederacy were concluded by treaty in 1831, but by the 1860s relations had again deteriorated to the point of war. The situation was worsened by Britain's determination to suppress the power of Kumasi over her neighbouring tributary states while refusing to fill the vacuum that this policy created. In January 1873 an Ashanti force crossed the Prah and advanced towards Cape Coast and in October Sir Garnet Wolseley arrived with a force composed from the Rifle Brigade, the Royal Welsh Fusiliers, the Black Watch and the Royal Engineers. In a swift advance Wolseley took and fired Kumasi and returned to the coast. The subsequent treaty signed by the Ashanti called for the paying of an indemnity in gold, the renouncing of their power over other states, and the opening up of the trade routes.

□ 48 PHOTOGRAPHER UNKNOWN. **Kwaku Dua II and The British Commissioner at Kumasi. February 1884.** The defeat of the Ashanti in 1873-74 led to a collapse of orderly rule in the Confederacy which came to a head when the Asantehene Mensa Bonsu was deposed in 1883. A year of anarchy ensued before Kwaku Dua II was installed as Asantehene in April 1884. Seated in the foreground of this photograph is Assistant Inspector Brandon Kirby of the Gold Coast Constabulary who travelled through Ashanti with letters from the Governor giving provisional support to Kwaku Dua's enstoolment, but refusing to visit Kumasi while human sacrifice was still practised. Kirby arrived in Kumasi on February 5 and was able to report that the town seemed more prosperous than on his previous visit, the inhabitants were 'exceedingly well satisfied with their choice of Quecoe Duah as their future King' and that there were no signs of human sacrifice. Unfortunately Kwaku Dua died of smallpox in June of the same year and civil order again collapsed until the enstoolment of Kwaku Dua III, better known as Prempeh I.

□ 49 PHOTOGRAPHER UNKNOWN. **The restoration of the Ashanti Confederacy. 1935.** In 1896 Prempeh I was exiled and after the war of 1900 Ashanti was formally annexed to the Gold Coast. Prempeh was permitted to return in 1924 and was installed as Kumasihene: at this time the government would not agree to his resumption of the title of Asantehene, although he was recognised as such by the people of Ashanti. He was succeeded in 1931 by his nephew Nana Osei Agyeman Prempeh II (1892-1970) and four years later the Ashanti Confederacy was officially restored and he was installed as Asanthene. Prempeh II was knighted in 1937 and in 1943 all the land in Kumasi which had been declared Crown land when Ashanti was annexed was returned.

Above: **Sappers cutting the 49th Parallel on the right bank of the Moyie River, British Columbia. 1860-61.** (C10/42)
Below: **Cook house, Turtle Mountain Depot. c1873.** (C10/46)

☐50 N. WALWIN HOLM. **Annexation of Ado to Lagos Colony. 1891.** From the mid 1880s British administration was steadily extended from Lagos towards the Yoruba interior, where years of inter-tribal strife were disturbing the trade routes to the coast. In 1891 the areas of Ilaro, Igbessa, Ado and Pokra were signed over to the Crown, a transfer that was accompanied by a durbar at each location, followed by a flag-raising ceremony. George C. Denton, acting Governor of Lagos in 1891, is here seen with the Chief of Ado and his own military and naval staff. In protest against this extension of British rule the Egbas closed the trade routes to Lagos and in the following year it proved necessary to mount a military expedition to restore order.

51 W.S. TURTON. **Meeting at Ogbomosho, Lagos Interior Expedition. 1893.** From January 3 to April 4 1893 the Governor of Lagos, Sir Gilbert Carter, travelled to Jebba and back with a group of officers and an escort of 100 Hausas in order to negotiate with the Egba and Jebu chiefs still disrupting the trade routes from Yorubaland to the coast. Another purpose of the expedition was to end the long-standing war between the Ibadans and the Ilorins: both these tasks were successfully accomplished, although to Carter's intense disappointment, the Balogun Ajaye of Ibadan could under no circumstances be persuaded to accept a British resident. Carter remained at Ogbomosho from February 6-19. Not only was the mission important in its immediate extension of British influence, but during the journey investigations were also made as to the possible route for the railway which in later years was to open up the country. Seated (l. to r.) in this photograph are: the Balé of Ogbomosho; Sir Gilbert Carter (1848-1927), Governor of Lagos 1891-97; Captain R.L. Bower, commanding the Hausa detachment; (later Sir) George Basil Haddon-Smith (1861-1931), A.D.C. to the Governor; Dr. J.W. Rowland, botanist to the expedition or Grant Fowler, the geographer; and Lieutenant W.R. Harding, Lagos Constabulary Paymaster.

C12 TRANSVAAL & ZULU WAR

52 H.F. GROS. **The Transvaal Annexation Commission at Ulundi House, Pretoria. May 24 1877.** Following the annexation of Natal in 1843 and the extension of British influence over the Orange Free State, the Transvaal remained the last outpost for the fiercely independent Boers, but it was not until 1864 that the Republic was formally constituted. The small republic's position was precarious however, in the face of British ambitions for South African federation and the influx of outsiders eager to exploit the mineral wealth of the Transvaal, and in late 1876 Theophilus Shepstone was appointed Special Commissioner to the Transvaal with orders to carry out the annexation. This was formally announced on April 12 1877 and on May 24, the Queen's Birthday, the young Rider Haggard (lying on the ground at front of group) and Colonel Brooke hoisted the Union Jack in the Pretoria Market Square.

53 H.F. GROS. **The Pretoria Rifles, Convent Redoubt Garrison, Pretoria. 1881.** The ignominious rout of British forces at Bronkhorst Spruit on December 20 1880 signalled the outbreak of the First Boer War, and Pretoria found itself blockaded in enemy territory. The Pretoria Rifles were one of a number of volunteer units raised during the siege and disbanded at the cessation of hostilities on March 28 1881. Keyed in the background of the photograph are Fort Commeline, a fortified look-out post on the hills south of the town, and the military camp, which also housed the civil population during the siege.

☐54 H.F. GROS. **Editorial offices of 'News of the Camp,' Pretoria. 1880-81.** As the patriotic fervour of the inhabitants of Pretoria gave way to the despondency of inaction, some relief was to be found in the pages of *News of the Camp,* a 'journal of fancies, notifications, gossip and general chit chat,' founded and edited by Charles du Val (1854-1889), a touring showman who had arrived in Pretoria on November 18 1880. The plant and type used belonged to the *Transvaal Argus,* and the paper forms a lively commentary on the life of the beleaguered garrison as well as a valuable, if partisan, record of military actions in the area. After the ending of hostilities du Val compiled a limited edition of the complete file of the newspaper (40 issues from December 25 1880 – April 9 1881) illustrated with tipped-in photographs selected by the purchaser.

☐55 Prob. J.R. MEE. **Commissariat stores, Lower Tugela, Natal. 1879.** The rise of Zulu power and its expansionist nature under a line of warrior kings from Shaka to Cetshwayo was bound to come into conflict ultimately with the growing European presence in South Africa. The arrival of Sir Bartle Frere as Governor of the Cape in 1877, with instructions to pursue the cause of South African federation, made a confrontation inevitable. The repudiation of demands clearly aimed at the destruction of Zulu autonomy formed the pretext for war and three invasion columns moved across the Natal border into Zululand in the new year of 1879. The forces stationed at Fort Pearson on the Lower Tugela formed the eastern wing of the advance, and crossed the river into Zululand on January 12 1879.

56 JAMES LLOYD. **The battlefield at Isandhlwana, Zululand. May 21 1879.** The disastrous defeat of the central column of the Zululand force under Colonel Richard Glyn on January 22 1879 stopped the invasion in its tracks, only a few fugitives managing to escape the massacre at Isandhlwana. Beyond the abandoned wagons of the original force, men under Colonel Drury-Lowe search the battlefield in order to bury the English dead. This took place during Chelmsford's second invasion of Zululand in May: on July 4 his force invaded Cetshwayo's stronghold at Ulundi and in a battle which lasted 30 minutes, lost 10 of his men to well over 1000 Zulus.

Previous left hand page:
Above: **Steam engine for the Ashanti Expedition. 1873.** (C11/47)
Below: **The British Commissioner at Kumasi. February 1884.** (C11/48)

Previous right hand page:
Above: **The restoration of the Ashanti Confederacy. 1935.** (C11/49)
Below: **Annexation of Ado to Lagos Colony. 1891.** (C11/50)

Above: **Editorial offices of 'News of the Camp,' Pretoria. 1880-1.** (C12/54)
Below: **Commissariat store, Lower Tugela, Natal. 1879.** (C12/55)

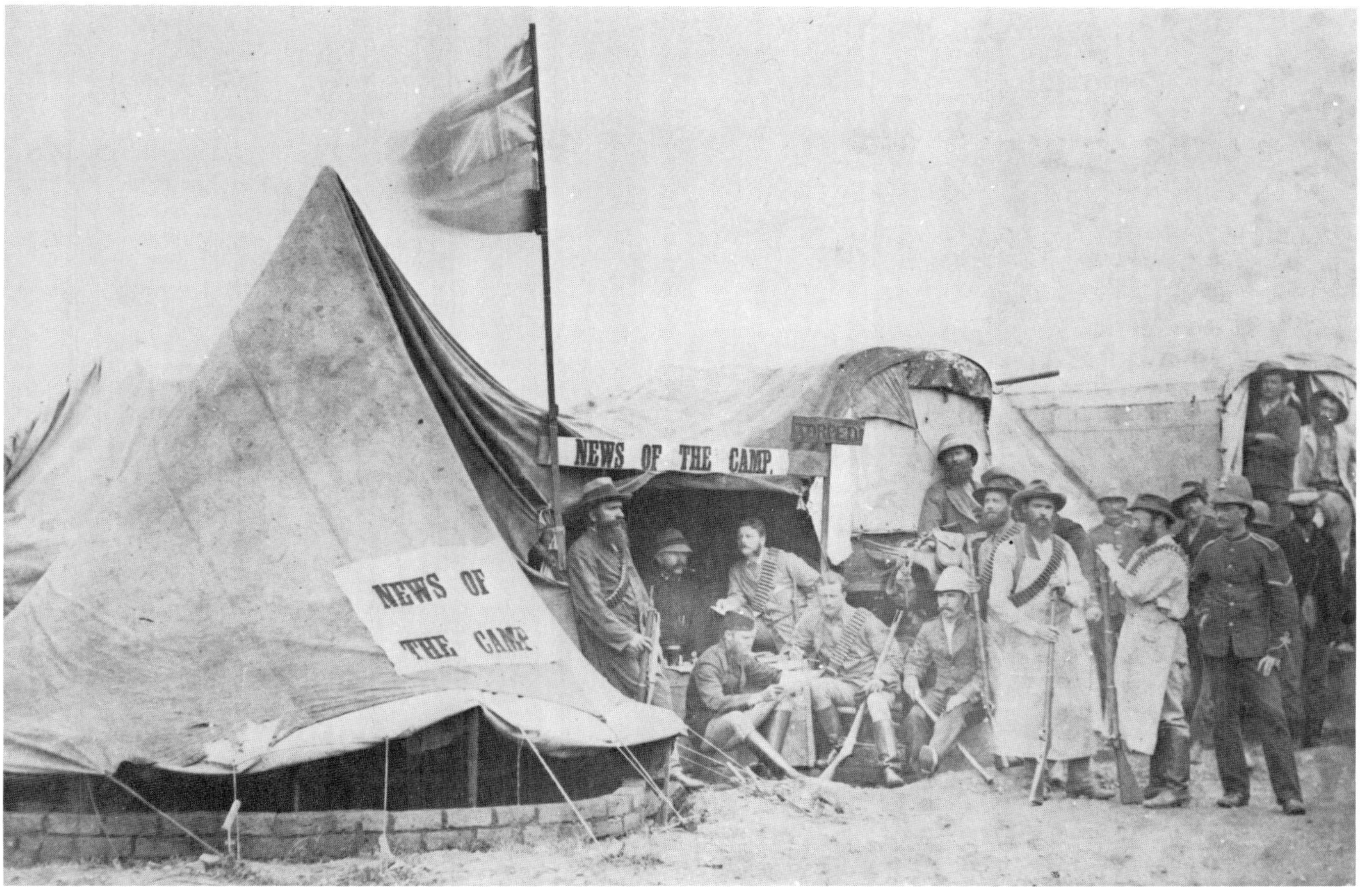
NEWS OF THE CAMP.
NEWS OF
THE CAMP

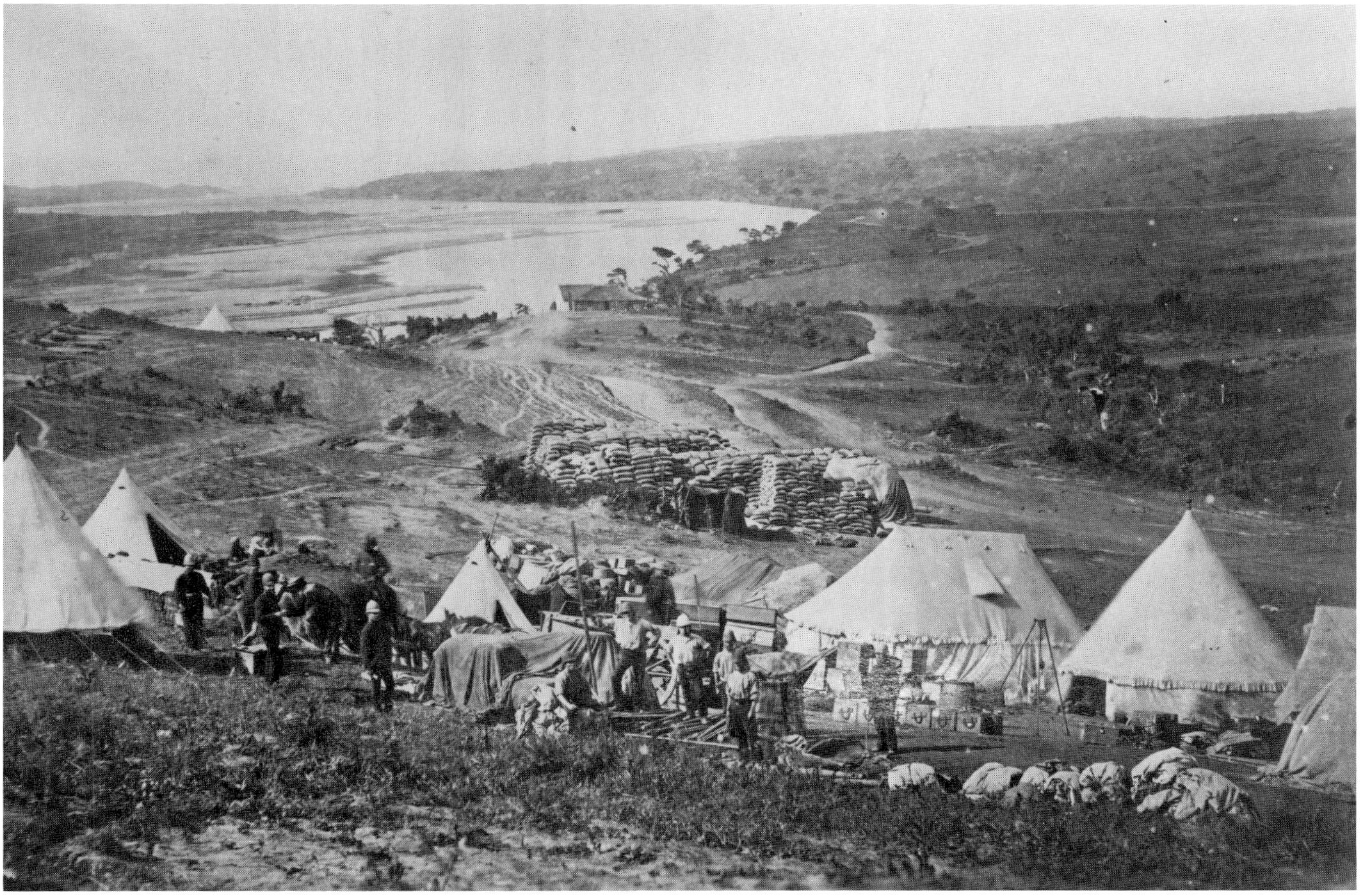

C13 NEW ZEALAND, NEW GUINEA, SAMOA, BURMA

57 D.L. MUNDY. **Captain Gilbert Mair with Arawa soldiers at Kaiteriria, Te Kooti Campaign. February 1870.** The signing of the Treaty of Waitangi in 1840 had guaranteed the Maoris possession of their lands and equality before the law, but the European colonists' hunger for new lands exacerbated tensions which first broke out into a war in February 1860 which was to last until 1872. Te Kooti was a renowned Maori warrior and from 1868-70 pursued a guerilla campaign against European settlers and settlements. After his defeat by Captain Mair (standing beside the spades at the left of the photograph) near the Arawa settlements at Rotorua, Te Kooti retreated to the King Country where he was given refuge by Ngatimaniapoto. The flag in the background was captured from Te Kooti at Te Pourere, his last fortified stronghold. This photograph of Mair's Arawa flying column was taken at Kaiteriria (green Lake), Rotorua.

□58 PHOTOGRAPHER UNKNOWN. **Proclamation of the British Protectorate over south-east New Guinea at Port Moresby. November 6 1884.** In April 1883 fears over increasing German influence in the South Pacific had led to the proclamation of a protectorate over parts of New Guinea by Henry M. Chester on behalf of the Queensland government. This action was repudiated by the British government, but the Australian outcry eventually forced it to take action and on November 6 1884 Commodore James Erskine proclaimed a British Protectorate from the verandah of the L.M.S. mission house of Revd. Lawes. The ceremony was then repeated at various locations within the British territory over the next month. Two unnamed photographers were brought up from Sydney to record the event, which was officially described as being suitably awe-inspiring. Hugh Hastings Romilly however, who had mistakenly hoisted the Union flag some days earlier, offers in his letters a more convincing description of the ceremonies of Empire: '(The marines) fired repeated *feux de joie* and made us stand bare-headed in a frightful sun. I don't think I was ever so hot in my life, and we were very glad when it was over. The natives, who were beginning to get accustomed to seeing the flag hoisted, were apathetic, and only a few stragglers turned up. The distribution of knives and tobacco on the previous day amused them far more'. (Letter of November 11 1884).

59 A.J. TATTERSALL. **Consuls of the three powers in Samoa. c1893.** In 1893 the English, American and German consuls in Samoa became joint advisors to the king in an attempt to protect their own interests and to stabilise the complicated and often chaotic framework of the Samoan political scene. This portrait of (Sir) Thomas Cusack-Smith (1859-1929), William Churchill (1859-1920) and Herr Basci was taken during this period. The Berlin Conference of 1889 had agreed to preserve Samoan autonomy under international supervision, but the uneasy co-existence of the various foreign interests, each seeking to promote their own contender to the throne, sparked off a series of revolts which led to the civil war of 1899.

Above: **Proclamation of the British Protectorate over south-east New Guinea at Port Moresby. November 6 1884.** (C13/58)
Below: **Assault on the Kyaing-Kwintaung Stockade by the 2nd Battalion, Devonshire Regiment, Wuntho Sawbwa Campaign, Burma. February 22 1891.** (C13/62)

60 PHOTOGRAPHER(S) UNKNOWN. **Three Kings of Samoa. 1890s.** During the period leading up to the civil war three Samoan rulers acted variously as allies of, or in opposition to the international powers. Malietoa Laupepa first came to the Samoan throne in 1858 and after being deposed and reinstated several times, was reigning at the time of his death in 1898. Matafa'a, his most powerful rival, returned from exile the following year and after the partition of Samoa in 1900 became Paramount Chief (the Kaiser retaining the title of Paramount King). Matafa'a died in 1912. Malietoa Tanumafili, the son of Malietoa Laupepa, was the young English candidate for the Samoan kingship. His reign was brief, however: crowned on March 23 1899 (and here seen in his coronation uniform), he left Samoa when Matafa'a came to power to continue his education in Fiji.

61 BURTON BROTHERS. **American gatling gun at Point Mulinu'u during the Samoan Civil War. 1899.** Point Mulinu'u was the scene of an attempted occupation by Matafa'an forces on March 14 1899 after Rear Admiral Kautz of the U.S.S. *Philadelphia* had peremptorily dissolved the provisional government. The action signalled the start of renewed hostilities: the attack on the Tivoli Hotel, the bombardment of Matafa'an villages and the battle outside Apia on April 1. By mid May hostilities had largely ceased after a commission had been sent to resolve the situation. The subsequent partition acknowledged Germany's commercial pre-eminence, gave the Americans one of the finest harbours in the Pacific in Pago Pago, and gave Britain concessions in other areas in return for any losses sustained in Samoa.

□62 (?) FELIX BEATO. **Assault on the Kyaing-Kwintaung Stockade by the 2nd Battalion, Devonshire Regiment, Wuntho Sawbwa Campaign, Burma. February 22 1891.** British concern for the security of India's eastern borders and, later, suspicion of growing French influence westwards from Indo-China had led to a series of wars against Burma which consolidated British control of Lower Burma and culminated in the annexation of the whole country. For several years after the campaign of 1885-86 however, areas of resistance – notably in the Shan States – remained: the Wuntho Sawbwa, Nga Aung Myat, whose territory lay in the hilly country between the Katha district and the Chindwin River, had never acknowledged British authority and persistently refused to allow British troops to cross his lands. Open rebellion broke out in February 1891 and on the 16th Kawlin was attacked. On the 22nd, 400 men under Captain Davies of the Devonshire Regiment took the heavily fortified stockade at Kyaing-Kwintaung and an action at Okkan on the same day stamped out the rebellion in the south of the territory.

63 (?) FELIX BEATO. **Wuntho Sawbwa's troops surrendering arms to the British at Wuntho. March 1891.** While the military engagements at Kyaing-Kwintaung and Okkan were taking place a military expedition under the command of Brigadier General George Wolseley was meanwhile being organised at Mandalay. The three columns were involved in some minor engagements and by March 9 the financial commissioner was able to report that the state of Wuntho had been annexed and was being brought under direct administration. With the occupation of Wuntho a general amnesty was declared to those of the Wuntho Sawbwa's followers who came in and surrendered their arms. The deposed Sawbwa remained free however, and despite a reward of Rs. 5000 offered for his capture, escaped to China where he stayed for a year before returning to the Sadon area to again organise resistance against the British.

Settlement, trade & transport

The public announcement of the invention of photography coincided with landmarks of military conquest and colonial settlement which heralded an era of unparalleled imperial expansion and consolidation which photography was uniquely fitted to document: in 1839 East India Company forces entered Kabul in the later stages of the First Afghan War and the same year saw the start of a series of opium wars with China as Britain sought to protect her market for Bengal-grown opium; Tasmania was being explored and there was a land boom in Melbourne. At the Treaty of Waitangi the following year Maori chieftains signed over the sovereignty of parts of New Zealand to Queen Victoria and in Ceylon the construction of the first metalled roads was commenced. As photography spread overseas from Europe these were the sort of events which the photographer would attempt to record, whether as contributions to knowledge, visual propaganda or simply from pride in the architecture and engineering constructions of newly opened lands.

In the young cities of Australia, Canada and New Zealand there was in the early days rarely either a large enough or sufficiently wealthy population to ensure a photographer's livelihood in one location and many of the pioneer photographers earned their living touring from town to town, staying only as long as they were in demand and then moving on to another untapped settlement. For John Thomson in Penang in the 1860s such a life formed 'a congenial, profitable, and instructive occupation', with his photographs 'of characteristic scenes and types . . . in constant demand among the resident European population', but for the majority photography was often an unremunerative profession, although to many craftsmen and traders it appeared as an opportunity to break into a new market while maintaining their former businesses. Several early photographers took up the craft from professions in a related area of expertise, Adolphe Duperly in Jamaica, for example, used the daguerreotype and combined it with his trade as a printer, publishing around 1844 his *Daguerian excursions* containing 24 lithographs from his own photographs. In India Frederick Fiebig followed a similar path, having been a lithographer before becoming a photographer, while in Tasmania Thomas Browne advertised his three lines of business – photography, lithography and stationery – in the *Hobart Town General Directory* for 1847. The skills of the cabinet maker were also useful in the construction of cameras and there are several instances of practitioners of this craft taking up photography, while G.L. Pairaudeau offers perhaps the most eccentric but entirely logical range of skills to his customers in *The British Guiana Directory and Almanac* for 1876, advertising his watchmaking establishment, photographic gallery and dental surgery from a single premises in Main Street, Georgetown.

As photographers set up permanent establishments in the economically expanding settlements a staple photographic subject was the recording of the trade, agriculture and communications of the various colonies – subjects which would find a steady sale among settlers for transmission to Europe as a more telling impression of their lives and environment than verbal description could supply. Skeen and Co. in Ceylon produced particularly interesting sets of such views, advertising as early as 1864 'Wilshaw and Skeen's series illustrative of coffee culture in Ceylon, from the felling of the forest to the shipment of the berry.' Skeen and Co. made this branch of documentation a speciality; with the collapse of the coffee industry from 1869 onwards and the subsequent growth of tea cultivation, they brought the same technique to bear, producing in the 1880s a series of 30 photographs illustrating all aspects of the new industry. The firm's particular forte is evident in these prints in the unpretentious use of the camera to demonstrate with great clarity the various stages of production, with each figure in the photograph meticulously arranged in the attitude most revealing and characteristic of his job. The same clear documentation was also applied to the cinnamon, cocoa, rubber, cardamom and plumbago industries.

Much of the work of photographers like Skeen and Co. reached its largest audience at the international exhibitions where, since the Great Exhibition of 1851, photography had held an honourable place, and pictures such as these were used to illustrate both the commercial growth and potential of the colonies. Herbert Deveril had been specially commissioned by the New Zealand Government to take photographs showing the development of the colony for the Philadelphia Exhibition of 1876, and Robert Harris emphasised the mineral resources of South Africa when he published his *South Africa illustrated in a series of one hundred and four permanent photographs* (1888), concentrating on mining scenes and remarking that 'he feels he places in the hands of subscribers a book not only of very general interest, but one which may be found of considerable value to those interested in the future welfare of South Africa.'

The documentation of the development of commercial and agricultural resources was also continued in the recording of great engineering projects, particularly railways, which to the Victorian mind stood at the helm of the onward march of civilisation (when the British North Borneo Company opened the first stretch of railway in its territories in 1898 the tiny locomotive was named, almost inevitably, 'Progress'). William D. Young, who had previously been a railway photographer in India, was employed by the Uganda Railway as official photographer (although on a freelance basis) and produced a vast number of pictures of the construction of the line, many of them purely technical but enough being of sufficient pictorial quality to sell commercially, advertised as 'camera pictures from Mombasa to Victoria Nyanza.' But perhaps the most interesting indication of the way in which photography was most explicitly used as evidence of colonial progress again comes from the firm of Skeen and Co., who recorded the building of the Ceylon railway from its beginnings until the end of the century. In 1867 the *Colombo Observer* published *An account of a trip from Colombo to Peradenia and back . . . on April 5th 1867,* which interspersed its description of the journey with comments on Skeen's photographs of the line, and whose highest praise was reserved for those pictures which most successfully recorded the difficulties of construction and underlined the moral that 'nothing is impossible to science and skill, when combined with industry and perseverance.'

D1 N.J. CAIRE. **A Gippsland selector. c1875.**

D2 MINING FOR GOLD & DIAMONDS

1 BEAUFROY MERLIN. **Mining claim, Hill End, New South Wales. 1872.** Gold was discovered at Hill End and Tambaroora in 1851 and for several years the two fields were among the richest gold producers in Australia. After the exhaustion of the alluvial gold, reef mining was resorted to and it was at Hill End in 1872 that the largest nugget of reef gold ever found up to that time was discovered in the mine of Louis Beyers and Bernard Holtermann. The Governor of New South Wales, Sir Hercules Robinson, who visited the town in 1873, remarked on the civilized appearance of a settlement with stores, churches, banks and a newspaper in place of the rough outpost he had anticipated.

2 NICHOLAS CAIRE. **View of Old Chum Hill, Bendigo. c1875.** Gold had first been found on a section of the Ravenswood Sheep Run in October 1851 and the influx of prospectors was such that by the time of the first census three years later the growing town could boast seven schools, three flourishing hotels and a regular Cobb & Co. stagecoach service to Melbourne. In August 1854 land allotments were auctioned and a survey laid out a regular street plan. By 1875 the shallow alluvial gold deposits were largely exhausted but quartz reef mining was now extracting huge quantities of gold. George Lansell (1823-1906), whose residence can be seen in the centre of the photograph, had come to Bendigo with his brothers in 1854 and after several years of unsuccessful investment in mining, made his fortune in the early 1870s with deep quartz reef mining. Known as 'Australia's Quartz King', he was largely responsible for the introduction of the diamond drill to Australia and in his heyday was the director of 38 mines.

3 PHOTOGRAPHER UNKNOWN. **The Revd. Alexander Don and Chinese gold miners, Tuapeka gold field, Central Otago. c1882.** The first important discoveries of gold in New Zealand were made west of Dunedin in 1861 and these were followed by finds in Otago and on the west coast. By 1874 there were some 5000 Chinese in New Zealand, most of them from South China, although some had moved on from Australian fields. The Revd. Alexander Don (1857-1934) came to New Zealand from Australia as a Presbyterian missionary in 1879. A period spent in China was followed by missionary work among the Chinese miners in New Zealand and in 18 annual tours of the gold fields he walked an estimated 16000 miles. His recollections, *Memoirs of the Golden Road,* were published in 1931. A scriptural text translated into Chinese hangs in front of the door of the miners' hut alongside devotional pictures.

□ 4 FREDERICK DALLY. **The Mucho Oro Claim, Stout's Gulch, Cariboo, British Columbia. 1867-70.** As takings declined for the thousands of prospectors who had flocked to the Fraser River in 1858, bands of diggers followed the river north to Cariboo in the search for a mother lode and by 1860 Quesnel was taking on the shape of a frontier town rather than a transient camp. Quesnel was swiftly eclipsed the following year by strikes east of the Fraser at William's Creek, near which the trio of gold towns of Barkerville, Richfield and Camerontown were soon to spring up. The lode at Stout's Gulch was discovered in 1861 by Edward Stout, who had been with William Dietz when gold was first found at William's Creek.

5 FREDERICK DALLY. **Barkerville, British Columbia. c1867.** The most famous of the three gold towns (with Richfield and Camerontown) which grew up around William's Creek, Barkerville was named after William Barker who, moving on from the claims at Stout's Gulch, found gold in August 1862 on land that was later to become the site of the town. Shortly after this photograph was taken Barkerville was almost completely destroyed by a fire in September 1868. The town has since been restored and is now preserved as an historical monument.

□ 6 JULIO SIZA. **Goldmining camp at Chinese Creek, British Guiana. 1880s.** Various unsuccessful attempts had been made to find gold in British Guiana since 1720, but it was not until 1865 that gold-bearing quartz was discovered at Wariri on the Cuyuni River. This project was abandoned because the location was in territory disputed by Venezuela and it was not until the 1880s that the gold industry became established. The first set of mining regulations was issued by the government in 1886, but the alluvial deposits were less rich than had originally been hoped and after an initial upsurge, production had begun to tail off by the turn of the century.

□ 7 PHOTOGRAPHER UNKNOWN. **The Kimberley diggings. c1872.** After the discovery of a diamond on De Beer's farm in July 1871, a wave of diggers moved from the alluvial sites in the Orange and Vaal River valleys to 'New Rush' (soon to be known as Colesberg Kopje). The photograph shows the mining plots in the very early days before the individual claims were bought out by Rhodes and Rudd and the Big Hole came into being. Before operations ceased in the Big Hole in 1914 an estimated 14½ million carats of diamonds had been recovered from the 25 million tons of blue ground excavated from the site.

□ 8 H.F. GROS. **Ferry on the Vaal River near the diamond mines. c1874.** A photograph possibly taken near the town of Christiana which had been laid out in 1870. The first diamonds to be found in the Transvaal proper were discovered in 1872 while a well was being dug on a farm near Potchefstroom; these were of small value but more were found on the banks of the Vaal at Christiana in the same year and many prospectors moved in from the diggings lower down river.

9 J.E. MIDDLEBROOK. **Sorting the gravel for diamonds, Kimberley. 1891.** The photograph is from an album compiled by Middlebrook in the hope that it would 'strikingly illustrate the importance and extent of the most valuable of Cape Colonial Industries', as well as being 'an interesting South African souvenir'. The photograph is accompanied by the following letterpress description: 'The Sorting Process is one of exceeding delicacy, requiring great practice and dexterity in the detection of a worthless fragment of illusive mica as compared with a genuine bit of 'rough goods'. The picture clearly enough shows how the gravel is spread out on the tables and in what manner the Sorters separate the valueless deposit from the gems so rich and rare'.

MUCHO ORO.

D3 & D4 SETTLERS

□ 10 NICHOLAS CAIRE. **View on the River Murray near Echuca, showing the railway wharf with steamers unloading. c1875.** No. 7 of Caire's *Views of Victoria (General series)* published by the Anglo-Australasian Photographic Company, Melbourne, the print was issued with the following letterpress description: 'The rapidly increasing traffic on the River Murray, with wool, timber, and other colonial produce, has called into requisition no less than 400 steamers and over 1000 barges. To meet this growing emergency the Victorian Government has expended several thousand pounds in the erection of a Railway Wharf which during the wool-season presents a very busy scene, the crowded steamers laden with the precious clip taxing to the utmost the powers of the Railway Department in the process of unloading. The River here is about a quarter of a mile wide, and is from 60 to 70 feet deep'.

11 (?) J.W. LINDT. **Lyrup Pumping Station, Murray River Settlements. c1892.** The Chaffey Brothers (who had pioneered the California irrigation system) and Alfred Deakin came to an agreement with the Victorian government to set up irrigation settlements on the Murray in 1886 and in the following year the South Australian government also supported the scheme, supplying 250,000 acres of land and founding the first settlement at Renmark. By the turn of the century nearly all the settlements were in financial trouble and in 1908 were reorganized under government supervision. Lyrup, with 700 acres given over to horticulture, was the only settlement to survive this crisis.

12 BEAUFROY MERLIN. **W.T. Lewis, undertaker, Gulgong, New South Wales. 1872.** Lewis stands at the door of his carpentry and cabinet making business in Herbert Street, Gulgong. Discoveries of gold had been made in the early 1860s in Gulgong (145 miles north west of Sydney), but although the goldfield had been declared in 1868 it was not until April 1870 that the first payable find was announced. For the next five years it was the most productive field in the colony, producing almost 13¼ tons of gold and attracting a population of several thousands. In the peak year of 1872 finds of 134,455 oz. were declared.

13 SAMUEL CLIFFORD. **Bush settlement, Tasmania. c1865.** This newly founded settlement among thick forest was situated near the Huon Road about five miles from Hobart.

□ 14 C.H. MOORE. **The Mount Perry Hotel, Heusmann Street, Mount Perry, Queensland. c1872.** Copper was discovered in 1869 in an area originally given over to scattered sheep runs and by the turn of the century Mount Perry had a population of around 4000, making it one of the ten or twelve largest towns in the state. After the First World War, when the Queensland Copper Company shut down operations, the town declined. The Mount Perry Hotel was erected in early 1871 by Tim Maher, who held the licence until the beginning of the following year.

15 D.L. MUNDY. **Hunt's Claim or Shotover, Thames Gold Fields, New Zealand. c1870.** The Shotover Reef, discovered by William Hunt in August 1867, was the first important reef to be found in the Thames area south east of Auckland: in 1871 the reef produced nearly £2,000,000 worth of gold.

□ 16 D.L. MUNDY. **Flax rope making at Hokianga, North Auckland Peninsula. c1870.** This early photograph of a flax mill shows workers winding and spinning flax into lengths of rope while in the background the stripped flax dries on lines. The last few feet of a water race can be seen at roof level beside the mill. From the 1820s until the Second World War flax was an important New Zealand export.

□ 17 D.L. MUNDY. **Whitianga, Mercury Bay, New Zealand. c1870.** The view from the jetty shows the Whitiangi Hotel and the Whitiangi Music Hall situated on the waterfront. It was east of Whitianga, at Cook's Beach in Mercury Bay that Captain Cook observed the transit of Mercury and on November 15 1769 raised the British flag. The area was later settled by traders in kauri wood and gum.

18 JAMES BRAGGE. **Eketahuna, northern Wairarapa, New Zealand. 1878.** Founded in 1872, Eketahuna was originally named Mellenskov by the Scandinavian immigrants who established the settlement and subsisted on contract bush felling. Farming districts developed with the clearing of the surrounding forest, but it was not until 1889 that the railway from Wellington reached the town.

□ 19 FREDERICK DALLY. **Ox team at Clinton with goods for the Cariboo mines, British Columbia. c1867.** 135 miles north of Yale, Clinton was the meeting point of the two routes to the gold fields, the Cariboo Road and the track from Lillooet. The Clinton Hotel, built in 1861, was the oldest surviving hotel on the British Columbia mainland until destroyed by fire in 1958.

20 FREDERICK DALLY. **The Great Bluff on the Thompson River Waggon Road, British Columbia. c1867.** The most enduring memorial to British Columbia's first Governor, Sir James Douglas (1803-1877), is the 400 mile Cariboo Road which he envisioned and saw through to construction. Following the course of the Fraser and Thompson Rivers the waggon road, clinging precariously to the cliffs along the water's edge, stretched north from Yale up to Quesnel and the Cariboo mines. Built between 1862 and 1864, part of the construction was undertaken by the Royal Engineers stationed in the colony, although the larger part was built by private contractors. By 1865, the year after Douglas relinquished the governorship, a further section had been added, taking the road to Barkerville and Richfield at the heart of the mining district.

21 ROYAL ENGINEERS PHOTOGRAPHER. **Trader McPherson and family, North West Angle, Lake of the Woods, Ontario. 1872.**

Previous left hand page:
Above: **The Mucho Oro Claim, Stout's Gulch, Cariboo, British Columbia. 1867-70.** (D2/4)
Below: **Goldmining camp at Chinese Creek, British Guiana. 1880s.** (D2/6)

Previous right hand page:
Above: **The Kimberley diggings. c1872.** (D2/7)
Below: **Ferry on the Vaal River near the diamond mines. c1874.** (D2/8)

Above: **View on the River Murray near Echuca, showing the railway wharf with steamers unloading. c1875.** (D3/10)
Below: **The Mount Perry Hotel, Heusmann Street, Mount Perry, Queensland. c1872.** (D3/14)

D5 COMMUNICATIONS

22 ZANGAKI. **Entrance to the Suez Canal at Port Said. 1880s.** The idea of connecting Europe and Asia by a navigable waterway was not new, indeed the Pharoahs had succeeded in joining the Nile and the Red Sea by means of a canal. At the turn of the 19th century, with the growth of seaborne trade from the east tied to British mastery of the sea routes round the Cape, the idea of a canal once again became attractive to the European powers, especially the French; but it was not until 1854 that Ferdinand de Lesseps received the Viceroy's permission to form an international company to realise the project. Construction was started in April 1859 on the site of what would later become Port Said, and by 1862 the canal had been cut as far as Lake Timsah. By the summer of 1869 the 100 mile canal was completed and on November 17 the first flotilla of vessels successfully negotiated the waterway. The British, who had resolutely attempted to obstruct the construction of the canal at every opportunity, fully realised both its commercial and strategic importance and in a secret deal in 1875 Disraeli purchased the Khedive's shares in the Suez Canal Company for £4,000,000, thus placing France and Britain in joint ownership and paving the way for the Anglo-French condominium which was to control Egypt's financial and political affairs in later years.

23 ZANGAKI. **Troopships on the Suez Canal. 1880s.**

24 H.T. DEVINE. **Arrival of the first train from Montreal to Vancouver. May 23 1887.** From its first conception in the 1860s the difficulties attendant on building an ocean to ocean railway across Canada centred as much on economic and political factors as on the formidable physical barriers to be overcome. Even though one of British Columbia's conditions for joining a united Canada in 1871 was that construction would start on the line within two years, it was to be ten years before the Canadian Pacific Railway was incorporated and 14 before Alexander Smith drove in the last spike in Eagle Pass on November 7 1885. On July 4 1886 the first Canadian Pacific transcontinental train arrived at Port Moody after a journey from Montreal of 5¾ days. Although the official terminus of the line, Port Moody was to be superseded by Vancouver, where the first train arrived on May 23 1887, the year after its incorporation as a city.

25 PHOTOGRAPHER UNKNOWN. **Discharging mails at Salisbury, Southern Rhodesia. 1901.** This photograph shows the Bulawayo-Salisbury mail coach at the end of one of its last journeys: the connection of Salisbury to Bulawayo and the Cape in 1902 spelled the end of the old coaching days in Rhodesia.

26 NICHOLAS & CO. **Massulah boats at Madras. 1880s.** William Hickey, arriving in India in 1769, found the prospect of landing at Madras in a massulah boat, 'notwithstanding... the surf was very moderate that morning... the most terrific thing I had ever beheld'. Until harbour improvements were made in the 1880s these boats were the one method of landing passengers and their construction remained unchanged from Hickey's description: 'The boats are formed of broad planks, literally sewed together with twisted fibres of bark from the coconut tree, the bottom flat, the sides straight up to a certain height, and then inclining inwards to the upper edge...To prevent newcomers, especially women, from seeing the quantity of water constantly pouring in by the seams at her bottom, a weed, something like heath furze, is laid there more than a foot deep'. The massulah boats were accompanied through the surf by men in catamarans who attempted rescue in case of accidents.

27 PHOTOGRAPHER UNKNOWN. **Overland Telegraph workers and officers at Leichhardt Bar, Roper River, Northern Territory. August 1872.** In 1863, after his epic journey across the Australian continent, John McDouall Stuart had recommended his route as a potential one for an overland telegraph. In 1870 the Anglo-Australian Telegraph Company agreed, in the face of strong rivalry from Queensland, that the submarine cable from Java should make landfall at Port Darwin in the Northern Territory newly acquired by South Australia, but stipulated that the line must be ready for connection by the beginning of 1872. The Herculean task of building a line across 2000 miles of unsurveyed and largely unknown land did not quite meet this deadline, but in August the line was complete and on October 21 1872 the first direct message was transmitted between England and Australia.

28 PHOTOGRAPHER UNKNOWN. **Officers of the Overland Telegraph at Roper River, Northern Territory. August 1872.** Second from the right in this group is (Sir) Charles Todd (1826-1910), who more than any other individual was responsible for the success of the Overland Telegraph construction. Arriving in Australia in 1855 after an early career as an astronomer and telegraph engineer at Greenwich Observatory, Todd completed several smaller telegraph schemes in South Australia before planning and organizing the great overland route. Seen with Todd here are J.A.G. Little (Darwin's first postmaster), R.C. Patterson (Engineer in Charge of construction) and A.J. Mitchell (Chief Surveyor), who by March 1869 had found a route from Port Darwin to the Upper Adelaide River.

D6 FAR EAST

29 PHOTOGRAPHER UNKNOWN. **Tobacco estate manager's house. Borneo, 1880s.** The introduction of tobacco into Borneo received little initial support from the British North Borneo Company, but a sample bale sent to London in 1884 proved to be of very high quality and the following years saw the arrival of a rush of planters eager to exploit the untapped land. By 1890 61 estates growing tobacco were listed and *The Licensed Victuallers' Referee* of January 1899 was able to wax lyrical on future potential: 'Ten years ago Borneo was a mass of dense jungle; today Borneo stands in the front of the tobacco producing countries... In 1887 the tobacco crop of Borneo realised £400 sterling; in 1897 the crop realised over £165,000. This year it is vastly more... Borneo's inherent natural advantages should enable it in a very brief space of time to out-distance all its rivals'. This prediction proved over-confident, and after 1902 revenue started to decrease to the extent that by 1910 only 12 estates remained, and in 1929 production ceased altogether for a period.

30 PHOTOGRAPHER UNKNOWN. **Tobacco estate workers, British North Borneo. 1890s.** Chinese labourers sort tobacco in a shed on the Lanckton Estate, Marudu Bay.

Above: **Flax rope making at Hokianga, North Auckland Peninsula. C1870.** (D3/16)
Below: **Mercury Bay, New Zealand. c1870.** (D4/17)

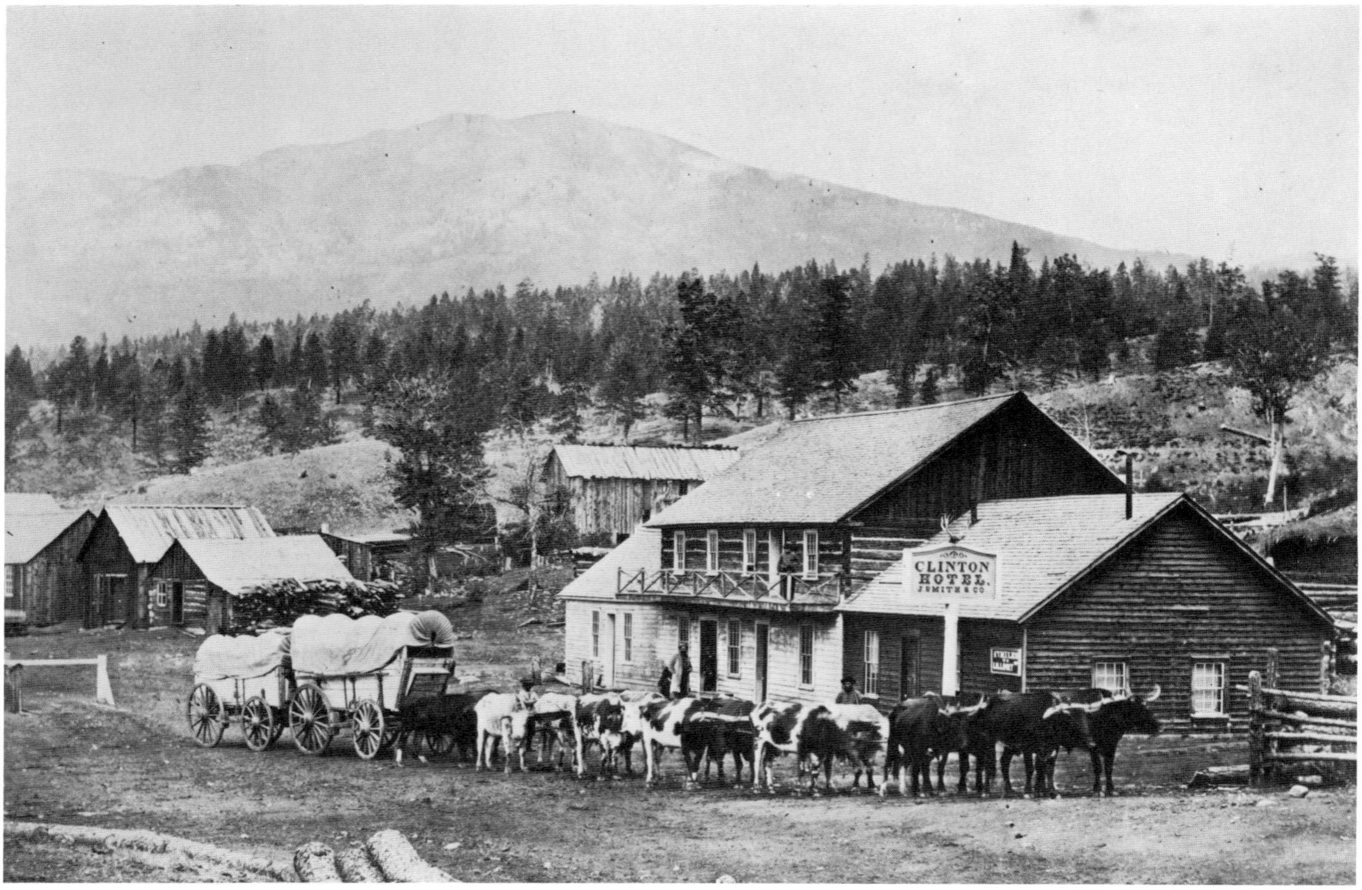
CLINTON
HOTEL.
J. SMITH & CO.

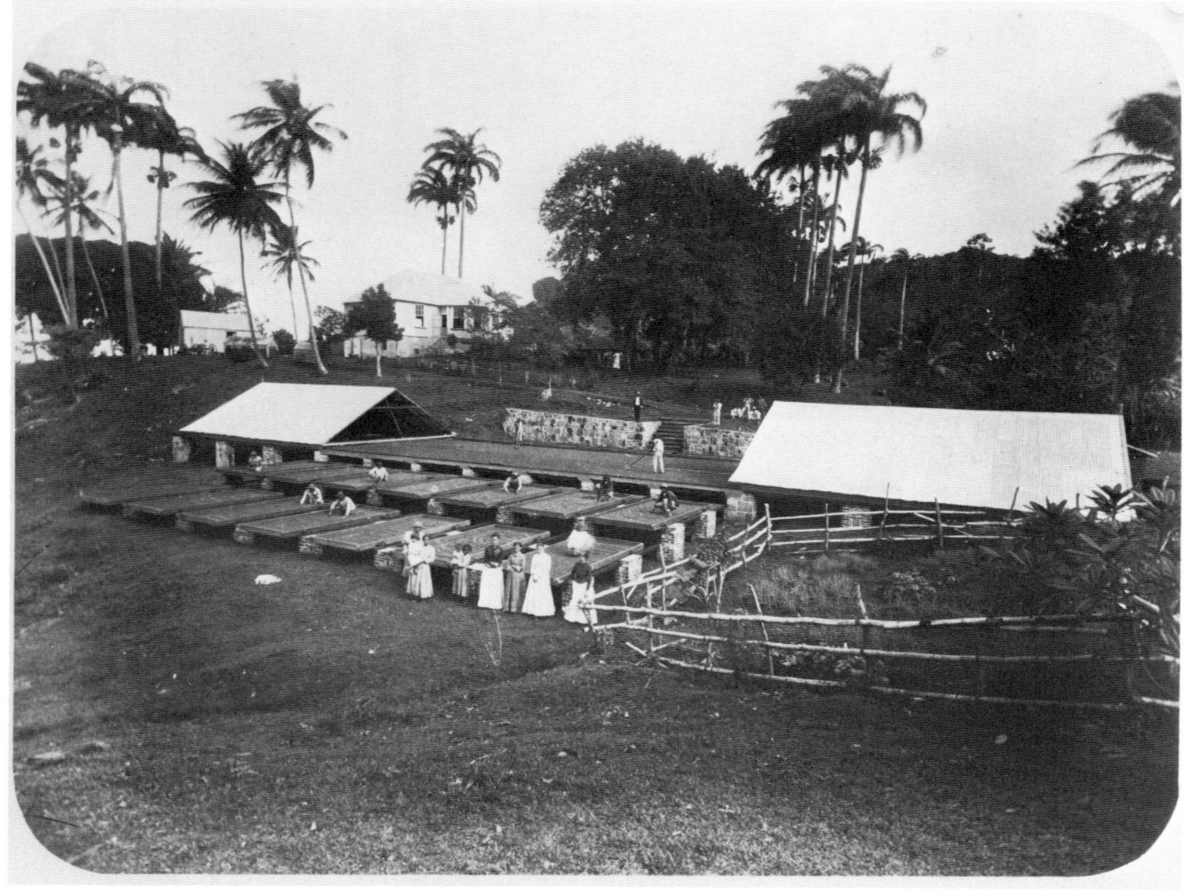

31 PHOTOGRAPHER UNKNOWN. **Kuala Lumpur Railway Workshops. c1888.** The first railway to be completed in Malaya ran from Port Weld to Taiping and was opened for public traffic in June 1885. In the following year the 21 mile line from Klang to Kuala Lumpur was finished and railway workshops built in 1887. The locomotive seen under repair here is the *Lady Clarke*, purchased by the government from the Sultan of Johore. After this bright start, the pace of construction slowed until a central administration came into being with the Federation of 1896. By 1909 the line running the length of the Malayan peninsula from Prai to Johore Bahru was completed.

32 PHOTOGRAPHER UNKNOWN. **Tin mine at Taiping, Perak. 1880s.** Tin had been exported from the Malay peninsula, mainly by the Dutch, for many years, but it was in the mid 19th century that its commercial importance reached a height that directly affected the political development of the states. The industry was almost entirely controlled by the Chinese who imported bands of labourers to work the open cast sites, paying duty to the Malay owners of the land. Not only did this situation lead to hostilities between Malay claimants to the tin duties, but the Chinese were also split into rival factions who fought bloody wars for the control of the industry. The ensuing chaos, together with piracy along the coastal waters, were the major factors leading to the appointment of a British resident in Perak in 1874. By 1883 the peninsula had become the world's largest tin producing centre. In 1896 the first European tin mining companies were floated and the introduction of technology into mining soon brought the industry under European control.

33 PHOTOGRAPHER UNKNOWN, **Tin mine in Larut. 1880s.** A European manager stands beside the Chinese coolie foreman at the edge of the open cast mining area.

D7 CARIBBEAN

□34 PHOTOGRAPHER UNKNOWN. **Drying the golden bean (cocoa), Grenada. c1890.** By far the most important export from Grenada at this period (in 1890 £228,889 worth of cocoa was exported, compared to £15,995 worth of spices, its closest rival), cocoa went through several stages of preparation before shipment. After being harvested by estate workers who knocked the pods off the trees with mitten-shaped 'hands' attached to poles, the beans were sweated in boxes for several days to remove the outer pulp. They were then spread out evenly on the racks illustrated here to dry in the sun before packing.

35 C.F. NORTON. **Wood cutting grant at Sacarara, British Guiana. 1878.** This photograph of William Bracey's wood cutting grant near the Essequebo shows logs squared-up and ready for shipment to Georgetown, with woodcutters' houses in the background. The picture is one of a series of 40 photographs taken by Norton while accompanying Everard Im Thurn on an expedition to the Kaieteur Falls in October-November 1878. The photographs were published in an album, *Scenes from the interior of British Guiana*, and carbon prints were also made of several for inclusion in the Norton Brothers' *Views of Guiana* (c1880).

36 PHOTOGRAPHER UNKNOWN. **Harvesting sugar cane, Vere, Jamaica. c1880.**

Above: **Ox team at Clinton with goods for the Cariboo mines, British Columbia. c1867.** (D4/19)
Below: **Drying the golden bean (cocoa), Grenada. c1890.** (D7/34)

D8 & D9 AUSTRALIA

37 SAMUEL CLIFFORD. **New Wharf from Salamanca Place, Hobart, Tasmania. c1870.** Blessed with the advantages of a sheltered deepwater harbour that allowed shipping to unload in the centre of the city which grew up around it, Hobart was able to develop its harbour facilities from mercantile interests rather than government subsidies.

38 PHOTOGRAPHER UNKNOWN. **Sandridge Pier, Port Melbourne. c1865-70.** Unlike Sydney, Brisbane and Hobart, Melbourne did not possess the advantage of good natural harbour facilities and for many years ships of deep draught had to anchor and unload off-shore. The inadequacy of the shallow and narrow River Yarra as the port for a growing city became acute after 1851 with the huge increase in the use of the port due to the discovery of gold in the colony. Little effective work had been done to remedy the situation when this photograph, showing the Melbourne and Hobson's Bay United Railway Company's pier, was taken, and it was not until Sir John Coode presented his scheme for harbour improvements in 1879 that work was put in hand to lay the foundations of the present-day port.

□39 PHOTOGRAPHER UNKNOWN. **Labour ship at Fiji. c1885.** In 1863 Robert Towns imported the first batch of 'Kanaka' labour from the South Sea Islands to work on his cotton plantation near Brisbane: in later years this was to develop into the notorious trade of the 'blackbirders', the band of seamen and adventurers who recruited, and often kidnapped islanders from the Solomons, the New Hebrides and Fiji to work as indentured labour on the cotton and sugar estates of Queensland. International agitation brought the trade under official scrutiny, but only after areas of Melanesia had become seriously depopulated. In 1901 the Commonwealth Government legislated against blackbirding and laid down that recruitment was to be ended by 1904, and by 1908 the last of the Kanakas had been returned to the islands.

40 J. WATSON & CO. **Raff's sugar plantation, Morayfield, near Caboolture, Queensland. c1873.** Sugar had been introduced into Australia from Tahiti as early as 1817, but was not grown in Queensland until 1862. A period of great expansion followed and in the peak year of 1886 59,000 tons were produced. George Raff (1815-1889) was a politician and mercantile businessman as well as a sugar producer and experimented with a number of crops on his Morayfield plantation. Like the great majority of sugar farmers, Raff employed Kanaka labour, but was commended by Revd. J.D. Lang for his treatment of the men, although this was disputed in some quarters.

41 PHOTOGRAPHER UNKNOWN. **Coffee plantation, Cairns, Queensland. c1910.**

42 PHOTOGRAPHER UNKNOWN. **Panoramic view of the Circular Quay, Sydney. 1870.** The task of reclaiming the tidal flats of the Tank Stream estuary was entrusted in 1840 to George Barney (1792-1862) who had arrived in Sydney on secondment from the Royal Engineers in 1835 and who acted as Colonial Engineer from 1837-44. This massive project was built by convict labour which transported the filling material in lighters from Cockatoo and Pinchbeck Islands. To cater for the rapid expansion of seaborne trade and passenger movement every coastal city had to develop its port facilities as extensively as possible to attract business, and the Quay was rebuilt in the 1870s to cater for the large wool clippers and extended in the 1890s for passenger steamers.

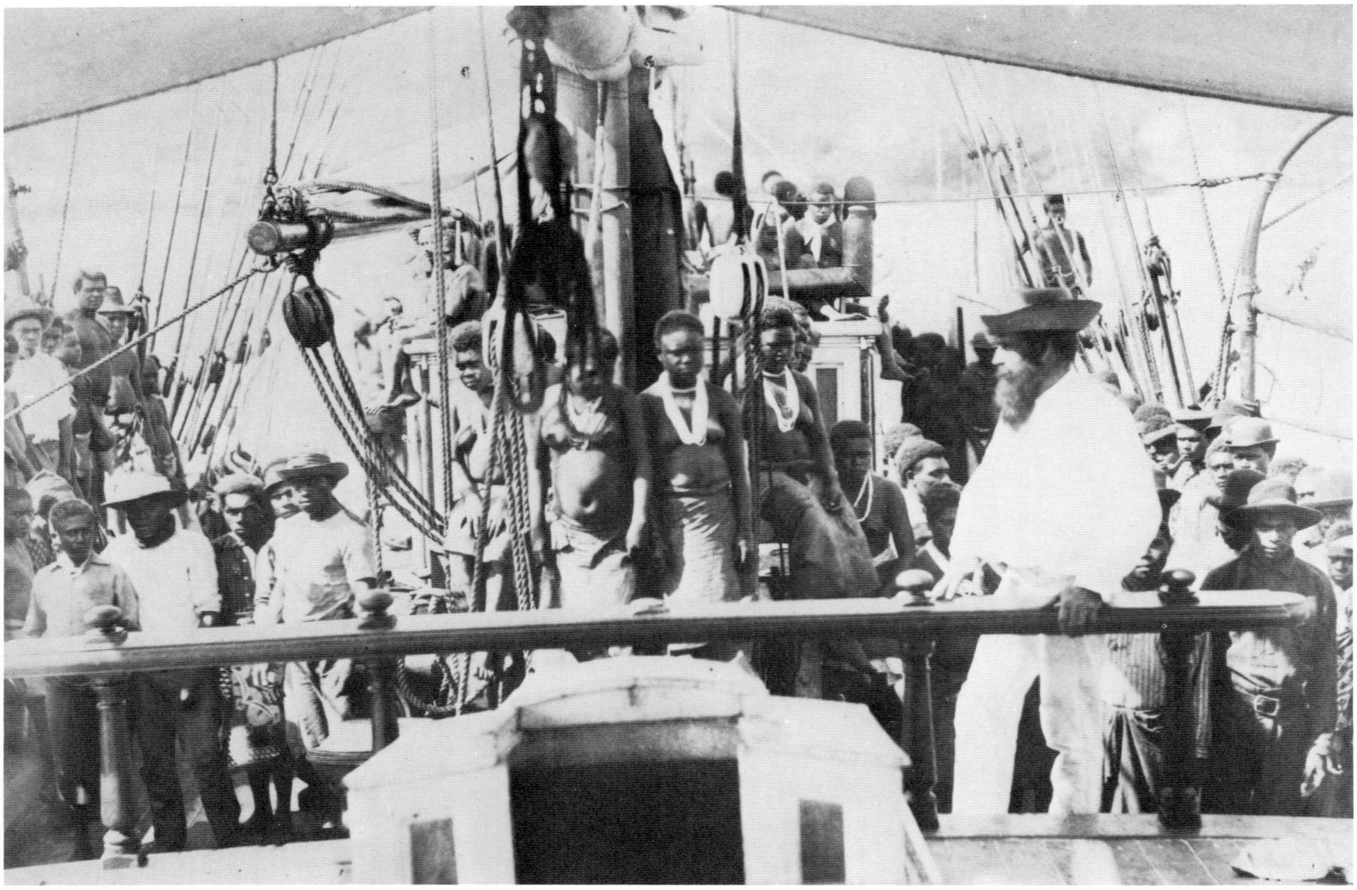

43 PHOTOGRAPHER UNKNOWN. **Locomotive workshops at Sydney. 1887.** The importance of the railway in the development of the colonies was fully appreciated in New South Wales and in 1846 a meeting was held in Sydney to discuss the question of a railway system. Three years later the Sydney Railway Company was incorporated. The first line to be started was from Sydney to Parramatta but in 1855 both the Sydney Railway Company and the Hunter River Rail Company, unable to operate without substantial subsidies, gave themselves up to government ownership and responsibility. The first line, from Sydney to Parramatta, was opened on September 26 1855. The economic importance of the railway in the early years is difficult to overestimate and between 1878 and 1886 1300 miles of line were opened. For profitable agriculture it was estimated that a farm some distance from a major centre needed to be within about 20 miles of the line, and the system was thus indispensable for the settlement and exploitation of southern New South Wales. As *The Railway Guide of New South Wales* (1886) argued: 'For very often a decaying inland town (like Parramatta, for instance, in this colony) will, through the action of a railway, gradually, and in the most astonishing manner, revive and receive a new and healthy impetus...For in many places (such as Lithgow and Blayney, for example, which but for the Railroad must have remained mere picturesque solitude), the arrival of the 'iron horse' has shown a really marvellous tendency to *create* industrial centres, thriving townships, and busy, populous communities..'

44 PHOTOGRAPHER UNKNOWN. **Petersham Station, Sydney. 1887.** The new station at Petersham on the Sydney to Parramatta suburban line was completed in 1885 to cater for the expanding commuter traffic into the city: 'On the southern side of the line, houses, villas, gardens and slowly developing streets are successively presented; where (not long since) there was nothing but open country, or shady 'bush'. On approaching Petersham Station a fine view over the country unfolds itself to the right – the celebrated 'Blue Mountains' becoming visible far away to the westward. Petersham Station is now the centre of a thickly populated suburban district, and on the slopes around it are many really delightful villas and gardens. Usual time of *trajet* from Sydney to Petersham, about twelve minutes.' (*The Railway Guide of New South Wales).*

45 PHOTOGRAPHER UNKNOWN. **Wool sorting shed, New South Wales. c1900.**

46 PHOTOGRAPHER UNKNOWN. **Shipping wool to the railway, New South Wales. 1890s.**

47 PHOTOGRAPHER UNKNOWN. **Travelling on the Tumut to Bega route, New South Wales. c1905.** The motor car was first introduced into Australia just before the turn of the century and by the 1920s was challenging the railway's primacy of the transport routes.

Above: **Labour ship at Fiji. c1885.** (D8/39)
Below: **Petersham Station, Sydney. 1887.** (D9/44)

D10 CEYLON

48 W.L.H. SKEEN & CO. **Train leaving Colombo Station. c1865.** The Ceylon Railway Company had been formed as early as 1845, but financial difficulties and a rebellion in the Kandy district in July 1848 resulted in the laying aside of the project. After much lobbying from the planting community, eager to open up the rich coffee land of the island's interior, the underwriting of the railway was secured and Governor Sir Henry Ward turned the first sod of the Colombo-Kandy line on August 3 1858. The first stage of the line, from Colombo to Ambepussa (34 miles) was open for traffic in October 1865; after a gruelling engineering struggle against savage gradients (rising 1385 feet in the 13 miles of the Kadugannawa Incline) the line was completed and the first train made the whole journey from Colombo to Kandy on April 30 1867.

49 CHARLES T. SCOWEN. **Tea estate bungalow, Ceylon. c1875-80.**

50 W.L.H. SKEEN & CO. **Packaging cinnamon, Ceylon. 1880s.** For hundreds of years a profitable export from Ceylon, cinnamon thrived most plentifully in the light sandy soil of the western maritime provinces, with some of the richest gardens situated around Colombo. The value of the spice was one of the principal reasons for both the Portuguese and the Dutch occupations of the island, and both powers exercised a jealous government monopoly over the harvesting of the plant, penalties for the transgression of which were particularly severe under Dutch law. The government monopoly remained in force under British rule until 1833, by which time the crop's importance was about to be superseded by coffee. Inferior foreign varieties and the use of cassia further undermined the industry, although it retains its reputation as the best quality cinnamon in the world. The separating of the bark from the wood was a skilled craft and these workers formed their own caste, the 'chalias'.

51 W.L.H. SKEEN & CO. **Sorting plumbago, Ceylon. 1880s.** From the beginning an industry almost wholly under Cinghalese rather than European control, plumbago (graphite) was Ceylon's major mineral resource and was first exported from the island in the 1820s. Although fluctuating markets often made the trade uncertain, the quality of Ceylon plumbago, allied to cheap labour and mining methods requiring little capital investment, allowed many fortunes to be made.

52 W.L.H. SKEEN & CO. **Coopers making barrels, Ceylon. 1880s.** The coopers' skills were in demand in Ceylon for the storage and transportation of a number of products, particularly coffee, which after the 1840s was shipped in barrels.

53 W.L.H. SKEEN & CO. **Newly cleared and lined land being planted out with tea bushes, Ceylon. 1880s.** Although tea is most immediately associated with Ceylon's plantation economy, the foundations for its success were in fact laid by coffee. Introduced to the island in 1824, the dominance of coffee not only determined the look of the land but was fundamental in shaping patterns of social organisation, legislation and immigration. The fungal disease of 'coffee rust' started to destroy the industry from 1869 onwards, but by this time the first steps had been taken towards the supplanting of coffee by tea. In 1867 the first 'tea gardens' were opened in the Ramboda district and by the perseverance of such pioneers as James Taylor, allied to tea's natural advantages as an evergreen crop capable of being successfully cultivated on a wider variety of terrain, it had by the 1880s completely overshadowed coffee's former importance.

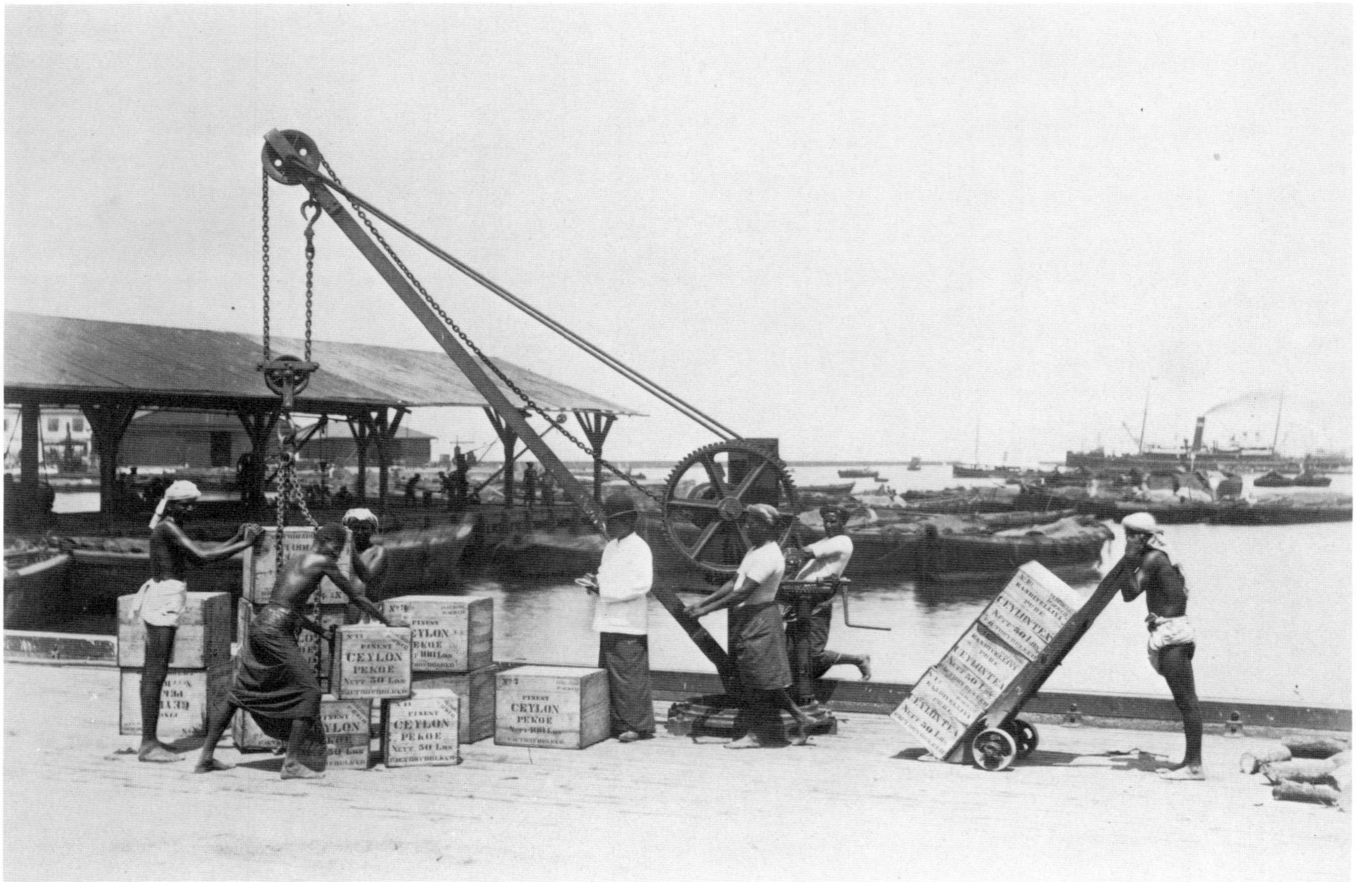
FINEST
CEYLON
PEKOE
NETT 50 Lbs

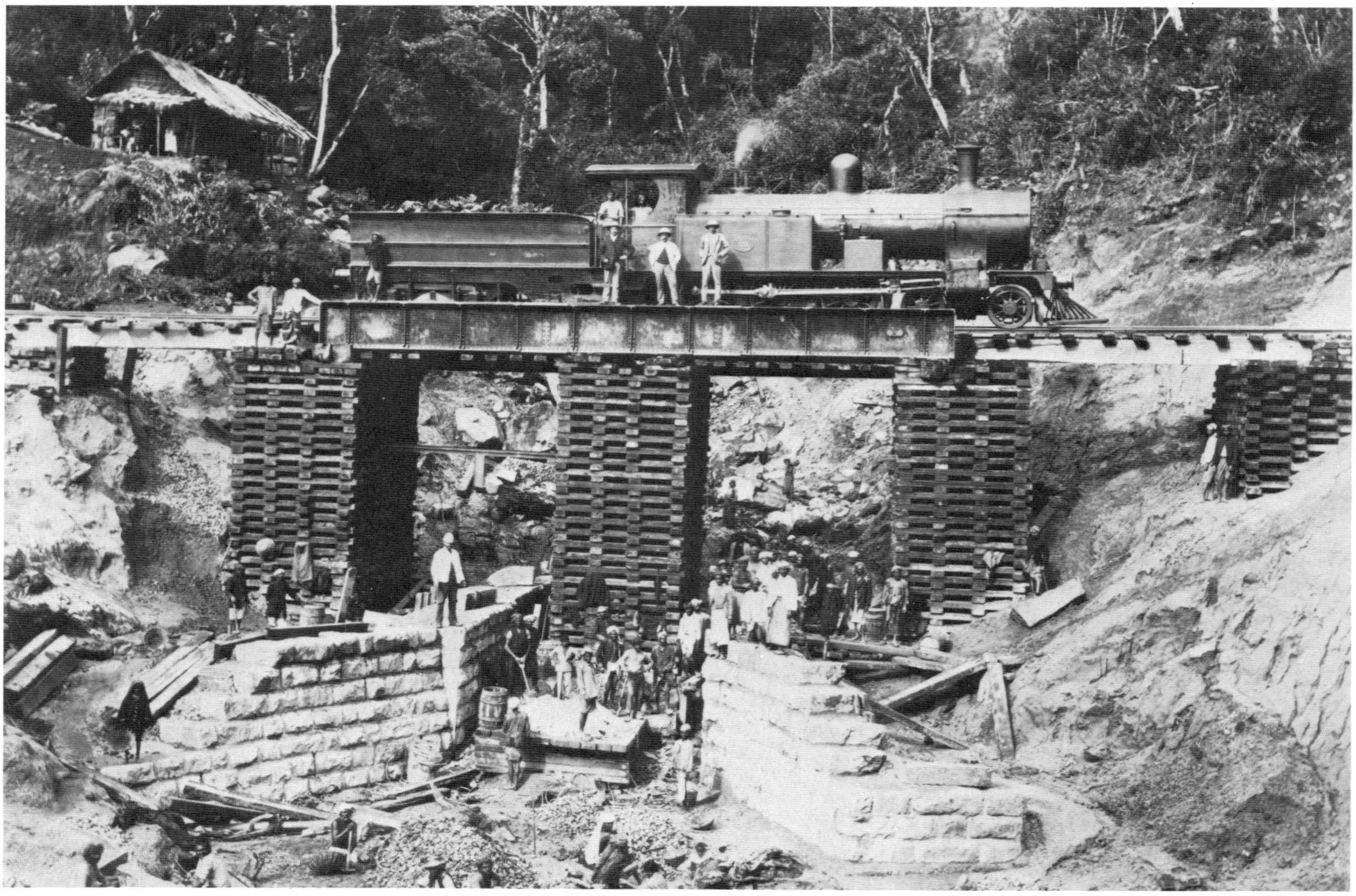

[54] W.L.H. SKEEN & CO. **Packing 50lb and 100lb chests of tea, Ceylon. 1880s.**

□[55] W.L.H. SKEEN & CO. **Packaged tea ready for shipment at Colombo. 1880s.**

□[56] W.L.H. SKEEN & CO. **Temporary bridge and new 16 foot culvert at mile 15¾ on the Haputale Railway. 1893.** The case for the extension of the Ceylon Railway to open up new land for cultivation and for strengthening the administration was forcefully argued by Sir Arthur Gordon, Governor from 1883-90 ('the first and most potent means of extending civilization is found in roads, the second in roads, the third again in roads'), and it was his vigorous championing of this cause to the Colonial Office which obtained the sanctioning of a line to the Uva country at a time when the colony's financial position was precarious. Work was begun at Nanuoya on December 1 1888 and the line was opened as far as Haputale on June 19 1893.

[57] W.L.H. SKEEN & CO. **Poloya Bridge, Matara Railway, Ceylon. May 1895.** The Galle-Matara line, a 25 mile coastal run to the southern tip of the island, was opened for traffic on December 17 1895.

D11 INDIA

[58] SAMUEL BOURNE. **Reversing Station on the Bhore Ghat Incline. 1860s.** The first section of the Great Indian Peninsula Railway, from Bombay to Thana, was officially opened in April 1853, but before the line could reach Poona and on to Madras, it had to cross the mountains of the Western Ghats. The task of designing the path up to the summit was entrusted to James Berkley (1819-1862), a former pupil of Robert Stephenson and Chief Resident Engineer of the G.I.P.R. from 1850-58. The Incline, rising 1821 feet in the 16 miles of its length, took 7½ years to build and was opened for traffic in 1863.

□[59] PHOTOGRAPHER UNKNOWN. **Viaduct construction on the Great Indian Peninsula Railway. 1868.**

□[60] SAMUEL BOURNE. **Shipping on the Hooghly at Calcutta. c1868.** With a ferocious tidal bore and dangerous, constantly shifting sand bars only passable at high tide, the 120 miles of the Hooghly between the Bay of Bengal and Calcutta made a perilous journey for merchantmen headed for the port, hazards increased by the possibility of cyclones such as those of October 1864 and November 1867 which left the harbour a mass of wreckage. Port facilities were improved in later years, but for a long period Calcutta was inaccessible to ships drawing more than 22 feet.

Above: **Packaged tea ready for shipment at Colombo. 1880s.** (D10/55)
Below: **Temporary bridge and new 16 foot culvert at mile 15¾ on the Haputale Railway. 1893.** (D10/56)

D12 EAST & CENTRAL AFRICA

[61] PHOTOGRAPHER UNKNOWN. **Coffee plantation washing house, Nyasaland. c1900.** The first of Nyasaland's export crops, coffee was introduced into the territory with plants brought to Blantyre from the Edinburgh Botanical Gardens in 1878. By 1885 there were forty acres under coffee and rising world prices led to rapid expansion so that by 1896 over 10,000 acres were being cultivated. This boom continued until the turn of the century when competition from Brazil saturated the world market and prices fell. This, coupled with a series of poor harvests in Nyasaland itself, spelt the end of the industry as a large scale concern. Its export importance was soon replaced by cotton, which in turn eventually gave way to tobacco and tea.

[62] PHOTOGRAPHER UNKNOWN. **On trek from Sunnyside Estate, Nyasaland. c1900.**

□[63] PHOTOGRAPHER UNKNOWN. **East African ivory traders. 1880s.** The real pioneers in the opening up of the East African interior were not the European explorers but the Arab caravans that pushed further and further westwards in search of the country's two most valuable export commodities, ivory and slaves. The two trades were intimately linked since the slaves taken to the coast for sale also transported the ivory that had been obtained. During the reign of Seyyid Said, who moved his court from Oman to Zanzibar in 1832, caravans pushed ever deeper into Central Africa and in the late 1840s the first Arab caravan reached Buganda. With the decline of the slave trade European merchants took over many of the ivory outlets on the coast.

□[64] PHOTOGRAPHER UNKNOWN. **Portrait of Tipu Tib. c1886.** Born in Zanzibar around 1830, Tipu Tib was the most powerful of the late 19th century traders and slavers in East Africa and played an important part in opening up the Congo interior to European administration. He was at first employed in his father's business enterprises but around 1850 struck out on his own organizing ivory and slaving caravans, and by the late 1860s was operating in the Congo basin and what is now north east Zambia. In 1883 he was appointed the Sultan of Zanzibar's agent in this area and in 1886 was persuaded by H.M. Stanley to accept the governorship of the eastern Congo. Committed to curbing the slave trade, he was unable to gain sufficient support from his employers and retired to Zanzibar in 1890 in the face of African and Arab hostility, losing much of his wealth in the process. His autobiography in Swahili was completed shortly before his death in 1905.

[65] A.C. GOMES & SON. **Train at Bububu Station, Zanzibar. c1910.** The narrow gauge line from Zanzibar Town to Bububu, a distance of five miles, was constructed by an American company in 1905. Taken over by the government in 1911, it continued in operation until increasing competition from road traffic forced its closure in 1928:
'The service is most popular and useful, and is largely used by the native population. A special first class coach is run for the benefit of those passengers from steamers who wish to obtain a glimpse of the island. The railway traverses some of the narrowest streets of the city, and it is a constant source of wonderment how passers-by escape being run over. Europeans resident in Zanzibar regard the railway with an amused tolerance.' F.B. Pearce, *Zanzibar, the island metropolis of Eastern Africa* (1920).

Bourne 1711

66 ALFRED LOBO. **Railway steamers at Entebbe Pier, Uganda. c1910.** Transport across Lake Victoria from the termination of the Uganda Railway at Port Florence (Kisumu) was by a series of steamers, many of which saw decades of service. The S.S. *Clement Hill* (left), named after a chairman of the Uganda Railway Committee, was launched in December 1906. In 1936, together with the *Winifred,* she was sunk to form a breakwater. The S.S. *Sybil,* launched at Kisumu in 1904, was converted to a lighter after damage in the First World War and was scrapped in 1967.

D13 WEST AFRICA

67 T.J. ALLDRIDGE. **Transporting produce in the Mende country in palm leaf hampers, Sierra Leone. 1890s.** Difficulties of transport along narrow jungle tracks were a major obstacle to the economic exploitation of the Sierra Leone hinterland before the start of railway construction in the mid 1890s. Using the traditional long cylindrical hampers attached to a wooden framework as seen here, it took 30 men, Alldridge estimated, to transport a ton of palm nut kernels.

68 PHOTOGRAPHER UNKNOWN. **Palm oil awaiting shipment at Calabar, Southern Nigeria. c1912.** With the abolition of slavery, the economic vacuum for merchants trading in West Africa was filled by the palm oil market and gradually the Southern Nigerian hinterland was opened up along the network of waterways that came to be known as the Oil Rivers, with their outlets at Calabar, Bonny, Opobo and other stations along the coast. Much of the trade was controlled by the British in the form of George Goldie's Royal Niger Company, which gained its Charter in 1886 and was used by Goldie to create a commercial monopoly backed by a recognized administration. The company's Charter was not surrendered to the Crown until 1899.

□69 PHOTOGRAPHER UNKNOWN. **The sternwheeler 'Hornbill' and trading canoes on the Eyong River at Okopedi, Southern Nigeria. 1909.** The *Hornbill* was one of a fleet of 19 sternwheelers, steam pinnaces and motor boats which transported produce and passengers to and from the hinterland and the coast. The Cross River Transport Service was run by Elder, Dempster & Co. and the *Hornbill* assisted in the service, carrying in 1909 6,233 passengers and 2,947 tons of cargo at a nett profit of £112. The *Hornbill* came into service in 1906.

Previous left hand page:
Above: **Viaduct construction on the Great Indian Peninsula Railway. 1868.** (D11/59)
Below: **Shipping on the Hooghly at Calcutta. c1868.** (D11/60)
Previous right hand page:
Above: **East African ivory traders. 1880s.** (D12/63)
Below: **Portrait of Tipu Tib. c1886.** (D12/64)

□70 PHOTOGRAPHER UNKNOWN. **Trader's warehouse at Opobo, Southern Nigeria. c1912.** Situated at the mouth of the Imo River, Opobo rose to a position of commercial importance under King Jaja who moved into the area in 1869. By controlling the middlemen who handled the shipments of oil from the interior, Jaja soon created a monopoly in the trade which was much resented by British interests. When Harry Johnston's demands that the British be allowed to buy their oil direct from up-river were ignored, Jaja was tried for blocking trade in 1887 and deported to the West Indies. Hereafter European merchants took over Jaja's markets.

71 PHOTOGRAPHER UNKNOWN. **Chiefs on the new Lagos Railway during the Jubilee celebrations. June 1897.** An added attraction of the grand Jubilee Durbar held in Lagos in June 1897 was the transportation of the participants on the new Lagos Railway. Sir Gilbert Carter's Interior Expedition of 1893 had convinced him of the vital importance of a railway to open up the hinterland. Surveys were made in 1894-95 and the 20 mile line from Lagos to Otta was started in March 1896 and completed in September 1897.
By December 1900 the line had been extended to Ibadan, a distance of 125 miles.

D14 UGANDA RAILWAY

72 WILLIAM D. YOUNG. **Survey Camp, Coast Section. 1896.** By the terms of the agreement reached at the Slave Trade Conference in Brussels in 1890, Britain was obliged to do all within her power to suppress slaving both on land and at sea. The most effective way of carrying out this work was seen as the construction of railways which would quickly wipe out the economic foundations of the caravans. The government therefore undertook to build a railway from the East African coast to Lake Victoria and in 1891-92 a preliminary survey led by Captain James MacDonald R.E. mapped out a feasible route. The survey party seen here is one of the later groups which made accurate plottings of the precise path of the line while building was actually in progress. Three main groups were engaged in this work, but it was not until 1900 that the complete line was staked out.

73 WILLIAM D. YOUNG. **Laying the first rail at Kilindini. May 30 1896.** George Whitehouse, the Chief Engineer of the Uganda Railway, arrived in Mombasa in December 1895 and set about preparing the island's facilities for the construction of a railway: a temporary viaduct had to be erected between Mombasa Island and the mainland (completed in August 1896), the port needed extensive improvements, and warehouses and accommodation for the labour force were non-existent. However, by the end of May sufficient progress had been made for work to start on the line across the island, and by the end of the year railhead stood 23 miles inland.

□74 WILLIAM D. YOUNG. **Incline on the Kikuyu Escarpment at Mile 363½. c. 1900.** Of all the natural obstacles confronting the railway builders the most serious was the descent down the steep sides of the Rift Valley. In order that construction need not be halted while permanent viaducts were built, temporary inclines were made which plunged straight down the precipitous slope of the Kikuyu Escarpment for the transportation of material and rolling stock.

Above: **The sternwheeler 'Hornbill' and trading canoes on the Eyong River at Okopedi, Southern Nigeria. 1909.** (D13/69)
Below: **Trader's warehouse at Opobo, Southern Nigeria. c1912.** (D13/70)

75 WILLIAM D. YOUNG. **Carriers crossing on Incline Ia, Kikuyu Escarpment. c1900.** Specially manufactured freight trolleys transported loads to the foot of the valley, lowered by wire ropes attached to cable drums, with the weight of a descending trolley counterbalanced by an ascending one. On the left of the group on the trolley stands George Whitehouse and on the right Ronald Preston, a foreman platelayer. The inclines, which were in use between May 1900 and October 1901, enabled the railway to advance more than 150 miles further before the permanent viaducts were erected.

❐76 WILLIAM D. YOUNG. **Indian platelaying gangs shifting camp to railhead. c1900.** Sparseness of population and the unwillingness of Africans to work on the line meant that the labour force had to be imported and the Indian Government was requested to supply this need. Apparently under the impression that the railway was a private enterprise, the Government of India imposed stringent conditions on emigration, demanding a minimum wage (Rs. 15 per month), free rations and forbidding task work. This latter stipulation, until reversed, considerably slowed the pace of construction. The first batch of 350 men arrived in Mombasa in January 1896 and over the period of construction from 1896-1903 nearly 32,000 Indians came to East Africa to work on the railway. Mortality was high throughout the labour force and the depredations of disease, accident and the celebrated man-eaters of Tsavo took a toll of 2,493 lives.

77 WILLIAM D. YOUNG. **Uganda Railway water supply train. c1900.** Beyond the open coastal plain the railway crossed many rivers from which the labour force's water supply could be obtained. Before this country could be reached however, the Taru Desert had to be crossed and ironically, this strip of land which offered level, bare ground ideal for railway work, was both waterless and devoid of game. To the gangs of labourers at railhead the daily appearance of the water supply train was the most important link with the base of the line.

Above: **Incline on the Kikuyu Escarpment at Mile 363½. c1900.** (D14/74)
Below: **Indian platelaying gangs shifting camp to railhead. c1900.** (D14/76)

From settlement to city

For the commercial photographer in the nineteenth century the growing cities and commercial centres not only offered the largest market for his product, whether portraiture, landscape or architectural views, but also supplied a readily available subject matter: photographs illustrating the spread of cities, notable new buildings and other indicators of civic pride found a steady sale to visiting travellers and to settlers to send back to England. Documentary evidence of the earliest commercial operators is sparse, but advertisements, newspaper reports and trade almanacs give some indication both of the numbers of early photographers who set up in business in the cities and their often precarious economic status within them.

When Daguerre announced his process to an eagerly awaiting world as a gift to mankind in August 1839 he was revealing something less than the truth: he had in fact patented the daguerreotype in England five days previously and his munificence therefore went largely unappreciated there, and this, together with Talbot's own patenting of the calotype when it was perfected in 1841 accounts in some measure for the fact that British photographers were rarely first on the scene in foreign countries. British dependencies however, were as quickly made aware as elsewhere of the discoveries, *The Malta Penny Magazine* of April 11 1840, for instance, publishing an account of the technicalities of the daguerreotype, which was demonstrated on the island by Horace Vernet and Frédéric Goupil Fesquet, 'an intelligent gentleman' who 'was so obliging as to take the pains to explain the process to any one asking for information.' Vernet and Goupil Fesquet were on their way back from a daguerreotype expedition to Egypt and already detailed news of the new art had travelled much further afield. In Calcutta Dr O'Shaughnessy, according to *The Asiatic Journal* of January-April 1840, had already been experimenting with photographic processes and at a meeting of the Asiatic Society on October 2 1839 'gave some details accompanied by specimens, of a new kind of photographic drawing, by means of the sun's light, of which the principle wholly differs from that of Europe . . . Professor O'Shaughnessy uses, it seems, a solution of gold, and produces many various tints, from a light rose colour through purple down to a deep black, and, what is more extraordinary, a green!' Daguerre's own discovery was also reported in great detail in the sub-continent, *The Bombay Times,* for instance, publishing three long descriptive articles (on December 14, 18 and 21 1839) which gave sufficient detail for those wishing to experiment with the process to do so. From the lack of available evidence to the contrary it seems likely that few amateurs in these early days would have had either the skill or patience to acquire the technique without tutors, and the spread of photography was an uneven progress left largely in the hands of the professional operator.

While American daguerreotypists visited Montreal in 1840, in India it was not until around 1849 that professional studios began to be advertised. In Australia G.B. Goodman was in business in 1842, but New Zealand had to wait until 1848 for H.B. Sealy to advertise his portrait and landscape establishment, and a further delay was occasioned 'in consequence of the necessity of procuring from Sydney certain drugs which he omitted to bring from England.' In the Far East photography first found its way to Singapore in the person of Gaston Dutronquoy, a portrait and miniature painter who had come to Singapore in 1839 and in December 1843 was advertising that 'Mr G. Dutronquoy respectfully informs the ladies and gentlemen of Singapore, that he is complete master of the newly invented and late imported daguerreotype. Ladies and gentlemen who may honour Mr Dutronquoy with a sitting can have their likenesses taken in the astonishingly short space of two minutes. The portraits are free from all blemish and are in every respect perfect likenesses. A lady and a gentleman can be placed together in one picture and both are taken at the same time entirely shaded from the effects of the sun. The price of one portrait is ten dollars, both taken in picture is fifteen dollars. One day's notice will be required.'

In Africa the pattern was even more fragmentary, with early and intense activity in the 1840s in Egypt and North Africa, while south of this area photographic activity all but ceases until one reaches the Cape where Jules Léger opened a studio in Port Elizabeth in 1846.

Throughout these early years photography was an expensive process and after the initial fascination businesses often lasted little longer than a season, the photographers themselves either setting up in a new, less risky profession or moving on in the hope of finding a more responsive clientele elsewhere. In South Africa the first recorded calotype photographer, A.W. Roghe from Frankfurt, arrived in 1849 but by 1850 had left for India where isolated references find him practising in Calcutta in 1851 and in Burma (possibly having abandoned photography altogether) in 1864. The more hapless John Paul arrived in Cape Town in 1850 and after six years of varying success left the colony, turning up again in India where he committed suicide in 1862.

By the late 1850s and 1860s the growing populations of the cities had begun to assure photographers of a steady income and from this period the documentation of the major centres is detailed and comprehensive. In New Zealand the growth of Dunedin from 1856 is covered by William Meluish while an even more exhaustive record of the changing face of Wellington is supplied by James Bragge. Charles Nettleton's immensely detailed panoramas of the Melbourne skyline and buildings under the construction were commissioned by a city council aware both of the rate of growth of the wealthy young metropolis and of the historical value of preserving a visual record of it. The economic opportunities offered by a city like Melbourne acted as a magnet to photographers compared to more static centres and thus received greater photographic attention, and it is interesting to note that while in the whole period between 1846 and 1870 only 48 professional firms are recorded as operating in Cape Town, in Melbourne on the other hand 43 photographers were advertising their services in 1867 alone.

E1 PHOTOGRAPHER UNKNOWN. **George Street, Sydney. 1880s.**

E2 FOUR OLDER CITIES

□ 1 JOHNSTON AND HOFFMANN. **The Bengal Secretariat, Calcutta. c1910.** Occupying the whole of the north side of Dalhousie Square, the Secretariat was erected in 1780 as the Writers' Buildings for the accommodation of junior East India Company servants on their arrival in India. Originally, in Montague Massey's words, 'a plain white stuccoed building utterly devoid of any pretensions to architectural beauty, and depending mainly for any chance claim to recognition on its immense length,' it was taken over by the Bengal government in 1880 and the decorated facade added in 1881-82. Electric trams were introduced in Calcutta in 1902.

2 FREDERICK FIEBIG. **South Park Street Cemetery, Calcutta. Early 1850s.** Maria Graham's comparison of South Park Street Cemetery in 1812 with its 'many acres covered so thick with columns, urns, and obelisks' to 'a city of the dead' was wholly in accord with the conception of the cemetery as a place of recreation, moral instruction, historical teaching and architectural diversity: a microcosm and salutary counterpart to the teeming city enclosing it. Opened in 1767, the grounds are, in the words of Cotton's *Calcutta Old and New* (1907), 'something more than mere fields where the dead are stored away unknown. They are a touching and instructive history, written in family burial plots, in mounded graves, in sculptured and inscribed monuments. They tell us of the past, its individual lives, of its men and women, of its children, of its households. We find no such records elsewhere of the price paid for Calcutta by generations of bygone Englishmen, who lived and died at their work.'

3 WILLIAM JOHNSON. **Panorama of Bombay Green from the Cathedral. c1856.** Acquired as a mission and trading settlement by the Portuguese in the 1530s, the island of Bombay came into British hands in 1661 as part of the marriage settlement between Charles II and Catherine of Braganza. Popularly known as 'The Gateway of India' in later years, something of its commercial pre-eminence can be glimpsed from the number of merchantmen crowding the harbour in the background. This view looks east from the Cathedral across the Green (seen here as it was before Elphinstone Circle was laid out in the early 1860s) towards the Town Hall which was completed after considerable delay in 1833. The Green had previously been the centre of the Bombay cotton markets, but in 1844 these were transferred to a new location on Colaba.

□ 4 JAMES ROBERTSON & FELIX BEATO. **Strada Vescovo from Strada Reale, Valletta. 1850s.** The Knights of the Order of St John of Jerusalem had settled in Malta in 1530, with their capital of Mdina. After the attempted Ottoman invasion of 1565 the necessity for a fortified stronghold led to the planning of the new city and the Grand Master Jean de la Vallette laid the foundation stone in the following year, the defences of the new city split into administrative 'languages,' each with its own auberge. With the diminution of the power of the Order, Malta came into British hands in 1800 after a two year occupation by the French. This view looks north along Strada Vescovo towards Marsamuscetto Harbour.

5 PHOTOGRAPHER UNKNOWN. **Adderley Street, Cape Town. 1870s.** Established in 1652 by Jan van Riebeeck as a victualling station for Dutch East India Company shipping *en route* for the spice trade of the east, Cape Town rapidly grew in economic importance during the flourishing years of the Company's fortunes during the 18th century. During the Napoleonic Wars it was held from 1795-1802 by the British and formally handed over to them in 1806. This view looks along Adderley Street from the corner of the Parade towards the Pagoda, Cape Town's first telegraph office.

E3 PANORAMIC VIEWS

6 CHARLES NETTLETON. **Panoramic view of Melbourne. c1868.** This section of a larger panorama looks eastwards along Lonsdale Street from its junction with Queen Street. Prominent buildings in the photograph include the Public Library (the present day portico not built until 1870), St Patrick's Cathedral (under construction), the Post Office and the Town Hall. The gold rushes of the 1850s had brought great wealth to Melbourne and the many small hotels seen in the panorama indicate the number of newcomers the city had to accommodate during the prosperous period leading up to the 'marvellous Melbourne' of the 1880s.

7 ROBERT HARRIS. **Kimberley morning market. c1888.** By the time Kimberley was officially designated a town in 1873 the diamond discoveries had already lured a population of 50,000 to the area. Kimberley's wealth continued to grow in succeeding years and the town's importance as a centre of distribution can be seen in this crowded market scene, taken during the last years of transport by the great spans of draught oxen. The railway from Cape Town reached Kimberley in 1885 and as the network increased so the demand for bullock transport lessened.

8 NORTON BROTHERS. **Panorama of Georgetown, British Guiana. 1870s.** As one of the earliest areas of attempted European settlement in the New World, the Guianas became important to the British from about 1740, when English settlers from the West Indian islands began to outnumber the Dutch. The settlement of Stabroek became Georgetown and after several changes of ownership the three colonies which were to form British Guiana were finally ceded to the British in 1814. Despite its reputation as a 'white man's grave' Anthony Trollope, writing in 1859 found Georgetown, with its wide streets and relaxed atmosphere, the most pleasant city in the Caribbean, and Demerara as a whole 'the Elysium of the tropics – the West Indian happy valley of Rasselas – the one true and actual Utopia of the Caribbean Seas – the Transatlantic Eden.' This view is taken from the top of the Demarara Lighthouse, with the Demarara River at the right.

E4 HOTELS & CLUBS

□ 9 J.N. CROMBIE. **The Greyhound Hotel, Queen Street, Auckland. c1865-70.** The Greyhound Hotel replaced the Greyhound Inn which was destroyed by fire in 1863.

10 J.E. BRUTON. **The Palmerston Hotel, Jetty Street, Port Elizabeth, Cape of Good Hope. c1873.** Conveniently situated near the landing beach and town centre, and later the railway station and North Jetty, the block of land occupied by the Palmerston has long been the site of a hotel. By 1840 the building had become the Pier Hotel (run by James Reed, who had come to Port Elizabeth as a child with the 1820 settlers) and after a number of changes of name, probably became the Palmerston shortly after the death of Lord Palmerston in 1865. James R. Rumsey was the proprietor from 1873-81. The building seen here was demolished in the 1880s, but the hotel retained its name until 1960, when it became the Campanile.

11 W.P. FLOYD. **The Hong Kong Club. c1870.** In May 1844, three years after the founding of the colony, a meeting was held to discuss the founding of a club 'to assist in producing a greater feeling of community among the, now becoming numerous, merchants, Civil Servants, Naval and Military men and others who were drawn to the newly formed Colony.' With rules based on those of the Madras and Bengal Clubs, the buildings (situated on Queen's Road and designed by Robert Strachan) were opened on May 26 1846 and served as the club's premises until the new buildings were occupied in 1897.

12 ADOLPHE DUPERLY & SON. **The Myrtle Bank Hotel, Harbour Street, Kingston, Jamaica. c1910.** Constructed in 'mission house' style after the previous building had been destroyed in the great earthquake of 1907, the hotel belongs to the breed of establishments designed to cater for the luxury tourist market of the early twentieth century: 'owned and operated by the United Fruit Company, (it) has become in Jamaica a synonym for everything associated with elegance and comfort in accommodation... On the verandahs of the Myrtle Bank more people take their ease and refreshments than in any other hotel in the island, and visitors... swiftly 'fall' for the rhythm of the rocking chairs that seem to swing more emphatically in the affirmative when the well-trained waiters answer the electric bells that are everywhere to hand..' (Allister Macmillan, *The West Indies Past and Present*, n.d., 1920s).

E5 & E6 CARIBBEAN

13 PHOTOGRAPHER UNKNOWN. **St George's, Grenada. c1890.** Founded as a French settlement in 1650, St George's is situated on a promontory overlooking the landlocked harbour known as the Carenage. With a population at this period of a little under 5000, St George's was a more flourishing centre than the decayed 'goodly English town' whose 'glory... has now departed' described by Trollope in 1859: 'Its appearance is singularly picturesque and interesting, as the steep slopes of the promontory, which projects into the sea in a southerly direction, are covered with brick houses, whose red-tiled roofs contrast pleasantly with the rich green tropical vegetation surrounding them. The ridge of the hills is crowned with three churches, and the highest point of the peninsula... is occupied by a fine old fort which dates from 1706; the two parts of the town are connected by a short tunnel which pierces the intervening hill.' *(The Grenada Handbook for 1896).*

□ 14 PHOTOGRAPHER UNKNOWN. **The suburbs of Port of Spain, Trinidad. 1870s.** Port of Spain replaced St Joseph as the capital of Trinidad 14 years before the Spanish surrendered the island to the British in 1797. The fine public architecture of Port of Spain dates from after 1808 however, when a huge fire left the largely wooden town in ruins. After 1845 the population was greatly increased by the immigration of East Indian labour and the old sugar estates on the outskirts of Port of Spain were opened up for building development. A few landmarks in the history of the city indicate its progress and growth during these years: the installation of a proper water supply for the town (1854), the opening of the public hospital (1858), the underground sewage system (1861), the introduction of horse drawn cabs (1862) and the building of the public baths and wash house (1866).

15 J.C. WILSON. **Market Square, Kingstown, St Vincent. c1910.** A few years before this photograph was taken, the eruption of La Soufrière in May 1902 devastated nearly a third of the island and killed 2,000 people. After the disaster the introduction of cotton helped in some measure to restore the island's economy and supplement the principal export, arrowroot.

Above: **The Bengal Secretariat, Calcutta. c1910** (E2/1)
Below: **Strada Vescovo from Strada Reale, Valletta. 1850s.** (E2/4)

□ 16 J.F. COONLEY. **Government House from George Street, Nassau, New Providence, Bahamas. 1890s.** British settlers from Bermuda in the early 17th century were the first permanent European inhabitants of the islands and in 1647 the Company of Eleutherian Adventurers was formed to promote systematic colonization. Nassau itself was founded on the site of the village of Charles' Towne and although its name was decreed in 1695, the town was not in fact laid out until 1729. The island became a Crown Colony in 1717 and in 1784 the population was doubled by the arrival of Empire Loyalists and their slaves from Georgia and Carolina. A good deal of the growth of the city of Nassau took place during the American Civil War when Nassau became the main supply base for blockade runners from the South. Government House was erected in 1801 during Governor Halkett's period of Office.

17 WILLIAM AVERY. **North Front Street, Belize, British Honduras. June 1897.** Although settled as early as the mid 17th century by English buccaneers trading in logwood and by the mid 18th century the chief port of the region, British claims to British Honduras were resisted by the Spanish until the Battle of St George's in 1798 and later by Guatemala. It was not until 1862 that a colony was officially constituted, with a Lieutenant Governor until 1884 subordinate to the Governor of Jamaica. The photograph shows the streets of Belize decorated in celebration of Queen Victoria's Diamond Jubilee.

□ 18 J.W.H. CAMPION. **High Street and Bay, Bridgetown, Barbados. c1872.** The view, looking west across the High Street, was probably taken from St Michael's Cathedral. Bridgetown has no natural harbour, although the open roadstead of Carisle Bay is well sheltered and there is a small Careenage protected by a mole. Founded in the late 1620s by the 'Windward Men' (a group of settlers who fought the 'Leeward Men' for possession of the island), Bridgetown was originally known as St Michael's Town.

19 PHOTOGRAPHER UNKNOWN. **King Street, Kingston, Jamaica. c1880.** This view looks south along King Street from the Parish Church, with the harbour and Palisadoes in the distance. The largest city in the West Indies, Kingston was founded in 1692 when Port Royal was destroyed in an earthquake, and the street plan laid out in 1695. The seat of government however, was not transferred from Spanish Town to Kingston until 1870. A great part of the city was destroyed by fire in 1882 and by earthquake and fire in 1907.

20 JOSE ANJO. **St John's, Antigua. c1912.** Settled by the English in 1632, three years after an abortive French attempt to colonise the island had failed through want of water, Antigua had a more peaceful history in the succeeding years than the majority of the West Indian islands, and was continuously administered by the British apart from a brief period (1666-67) when it fell into French hands. This photograph is taken from Rat Island, connected to St John's by a narrow causeway and at this period housing a signal station and leper asylum. Dominating the town are the twin towers of the Cathedral, completed in 1848 to replace its predecessor destroyed in the earthquake in 1843.

E7 SYDNEY

21 PHOTOGRAPHER UNKNOWN. **Darling Harbour from the Town Hall, Sydney. c1875.** The view looks south west over Sydney with the area around the junction of Kent Street and Druitt Street in the forground. The University of Sydney can be seen on the skyline in the distance. Crossing the harbour is the wooden Pyrmont Bridge, opened in 1858 as part of the 'Five Bridges Road' that gave access between the city and the northern suburbs.

22 PHOTOGRAPHER UNKNOWN. **French's Buildings, Darlinghurst, Sydney. 1870.** Until the late 1860s the eastern suburb of Darlinghurst remained sparsely populated with middle class villas, but the growth in Sydney's population (from 45,000 in 1846 to 137,000 in 1871) pushed the city outwards along the main highways and the path of the railway in the attempt to accommodate its working classes. These small terraced cottages commanded a rent of 8/- per week. By 1881 the suburban population of Sydney had overtaken that of the city itself.

23 PHOTOGRAPHER UNKNOWN. **The Metropolitan Intercolonial Exhibition grounds, Sydney. 1870.** 'The opening of the Intercolonial Exhibition yesterday was an occasion of general rejoicing. A public holiday was proclaimed, and a numerous and brilliant company assembled at noon to take part in the ceremony intended to celebrate the centenary of Captain Cook's landing on these shores, and afforded some indication of the wonderful progress made by Australia during the first hundred years of its existence as a portion of the British Empire... Among the crowd were numbers from remote parts of New South Wales and many from distant colonies. Flags of all nations floated in the breeze; the park – which bears the name of Prince Alfred – was partially covered with machinery of the most approved construction; stock of the best breeds, produce in great variety and of choice quality, shrubs and flowers of rare beauty and manufactured articles of various kinds; while the building challenged general admiration not only on account of its interior arrangements, but also as a splendid commemorative monument, affording evidence alike of architectural taste, mechanical skill and public spirit.' *(Sydney Morning Herald,* August 31 1870).

24 PHOTOGRAPHER UNKNOWN. **Sydney Gas Works. c1870.** From 1826 (when the first lamp was erected in Macquarie Place) until 1837 the streets of Sydney were lit by oil. In the latter year Ralph Mansfield formed the Australian Gas Light Company in Sydney and built a gasometer in a low-lying part of Darling Harbour at a cost of over £8,000, and the service was inaugurated on Queen Victoria's birthday, May 24 1841. 200 private customers subscribed to the initial supply which was at first only available to the relatively wealthy, and two years later the Sydney City Council took over the responsibility of providing public lighting.

□ 25 PHOTOGRAPHER UNKNOWN. **The Outer Domain, Sydney. c1875.** From early days the open land of the Domain was a popular pleasure spot for city dwellers and was described by B.C. Peck in his *Recollections of Sydney* (1850) as 'a favourite rendezvous of the inhabitants of Sydney, especially on Sundays, when the middle and poorer classes of society amuse a leisure hour by perambulating these extensive grounds, or the Botanic Gardens adjoining.' By 1888 the area had become an Australian Speakers' Corner and was recommended by the *Sydney Morning Herald* (January 24 1888) to those who 'would witness the fierce blaze of light a person can throw upon a subject of which he may know little.'

Previous right hand page:
Above: **The Greyhound Hotel, Queen Street, Auckland. c1865-70.** (E4/9)
Below: **The suburbs of Port of Spain, Trinidad. 1870s.** (E5/14)

Previous left hand page:
Above: **Government House from George Street, Nassau, New Providence, Bahamas. 1890s.** (E5/16)
Below: **High Street and Bay, Bridgetown, Barbados. c1882.** (E5/18)

□ 26 PHOTOGRAPHER UNKNOWN. **The Haslem's Creek Receiving Station, Rookwood Cemetery, Sydney. c1870.** The problems of the disposal of the dead of the growing cities greatly excercised the minds of architects, artists and town planners and was the source of much political agitation in England, culminating in the creation of the magnificent planned cemeteries of the mid-nineteenth century. Questions of hygiene dictated the removal of the necropolis from the centres of population and the idea of a cemetery serviced by the railway followed the example of Brookwood, near Woking, a huge necropolis (originally intended to cater for the whole country) connected with London by a terminus at Westminster Bridge Road. The Receiving Station at Rookwood was built in 1868 to the designs of J.J. Barnet (1827-1904) and was connected to a despatching station at Redfern. With the growth of motor transport in the present century, this branch line fell into disuse and in 1958 the complete structure of the Rookwood Station was dismantled and removed to Canberra where it was rebuilt as a church.

E8 NEW ZEALAND & CANADA

□ 27 (?) WILLIAM MELUISH. **Dunedin. c1858.** This photograph of the Dunedin waterfront taken from the hill overlooking Prince's Street shows the city at a turning point in its history. A small but growing town founded in 1848 by Scottish settlers and just beginning to experience some of the prosperity brought by the opening up of the rich farming lands of the Otago interior, it was to be transformed a few years later by the vast influx of gold prospectors who poured into the area as news spread of the Tuapeka gold finds of 1861. Photographs taken by Meluish in that year show almost every available space filled by a tent and the harbour crowded with ships. The harbour facilities at Dunedin caused problems for many years, with large ships unable to come close to shore, and for those that could, only a tiny jetty at which to moor. The arrival of gold diggers, as well as highlighting the inadequacy of the town's facilities, also in part provided the funds necessary to start the dredging and levelling process which has so altered the city waterfront.

□ 28 JAMES BRAGGE. **Newtown tram sheds, Wellington, New Zealand. 1879.** In 1878 Wellington became the first city in the southern hemisphere to install a steam tram service, 38 years after the original settlement of the area in 1840. This photograph shows the *Hibernia* and the *Florence* outside the Newtown tram sheds and was one of a series of prints prepared by Bragge for the Sydney International Exhibition of 1879. The city corporation bought out the Wellington Tram Company in 1900, replacing steam with horses, and in 1904 the line was electrified.

□ 28(A) FREDERICK DALLY. **Wharf Street, Victoria, British Columbia. c1867-70.** With the imminent partition of Oregon Territory, the Hudson's Bay Company sought a new headquarters for its trading operations in western Canada and the site of the future city of Victoria was first settled in 1843. Vancouver Island became a crown colony in 1849, but the settlement of Victoria remained a largely rural trading outpost until the gold rush of 1858 when it became the provisioning centre for prospectors travelling to the mainland. For two years after the union of the colonies of Vancouver Island and British Columbia, New Westminster was the capital, but after much discussion the centre of administration reverted to Victoria and when in 1871 British Columbia joined the Dominion of Canada it became the Provincial capital.

Above: **The Outer Domain, Sydney. c1875.** (E7/25)
Below: **The Haslam's Creek Receiving Station, Rookwood Cemetery, Sydney. c1870.** (E7/26)

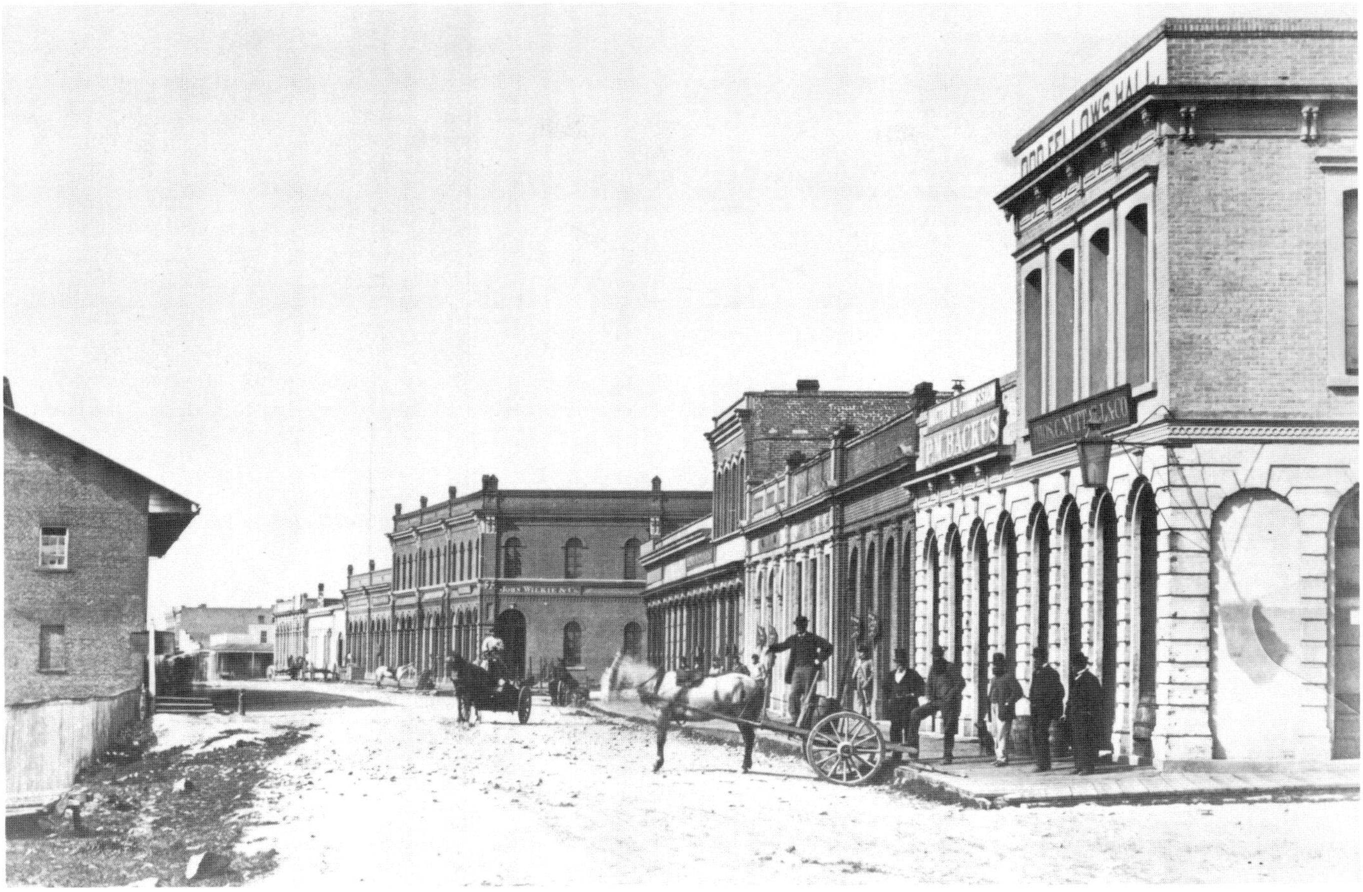
ODD FELLOWS HALL
P.M. BACKUS

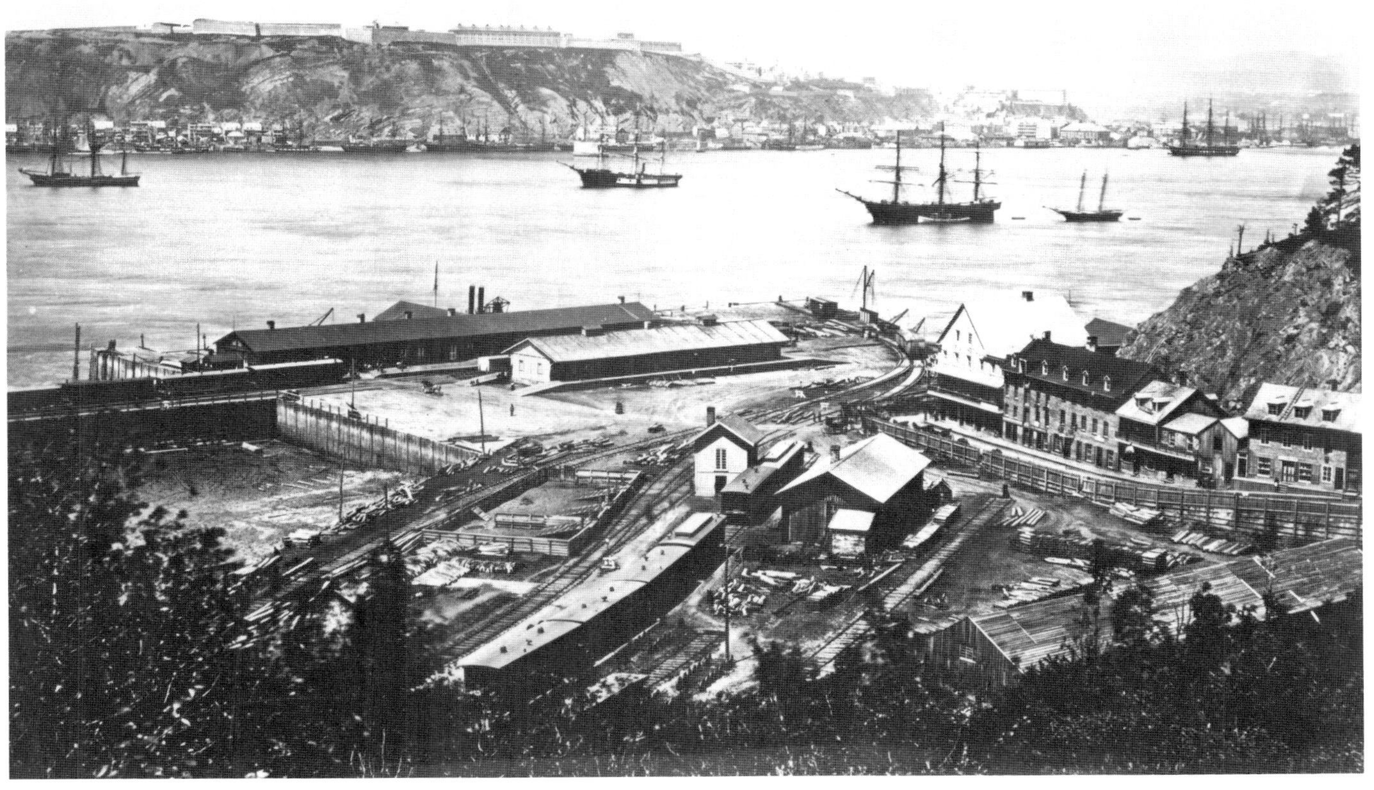

29 ARMSTRONG, BEERE & HIME. **King Street East, Toronto. Winter 1856.** Although a fur-trade settlement from the mid 17th century in an area contested between the French and the British, there was little real settlement until United Empire Loyalists moved into Toronto in 1793, renaming it York. Early growth was slow as the town was overshadowed by the commercial centre of Kingston, but by the time of its incorporation as a city in 1834 (reverting to the name Toronto), the opening up of the rich neighbouring farm lands had boosted the development of the town as a grain market and distribution centre. After the numerous changes of name and status in its history, Toronto became the capital of Ontario at Confederation in 1867.

□ 30 L.P. VALLÉE. **The town and Citadel of Quebec. c1870.** For short periods after the union of Upper and Lower Canada (1841) and before Federation (1867) Quebec, captured by the British in 1759, was the capital of Canada. The Citadel, built by the Imperial Government and completed in 1832, overlooks the St Lawrence, with the Point Lévis depot of the Grand Trunk Railway in the foreground.

E9 FIVE ISLANDS

31 PHOTOGRAPHER UNKNOWN. **Jamestown, St Helena. 1890s.** The view looking down from the hills enclosing the capital of St Helena remains little changed: Main Street runs north down to the Grand Parade with St James' Church at its corner and the prison behind, while the castle and courthouse occupy the other side of the square. Discovered by the Portuguese in 1502 and colonized by the East India Company in 1659, St Helena became an important watering and coaling point on the run round the Cape as well as a strategic base in the fight against the Atlantic slave trade. In 1834 it was taken over from the East India Company and became a Crown Colony. Like the Seychelles, its remoteness made it an ideal place of exile, its most famous prisoner being Napoleon (from 1815-21). The island also accommodated the Zulu king Dinizulu (1890-97), a deposed sultan of Zanzibar and Boer prisoners of war.

32 S.H. PARSONS. **The Cod Flakes at St John's, Newfoundland. c1900.** Claimed for England by Cabot in 1497, few attempts were made at permanent settlement in Newfoundland until the 17th century, although its rich fishing grounds were regularly visited by English, French, Portuguese and Spanish fleets. From 1675 the Newfoundland settlements were supervised during the fishing season by the Commodore of the Fleets: only in 1818 was the first resident governor appointed and Newfoundland raised to full colonial status. This photograph looks along the Straits, the narrow harbour entrance to St John's, with Newfoundlanders laying out gutted cod to dry on the wooden flakes.

33 PHOTOGRAPHER UNKNOWN. **Panorama of Port Stanley, Falkland Islands. c1905.** Discovered in 1592 by the English navigator John Davies, the Falklands were permanently settled by the British in 1833 and the Falkland Islands Commercial Fishery and Agricultural Association formed the following year. A formal civil administration was set up in 1841 and the seat of government moved to Port Stanley in 1843.

34 PHOTOGRAPHER UNKNOWN. **Levuka, the old capital of Fiji. c1880.** W.T. Pritchard, appointed the first British consul in Fiji in 1858, was based at Levuka and when the island was ceded to the Crown in 1874, it became the capital of the colony. The administration was transferred to Suva in 1882 however, and when much of Levuka was destroyed in the hurricane of 1886, few of the buildings were replaced and the town contracted in size in later years as Suva grew.

35 JOHN THOMSON. **Nicosia from the City Wall. 1878.** This view is reproduced in autotype in Thomson's *Through Cyprus with the camera in the autumn of 1878* (1879), where he was at pains to point the symbolic parallels between the architectural style of the city and the recent Turkish administration: 'These purely Eastern fortified dwellings afford a semblance of security against invasion, but sadly remind us of the despotic rule under which the people have struggled for centuries. They are for the most part built out of the soil on which they stand, and in this respect resemble huge ant-hills, under which the inhabitants were fain to burrow, unseen by their taskmasters, the Turks.'

E10 & E11 AFRICA

36 PHOTOGRAPHER UNKNOWN. **Steamer Point and Ordnance Bay, Aden. c1875.** As a strategically important coaling station on the Red Sea route between Egypt and India, Aden was annexed by Bombay in 1839 and continued to be governed from India until it became a Crown Colony in 1939. '...Steamer Point is arrived at, where there is a crescent (Prince of Wales Crescent) consisting of some fair-sized stone houses nearly all double and some treble-storied. Behind these again are several streets of double and single storied houses reaching to the hillside. Here are two hotels, a police station and the residences of a few consuls. Close by lie the coal grounds of the Government and the various steam navigation companies which have their depots at Aden. Not far from the crescent to the north-westward is the landing-pier...' (F.M. Hunter, *An account of the British Settlement of Aden in Arabia,* 1877).

□ 37 WILLIAM D. YOUNG. **Vasco da Gama Street, Mombasa. c1900.** A prosperous settlement since the sixteenth century occupied variously by the Arabs and the Portuguese, Mombasa was ruled from Zanzibar from the 1830s until its period as capital of the British East Africa Protectorate from 1888-1907. Vasco da Gama Street runs from Fort Jesus parallel with the waterfront, and part of the narrow gauge trolley line, in service on the island between 1890 and 1923, can be seen. In the foreground are the premises of Mr D.J. Dos Remedios' East Africa Stores, founded in Mombasa in 1898 and boasting 'a large stock of groceries, soft goods, liquors, and household goods; traveller's requisites are a speciality, and there is a splendid selection of glass and crockery.'

Previous left hand page:
Above: **Dunedin. c1858.** (E8/27)
Below: **Newtown tram sheds, Wellington, New Zealand. 1879.** (E8/28)

Previous right hand page:
Above: **Wharf Street, Victoria, British Columbia. c1867-70.** (E8/28A)
Below: **The town and Citadel of Quebec. c1870.** (E8/30)

Above: **Vasco da Gama Street, Mombasa. c1900.** (E10/37)
Below: **Central Freetown, Sierra Leone. 1890s.** (E10/41)

38 A.C. GOMES & SON. **Panorama of Zanzibar Town from the Harbour. c1905.** Zanzibar's strategic position as the base for the penetration of the East African hinterland and as the end point of the ivory and slaving routes from the interior had led to the installation of a British consul in 1840. Germany and France's recognition of Zanzibar as a British sphere of influence in 1890 in return for concessions elsewhere, led to the setting up of a Protectorate, a status the island retained until independence in 1963. Prominent at the left of the picture is the Beit el Ajeib ('House of Wonders') built for Sultan Seyyid Barghash in 1883 and badly damaged in 1896 when Seyyid Khalid briefly usurped the throne and the British mounted a bombardment of the waterfront. From 1911 the building housed government offices. In the centre of the panorama are the Old Consulate buildings, in use as such until 1874 when they were superseded by the buildings at the extreme right on Shangani Point. At this period the Old Consulate was used as a godown by the firm of Smith, Mackenzie and Co.

39 WILLIAM D. YOUNG. **Nairobi Hill. c1904.** Before the arrival of the Uganda Railway Nairobi was an uninhabited stretch of swampy and unhealthy but level ground. In 1899 it was selected as the headquarters of the railway so that sufficient stores and material would be readily available for the difficult engineering task of dropping the line down the Kikuyu Escarpment to the foot of the Rift Valley. The photographs shows residences on Nairobi Hill in the early days before the city was rebuilt on a modern town plan.

40 PHOTOGRAPHER UNKNOWN. **Salisbury market square, Southern Rhodesia. c1900.** The early years after the arrival of the Pioneer Column at Salisbury in 1890 were difficult ones for the settlers: gold deposits were not as extensive as had been expected and farming was a precarious occupation. Few remained solvent and the majority of the original pioneers left the country disappointed. The Matabele Rising of 1893, the war of 1896 and the growth of Bulawayo were additional setbacks, but in 1899 the Beira Railway reached Salisbury giving it an outlet on the coast, and its future prosperity was assured when, after delays caused by the Boer War, the railway link with Bulawayo and the Cape was completed in 1902.

□ 41 DIONYSIUS LEOMY. **Central Freetown, Sierra Leone. 1890s.** The view forms a section of a panorama taken from the tower of St George's Cathedral. The orderly lay-out of the streets reflects the origins of the city as a deliberately designed settlement. Chosen as a home for freed slaves, the first settlers arrived in 1787 and shortly afterwards the site was surveyed and the area divided into streets and house lots. The present lay-out of central Freetown dates from 1794 when the town was rebuilt after being destroyed by the French. The four storey house on the left on Gloucester Street is 'Horton Hall,' for several years the home of the doctor, educationalist and political thinker, James Africanus Horton (1835-1883). Oxford Street runs across the foreground of the photograph.

42 LISK-CAREW BROTHERS. **Hill Station, Freetown, Sierra Leone. c1908.** The visits to Freetown by Major (later Sir) Ronald Ross during his malaria investigations in 1899 and 1901 formed a convenient pretext for the growing racial segregation advocated by the Colonial Office between the Creole and European populations of Sierra Leone: of the 40 senior administrative posts in the colony in 1892, 18 were held by Africans; of the 92 such posts in 1912, the African representation had dropped to 15, five of which were later abolished. Ross' conclusions concerning the necessity for adequate drainage and the elimination of standing water near living quarters in the fight against the anopheles mosquito were largely ignored in favour of moving the city's European administrative staff to quarters in the hills south east of Freetown. Work started on the site towards the end of 1903 and three bungalows had been completed by April 1904. In the same year a railway connecting Hill Station with Water Street Station in Freetown was opened.

43 LISK-CAREW BROTHERS. **Wellington Street, Bathurst, The Gambia. c1913.** Saint Mary's Island was first occupied as a slave suppression post in 1816 with the hope that British traders would also set up in business. This hope was soon justified and by 1818 the population, including the garrison, stood at 600, although the town itself was 'nothing more than a number of thatched huts.' By 1820 'many elegant and substantial houses' had been built and the following year a government house, barracks and officers' quarters were erected. This photograph looks east along Wellington Street towards the junction with Russell Street. The Treasury and Customs buildings (commenced in 1849) are on the left.

44 J.W. ROWLAND. **Lagos looking east from the church tower. c1885.** A Protectorate was established by the British in Lagos, an important slave market until the mid 19th century, in 1851, and the area ceded to the Crown in 1861. The island and its hinterland formed a colony (administered at various periods by Sierra Leone and the Gold Coast, and for a time forming part of the Oil Rivers Protectorate) until its absorption into Southern Nigeria in 1906. In the foreground of this photograph are the government steamers *Gertrude* and *Ekuro,* moored at the Government House pier.

45 PHOTOGRAPHER UNKNOWN. **Marina Embankment, Lagos, during construction. 1880s.** The Expanding Commercial importance of Lagos highlighted the poor facilities of the town, particularly along the Marina where the principal business premises were situated. Work on reclaiming the island's swamps and the unhealthy foreshore was carried on in a piecemeal fashion for many years, but only in 1880 was work started in earnest. 1370 yards of waterfront had been rebuilt by the end of 1890 and the work continued well into the present century.

46 PHOTOGRAPHER UNKNOWN. **James Town, Accra. c1885.** The city of Accra grew in the 19th century from the three fortified trading posts built in the preceding two centuries by the Dutch (Fort Crèvecoeur, later renamed Fort Ussher), the Danish (Christianborg Castle) and the British (Fort James), and was selected as the capital of the Gold Coast in 1876. James Town was the European residential section of the city, which developed rapidly after 1909 when railway construction began to open up the rich cocoa growing areas of the hinterland.

Above: **Raffles Square, Singapore. c1875-80.** (E12/48)
Below: **Pedder Street from the Wharf, Hong Kong. c1889.** (E12/49)

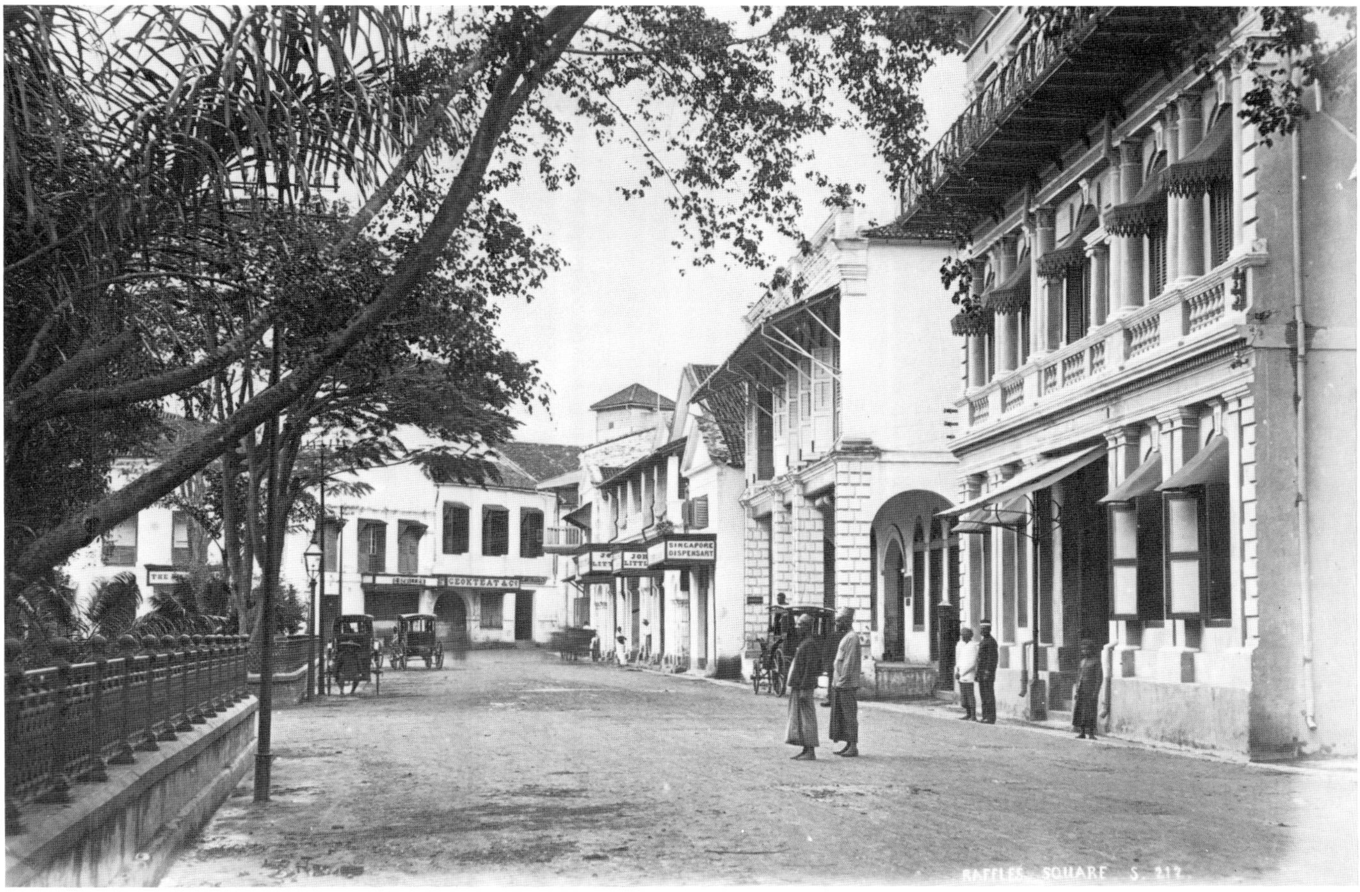
SINGAPORE DISPENSARY
RAFFLES SQUARE

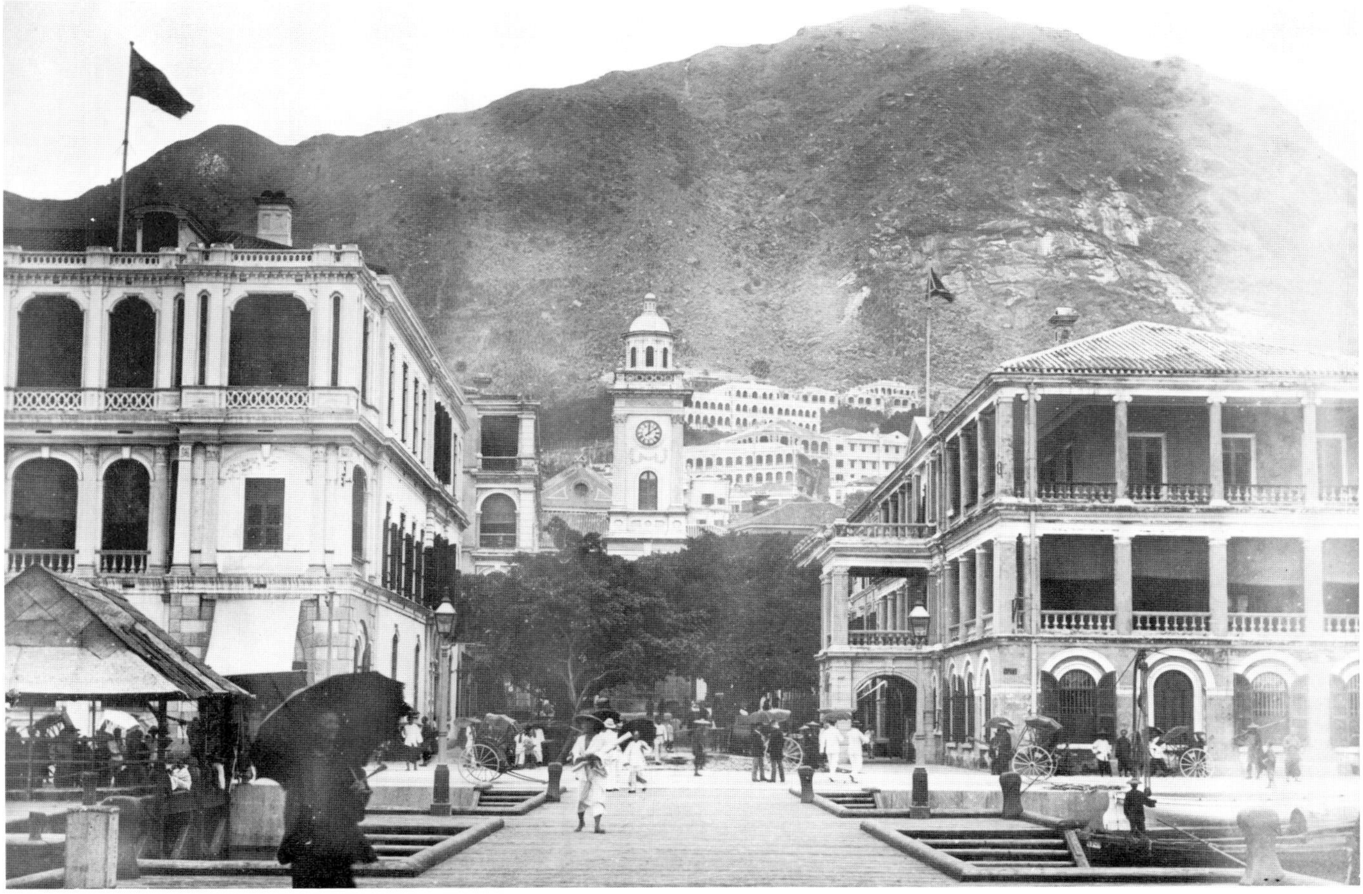

E12 INDIA & FAR EAST

47 NICHOLAS & CO. **The sea front at Madras. c1880.** This view looks north along the sea front at Madras with the buildings comprising Fort St George at the left. The earliest of the East India Company's stations on the east coast, Madras was first settled in 1639 and the original portions of Fort St George built in the mid 1640s. The commercial expansion of the city was hampered by the lack of a good harbour and ships had to anchor in the open roadstead while landing passengers braved the ferocious surf of the foreshore in the deep-bottomed massulah boats. Improvement of the situation began with the construction of a 1000 foot screw-pile pier (visible in background) which was opened in 1862. Work on a protected artificial harbour to the north of Fort St George was started in 1875, but six year's work was largely destroyed by the cyclone of 1881 and the project was not completed until 1896.

□ 48 G.R. LAMBERT & CO. **Raffles Square, Singapore. c1875-80 and c1900.** The phenomenal rise of Singapore in the years after 1819 when Thomas Stamford Raffles obtained the swampy island for the British was the result of a combination of factors: its central position on the routes to and from the Far east, its policy of free trade and the encouragement of settlement, and the commercial acumen of Chinese immigrants all played their part. Raffles Square or Place (also known as Commercial Square) was the business centre of the city and its changing, ever more prosperous face can be seen in these two photographs. The premises of John Little and Co., one of Singapore's largest general retailers, can be seen in both prints. The business had occupied the same site since its establishment in 1845, and by 1908 another extension was being planned.

□ 49 PHOTOGRAPHER UNKNOWN. **Pedder Street from the Wharf, Hong Kong. c1889.** The clock tower, erected by public subscription in 1862, stands at the junction of Pedder Street and Queen's Road. The latter was named shortly after the founding of the colony in 1841 and land plots were surveyed and auctioned off in the July of that year. The buildings at the right were the premises of Jardine, Matheson and Co., traders in the east since 1834 and who moved their headquarters from Macao to Hong Kong in 1842. These officers were occupied by the business from 1864 until their demolition in 1907. At the time this photograph was taken, the road running across the foreground was the Praya, directly on the waterfront. Between 1890 and 1904 a 250 yard wide section of the waterfront was reclaimed and the old Praya became Des Voeux Road, named after Sir William Des Voeux (Governor 1887-1891).

E13 THREE GOVERNMENT HOUSES

50 SAMUEL BOURNE. **Government House, Calcutta. c1869.** Built at Wellesley's instigation and designed by Lieutenant Charles Wyatt of the Bengal Engineers, the house had as its prototype Kedleston Hall in Derbyshire, the home of one of its later and most distinguished occupants, Lord Curzon. Conceived by Wellesley as an imperial symbol of British government in India, the building was erected between 1799 and 1803 and this view looks across the garden towards the south facade: the dome was a later addition to the building, added to give some visual relief from the horizontal line of the roof (it served no practical function and was invisible from the interior). The unauthorised expense incurred in building the house was partly responsible for Wellesley's recall from his post as Governor General.

51 JOHNSTON AND HOFFMANN. **The Throne Room, Government House, Calcutta. c1905.** Adjoining the Marble Hall is the Throne Room where, in addition to Viceregal durbars, dinner parties for not more than 50 guests were held. Beneath the canopy at the left is the throne which had once belonged to Tippu Sultan.

52 ALFRED LOBO. **Government House, Entebbe. 1908.** Designed by Captain Usborne of the Royal Engineers and completed in July 1908, Sir Henry Hesketh Bell's chosen residence offers a surprisingly suburban contrast to the majority of Government Houses. In replacing the Administrator's former residence, 'a very large bungalow of wood and iron, raised high on piles,' Bell, in the absence of a suitable indigenous architectural style from which to borrow, decided on 'a really comfortable English house...The house is therefore of the big 'villa' type with very spacious verandahs on the ground floor. The reception rooms are large and lofty and nearly every bedroom has its own entirely private little balcony commanding views over the lake that will make early breakfast a pure delight.' (Sir Henry Hesketh Bell, *Glimpses of a Governor's Life,* 1946). Bell's two pet lion cubs roam the garden in the foreground.

53 SIR HENRY HESKETH BELL. **Government House, Entebbe interiors. 1908.**

54 A.C. GOMES & SON. **The Residency, Zanzibar. c1905.** The Residency was built in 'saracenic' style in 1903 for the Regent of Zanzibar, A.S. Rogers. J.H. Sinclair, the architect, also designed the Government House at Dar es Salaam, a more imposing mansion in similar style.

55 (?) A.C. GOMES & SON. **Interior, the Residency, Zanzibar. c1905.**

Rule & recreation

'What would one not give to have photographs of the Pharoahs or the Caesars, of the travellers, and their observations, who supplied Ptolemy with his early record of the world, of Marco Polo, and the places and peoples he visited on his arduous journey? We are now making history, and the sun picture supplies the means of passing down a record of what we are, and what we have achieved in this nineteenth century of our progress.'

This expression of faith in the importance of photography as a recorder of history's onward march was given by John Thomson in a talk on exploration and photography delivered to the Geographical section of the British Association in Cardiff on April 24 1891. Photography's potential as a documenter of imperial achievement was well understood by this time, however: in 1884 Commodore Erskine had brought up two Sydney photographers to record the events connected with the proclamation of a British protectorate over South East New Guinea, and in the same year that Thomson made these remarks, Major G.C. Denton had commissioned N. Walwin Holm to photograph the raising of the British flag in the territories of Igbessa, Ado, Ilaro and Pokra on the Lagos mainland.

Thomson himself ranks among the most accomplished of an intrepid group of travelling photographers whose journeys in search of the picturesque, the exotic and the unknown introduced a public both to other civilizations and to the impact of Britain's colonial presence among them. The greatest of Thomson's photographic journeys of exploration was his penetration of the Chinese empire in a number of forays from his base in Hong Kong between 1868 and 1872. The results of these travels were issued in four folio volumes entitled *Illustrations of China and its people* (1873-74) and lavishly illustrated with collotypes from Thomson's photographs. There was little doubt in Thomson's mind that China lay ripe for commercial exploitation and for the benefits of European ideas, and his descriptive text is at pains to point out, for instance, the instructive contrast in the treaty port of Shanghai of the 'native dwellings huddled together as if pressed back to make way for the higher civilization that has planted a city in their midst.' A few years later the point was made yet more explicit when Thomson travelled to Cyprus to photograph the island and its people shortly after Britain had taken over the administration from the Ottoman Empire. In the introduction to *Through Cyprus with the camera in the autumn of 1878* (2 vols, 1879), illustrated with sixty woodburytypes and autotypes, Thomson states that as well as providing 'a faithful souvenir' of an island 'woefully wrecked by Turkish maladministration,' his photographs will supply 'incontestable evidence of the present condition of Cyprus, and they will also afford a source of comparison in after years, when, under the influence of British rule, the place has risen from its ruins.'

Thomson's belief in photography's importance was practically expressed in his appointment, at his own suggestion, as instructor in photography to the Royal Geographical Society, so that African explorers in particular might return from their travels with accurate illustrated records; but his greater influence lies in the way in which he married photography and descriptive text in his books to emphasize the instructive elements in the picture and the progressive benefits of British rule as he saw them. Thomson's were by no means the first printed books to utilize photography extensively (indeed, particularly in India, they had been produced since the 1850s), but his particular style created a *genre* which is continued in such works as J.W. Lindt's *Picturesque New Guinea* (1887). Like most of Thomson's books, this too was published by the firm of Sampson Low who themselves, in association with the fine collotype printing of the Autotype Company of London, were to produce a succession of photographically illustrated travel books.

The celebrations attending the Diamond Jubilee of 1897 stand as an apogee of imperial pride and photographers were quick to take commercial advantage of the pictorial opportunities offered by the occasion, while the resulting photographs were used as incontrovertible evidence of progress and harmonious government under the British flag. In Hong Kong in 1896 the unveiling of Queen Victoria's statue was ceremoniously celebrated and extensively photographed, while a gathering of chiefs for the Jubilee celebrations in Lagos was photographed as concrete proof of new found amity under British rule. Commercially also the events connected with the Jubilee brought forth numerous publications which unambiguously commandeered photography as an ally to progress. Thus R.C. Hurley produced *Sixty Diamond Jubilee photographs of Hong Kong,* a small album of prints prefaced with an explanation of its imperial significance: 'In publishing, on the occasion of the Diamond Jubilee of Her Most Gracious Majesty Queen Victoria, this collection of pictures of Hong Kong – the first of which displays the island in all its primitive barrenness and desolation – the Author would venture to draw attention to the fact, that the extraordinary transition here illustrated lies wholly within the period of the sixty years covered by Her Majesty's Glorious Reign . . . This unpretending collection of illustrations is offered to the public as a suggestive and lasting memorial to the Grandest Jubilee the world has ever witnessed.'

More substantial publications also appeared in England, one such being *The Queen's Empire* (1897), a collection of nearly 300 photographs printed in half-tone with descriptive captions and an introduction by H.O. Arnold-Foster M.P. With pictures grouped into sections comparing life in the various colonies with corresponding scenes from British life, the volume was both propagandist and sincere in tone, painting an idealised picture of unity in diversity where, 'with all the variety and all the novelty there is yet, happily, one bond of union, one mark of uniformity. In every part of the Empire we shall find some trace of the work which Britain is doing throughout the world – the work of civilising, of governing, of protecting life and property, and of extending the benefits of trade and commerce.'

The Queen's Empire, and its many subsequent variant editions, form a culmination of the realisation of photography's power, graphically expressed through Samuel Bourne's revealing use of military metaphor thirty-five years before: 'From the earliest days of the calotype, the curious tripod, with its mysterious chamber and mouth of brass, taught the natives of this country that their conquerors were the inventors of other instruments beside the formidable guns of their artillery, which, though as suspicious perhaps in appearance, attained their object with less noise and smoke.'

F1 PHOTOGRAPHER UNKNOWN. **Hausa Officers, Gold Coast. 1880s.**

F2 DURBARS

1 PHOTOGRAPHER UNKNOWN. **Sir Richard Temple's camp at the Imperial Assemblage, Delhi. January 1877.** 'A happy opportunity of celebrating an important political and historical event,' the Assemblage at Delhi was held to ratify the act of the Crown's assumption of sovereignty over India and to formally proclaim Queen Victoria as Empress of India. A city of tents and pavilions was set up on the plains surrounding Delhi (the English camp being on the site occupied by the army in 1857) and on December 23 1876 the Viceroy Lord Lytton arrived to inaugurate the ceremonial festivites. Proclamation Day was on January 1 1877 and the Assemblage broke up on the 5th. One of the most important aspects of the Durbar was the convening of meetings to discuss means of fighting the famines then raging in the Madras and Bombay Presidencies. Sir Richard Temple (1826-1902), newly appointed Governor of Bombay, was made a special commissioner by Lytton to investigate and formulate measures for famine relief.

2 BOURNE AND SHEPHERD. **The Khan of Khelat with chiefs and ministers at the Imperial Assemblage, Delhi. January 1877.** By treaty of 1876 the Khan of Khelat was established by the British as the leader of the confederacy of Princely States comprising Baluchistan and his presence at the Durbar was seen by J. Talboys Wheeler in his *History of the Imperial Assemblage at Delhi* (London 1877) as a vindication of the extension of British rule on the North West Frontier: 'The Khan of Khelat came in person with a large body of his chiefs and followers. The arrival of these men was one of the most interesting and curious episodes in the Assemblage. They had been fighting one another for many years: Khelat had been in terrible disorder. The intervention of the British Government became an absolute necessity. No sooner was the intervention put in force than the whole country quieted down. The Khan and his Sirdars ceased to breathe vengeance against each other. They arrived in Delhi in the same train like a happy family. The pacification of Khelat was inaugurated at Delhi by the Khan and his Sirdars. Their visit was one of the most important incidents in the history of the Assemblage.'

□ 3 LALA DEEN DIYAL. **The Prince of Wales replying to the municipal address on his arrival in Bombay. November 9 1905.** Almost 30 years to the day after his father's visit to the sub-continent, the Prince and Princess of Wales arrived in Bombay on November 9 1905 for a five month tour of India. The Prince is here seen replying to the speech of welcome given by the President of the Corporation of Bombay, Sir Pherozeshah Mehta. The Prince's entourage travelled north to Peshawar, and then to Calcutta and Burma. Returning to India at Madras, the tour proceeded north to Quetta and Chaman, finally departing from Karachi on March 19 1906.

4 PHOTOGRAPHER UNKNOWN. **The Central Pavilion at the Delhi Durbar. December 12 1911.** His interest in India stimulated by the tour of 1905-06, George V determined to visit the sub-continent again to announce in person his coronation. In addition, he hoped that his own presence might revive and consolidate Indian loyalty to Britain in the face of growing nationalism. Originally his intention had been to actually crown himself in Delhi, but unforseen difficulties arose: it was discovered that no one was entitled to remove the crown from England, the Archbishop of Canterbury voiced religious reservations, and the matter of creating a precedent was discussed. Ultimately it was decided that the King would attend the Durbar wearing a crown specially made for the occasion. The royal party arrived in India on December 2 and at the ceremony itself the King, after receiving the homage of the Indian princes, made two important political announcements: the revision of Lord Curzon's partition of Bengal and the transfer of the capital from Calcutta to Delhi. After a programme of ceremonial, sightseeing and hunting, the King and Queen left India on January 10 1912.

□ 5 W. BEATTIE. **Meeting of Prime Minister Seddon of New Zealand and King Mahuta at Huntly. April 5 1898.** Richard John Seddon was Premier of New Zealand from 1893 until his death in 1906 and during this period made several tours through Maori districts attempting to persuade the Maoris away from the separatism which had been dominant since the wars of the 1860s and 70s. In April 1898 he visited King Mahuta at Huntly to discuss proposed land legislation and is seen here with his entourage and the members of Mahuta's Kauhanganui (Great Council), the whole group flanked by a Maori and a colonial policeman. Gilbert Mair, who had played a prominent part in the defeat of Te Kooti in 1870, acted as interpreter during the meeting.

6 AFONG. **Celebrations of the Coronation of King Edward VII at Wei Hai Wei. August 9 1902.** A secluded outpost of the Empire on the north China coast, Wei Hai Wei was leased as a treaty port by the British from 1898-1930 and served as a sanatorium and flying naval base for the China Squadron. (Sir) Reginald Fleming Johnston (1874-1938), seen here at the right of the picture, served a large part of his career in Wei Hai Wei and wrote a history of the area entitled *Lion and dragon in northern China* (1910). In honour of the Coronation the chief port of the dependency was renamed Port Edward, naval and military reviews were held, the King's portrait was taken in procession around the town and the Chinese headmen presented ceremonial scrolls before which they kowtowed, 'the most striking testimony of respect for a foreign ruler,' in the words of the Administrator James Haldane Stewart Lockhart, 'on the part of the Chinese that I have ever witnessed.'

Above: **The Prince of Wales replying to the municipal address on his arrival in Bombay. November 9 1905.** (F2/3)
Below: **Meeting of Prime Minister Seddon of New Zealand and King Mahuta at Huntly. April 5 1898.** (F2/5)

F3 DIAMOND JUBILEE

☐ 7 N. WALWIN HOLM. **Chief Olowa and retinue at the Jubilee Durbar, Lagos. June 22 1897.** As well as a celebration of the sixty years of Queen Victoria's rule, the Diamond Jubilee was seen as an opportune occasion for furthering the aims of Empire: 'The celebration...was utilized...as the occasion for bringing together at headquarters a representative gathering of native kings and chiefs, collected from all parts of the Colony and Protectorate, that was probably unique in the history of Lagos for numbers and importance. Many distant and widely separated people met at Government House in June last, to find for the first time that they had one interest and sentiment in common – that of allegiance and loyalty to the Queen – and it cannot be doubted that such a gathering of the clans, some of them perhaps not over-fond of one another, under one standard, must have a vast and most important effect upon the Colony.' *(Lagos Colony, Annual Report for 1897).*

☐ 8 W.L.H. SKEEN & CO. **Governor's enclosure at the Jubilee celebrations, Bogambra Ground, Kandy. June 29 1897.** 'The weather was brilliant, old King Sol smiling most approvingly on the demonstration of loyalty to Queen Victoria... several photographic views were taken of the enclosure and its surroundings. His Excellency in a clear voice read the loyal address of the inhabitants of Ceylon to Her Gracious Majesty... Immediately after the reading a salute of 60 guns was fired; the Lancashire troops presented arms and the band played the National Anthem.' *(Ceylon Overland Observer,* July 1 1897). The elephants in the foreground knelt as Governor Ridgeway's entourage passed on its way to the dais.

9 MEE CHEEUNG. **Inauguration of the Queen Victoria statue, Hong Kong. May 28 1896.** Statues in celebration of the rule of Queen Victoria appeared at some stage of the reign in the capital cities of almost every colony and the approach of the Diamond Jubilee of 1897 produced an upsurge of this form of homage. The Hong Kong statue was situated on reclaimed land at the junction of Chater and Wardley Streets (later Statue Square) and was unveiled with due ceremony on May 28 1896. In the background scaffolding can be seen on the nearly completed new Hong Kong Club.

F4 ROYAL VISITS

10 JOHN THOMSON. **Arrival of the Duke of Edinburgh at Pedder's Wharf, Hong Kong. November 2 1869.** Prince Alfred, Duke of Edinburgh, after entering the navy in 1858 was commissioned Captain of the *Galatea* in 1867, and during a number of royal visits made while commanding the ship arrived in Hong Kong on October 31 1869, although it was not until November 2 that the official landing was made. The ceremony at the landing is described by the Revd. William Beach in *Visit of H.R.H. the Duke of Edinburgh to Hong Kong in 1869* (illustrated with tipped-in prints by John Thomson): 'Precisely at the hour fixed, 11 o'clock, closely copying the punctuality for which our Sovereign Lady is so celebrated, His Royal Highness made his official landing at Pedder's Wharf... One of the most striking spectacles connected with the Royal visit was presented to the eye as His Royal Highness approached the shore, followed by the multitude of boats, which, as soon as he had passed them, closed in and took their places behind the Royal barge.' After being met by the Governor, the Duke passed under the triumphal arch and travelled to the City Hall in a state sedan chair of yellow velvet embroidered with silver and with a silk canopy, 'amidst the booming of guns and the loud cheers of the large crowd assembled to do him honour.' After two weeks of festivities and ceremonial, the Duke departed on November 10.

11 W.L.H. SKEEN & CO. **The Duke of Edinburgh and party at the Pavilion, Kandy. April 1870.** In contrast to the civic festivities at Hong Kong, the Duke of Edinburgh's stay in Ceylon from March 30-May 10 1870 was devoted to outdoor pursuits: a visit to the elephant kraals was arranged and much of the visit was taken up with hunting. Seen here with Prince Alfred are Sir Hercules Robinson (Governor of Ceylon 1865-72) and family; Lieutenant (later Admiral) Charles Beresford (1846-1919), a brother officer on the *Galatea;* and Hon. Eliot Yorke (1843–1878), an equerry to the Duke.

☐ 12 JOSE ANJO. **Visit of Princess Marie Louise of Schleswig-Holstein to Antigua. March 1913.** The Governor of the Leeward Islands, Sir Henry Hesketh Bell, stands beside Princess Marie Louise as an address of welcome is read out on her arrival at St John's. A grand-daughter of Queen Victoria, the Princess was asked to convey a message of goodwill from George V to his West Indian subjects and during her visit also opened an inter-colonial exhibition in Barbados. She stayed in Antigua for two days, visiting English Harbour, the Central Sugar Factory at Gunthorpes, and the hospital and poor house.

13 PHOTOGRAPHER UNKNOWN. **The Duke and Duchess of York in Uganda. 1925.** The Royal visit to Uganda by the Duke and Duchess of York, later King George VI and Queen Elizabeth, lasted from February 13 to March 4 1925. As well as the ceremonial inspections and festivities a good deal of the tour was spent on safari.

F5 & F6 RECREATIONS

☐ 14 (?) A.J. TATTERSALL. **Sailors from H.M.S. 'Katoomba' entertained by Robert Louis Stevenson at Vailima, Samoa. September 12 1893.** Stevenson recorded this entertainment in his journal as 'being perhaps the brightest in the annals of Vailima.' After a meal of chicken, ham, fruits, lemonade and claret negus flavoured with rum and limes, 'they played to us, they danced, they sang, they tumbled... and so they wound away down the hill with ever another call at the bugle, leaving us extinct with fatigue, but perhaps the most contented hosts that ever watched the departure of successful guests.' Among the members of Stevenson's Samoan household seen in the photograph are Graham Balfour, R.L.S.' cousin and later his biographer (standing behind the novelist), and Bazett Haggard, brother of Rider Haggard, standing with Isobel Strong in front of R.L.S.

15 PHOTOGRAPHER UNKNOWN. **Amateur theatricals, Darjeeling. 1872.** Major Lance, Captain Lemessurier, Captain Henderson, Major Woodward, Miss E. Judge and Miss Vice are posed in their costumes for a performance of *Slasher and Crasher* at the hill station of Darjeeling.

Above: **Chief Olowa and retinue at the Jubilee Durbar, Lagos. June 22 1897.** (F3/7)
Below: **Governor's enclosure at the Jubilee celebrations, Bogambra Ground, Kandy. June 29 1897.** (F3/8)

16 PHOTOGRAPHER UNKNOWN. **Admiralty House, Clarence Hill, Bermuda. c1870.** Although Bermuda became the headquarters of the North America and West Indies Squadron in 1767, early commanders had no official residence until 1816 when the colony passed over to the Crown the building and land in north west Pembroke which became Admiralty House. Plans were put forward for rebuilding the house at various times between 1822 and 1844, but it remained in use as such (with a number of additions and alterations) until 1956.

□17 PHOTOGRAPHER UNKNOWN. **Band in the Parade Gardens, Kingston, Jamaica. c1880.** A mixed European and Jamaican band poses for the photographer in the Parade Gardens in front of the Coke Methodist Church. In 1914 the gardens were renamed the Victoria Park by Princess Marie Louise and in 1979 became the Sir William Grant Park.

18 A. HUGH FISHER. **An up-country picnic in British North Borneo. 1907.**

□19 SAMUEL BOURNE. **Hunting party in camp, Srinagar. 1864.** Intersected by canals and waterways, Srinagar in the Vale of Kashmir abounds with waterfowl; its main importance from the big game hunter's viewpoint however, was as a staging post on the route to the Himalayas where stores could be purchased, porters hired and licences obtained.

20 WILLIAM NOTMAN. **Caribou hunters resting, Canada. 1866.** The photograph is one of a series produced by Notman and sold as a set entitled *Sports, Pastimes and Pursuits of Canada: Cariboo Hunting.* These series of studio tableaux were considered marvellously realistic although to the modern eye they have a somewhat wooden air of unreality. In the 1870s Notman moved on to even more ambitious scenes, illustrating, by the use of montage and composite photographs, such activities as sledging, camping and curling, and producing large group photographs from individual portraits.

21 PHOTOGRAPHER UNKNOWN. **Hunting party in Kedah. October 1889.** A hunting party poses on the verandah of the Astana Anak Bukit, the country house of the Sultan of Kedah. At the right, Frank Swettenham stands beside the Raja Muda, Tunku Abdul Aziz. Robert William Duff (1867-1937), founder in 1903 of the Duff Development Company, stands at the left of the group.

22 PHOTOGRAPHER UNKNOWN. **Shanghai Race Course. c1875.** Taken by the British in 1842, Shanghai became one of the original treaty ports by the terms of the Treaty of Nanking, with English, French and American concessions. The European community soon set about organising a turf club and the first recorded meeting took place in the autumn of 1850. The grounds seen here were purchased in 1858. Prior to 1854 English thoroughbreds were imported, but after that date Mongolian ponies were raced.

Previous left hand page:
Above: **Visit of Princess Marie Louise of Schleswig-Holstein to Antigua. March 1913.** (F4/12)
Below: **Sailors from H.M.S. 'Katoomba' entertained by Robert Louis Stevenson at Vailima, Samoa. September 12 1983.** (F5/14)

Previous right hand page:
Above: **Band in the Parade Gardens, Kingston, Jamaica. c1880.** (F5/17)
Below: **Hunting party in camp, Srinagar.** (F5/19)

23 JOHNSTON AND HOFFMAN. **Royal Calcutta Turf Club's Race Stand: Viceroy's Cup Day. c1910.** The first race meetings took place in Calcutta in 1803 in the face of Governor General Wellesley's disapproval, and by the end of the century Viceroy's Cup Day had become one of the most important social occasions of the Calcutta season: '...Racing, which appeals to the Indian no less than to the European, and on Viceroy's and King Emperor's Cup days draws to the race-course a crowd of enormous proportions...Society is there in all its 'glad rags' – Maharajahs, Rajahs and princelings of nearly every state in India, Europeans, official and non-official; ladies of every grade, 'in the swim' and out of it throng the enclosure...' (Allister Macmillan, *Seaports of India and Ceylon,* 1928).

24 HARVIE AND SUTCLIFFE. **The Terrace and Carriage Paddock, Flemington Race Course, Melbourne. c1900.** The first races were held in Melbourne in 1841 by the newly organised Port Phillip Turf Club, which was superseded in 1864 by the Victoria Racing Club. The great event of the racing season, the two mile Melbourne Cup, was instituted in 1861 and is held on the first Tuesday of November.

□25 A. SYLVESTER TAYLOR. **The Barbados Bicycle Club in front of the billiard room at Government House. c1882.** The penny-farthing, or 'ordinary,' bicycle remained in vogue from about 1872-85, during which period an extraordinary cycling craze swept England and eventually reached her overseas possessions. For the smaller man the tricycle obviated the difficulty of reaching the pedals from the high saddle. The date of the formation of the Barbados Bicycle Club has not been determined, although the presence of the Governor Sir William Robinson in this photograph (standing in the centre of the group in the portico of the billiard room) dates this print to between 1880 and 1885. Cycling retained its popularity in the island: sufficient support existed for Frederick Martinez to organise a marathon race in 1909 and *Da Costa's Barbados Illustrated* was able to report in 1911 that 'cycling is a favourite exercise with all classes in the community. There are hundreds of machines on the island, and the cyclist is everywhere in evidence.'

□26 PHOTOGRAPHER UNKNOWN. **Tennis party at Government House, Grenada. c1890.** In the foreground stands Sir Walter Francis Hely-Hutchinson (1849-1913), Governor of the Windward Islands from 1889-93 and later of Natal and Zululand (1893-1901) and Cape Colony (1901-10).

□27 PHOTOGRAPHER UNKNOWN. **Cricket match at the Tanglin Barracks, Singapore. 1869-70.** Evidence of the playing of cricket in Singapore dates back to 1837 when complaints were made of Europeans playing the game on the Esplanade on Sunday afternoons, but the first recorded match was played on October 14 1852 between 'a picked eleven v. the Club,' when six men on one side and nine on the other played, the picked eleven making 11 in the first innings and 1 in the second, only to be beaten by the Club who made 14 and 12. After this inauspicious start cricket gained popularity rapidly and several clubs were formed. The Tanglin Barracks were the home of the Singapore Volunteers (raised at the outbreak of the Crimean War) and were built during Governor Cavenagh's period of office (1861-67).

Above: **The Barbados Bicycle Club in front of the billiard room at Government House. c1882.** (F6/25)
Below: **Tennis party at Government House, Grenada. c1890.** (F6/26)

28 PHOTOGRAPHER UNKNOWN. **The Straits Settlements Cricket Team of 1897.** The popularity of cricket in the Straits Settlements led to regular tours being arranged by the Singapore Cricket Club against other colonial teams. The first of these was to Hong Kong in 1890. Thereafter regular fixtures took place with Ceylon and Hong Kong. The 1897 team, probably the strongest ever fielded by the Straits, visited Hong Kong in November, easily beating the colony, the Shanghai team and a combined Hong Kong and Shanghai team. In the Shanghai game, R.M. McKenzie took ten wickets for 57 runs.

F7 AT WORK

□29 PHOTOGRAPHER UNKNOWN. **H.H. Davies and E.A. Richardson outside the Principal's bungalow, Colvin Taluqdars' School, Lucknow. c1905.** The Taluqdars were the landowners and minor rajahs of Oudh, mostly related to the deposed King of Oudh, and the school was created by Sir Auckland Colvin for the education of their sons. Herbert Howel Davies (1872-1910) was selected as principal by Colvin in 1902 and under his care, according to his obituary in the *Mussoorie Echo*, 'one would have to search far before finding a school in which there is a healthier, manlier tone, or in which there is a more honourable feeling of esprit de corps amongst the pupils past and present.'

30 W. BUCHANAN SMITH. **On tour in the British Cameroons. c1927.** For colonial administrators acting as residents and district officers much of the year was spent on tour visiting outlying areas, settling disputes and collecting taxes. The German Cameroons, conquered by British and French forces in 1916, were administered after the First World War under mandates from the League of Nations. Britain's portion, the smaller western section, was governed as part of Nigeria from 1923 and in 1927 Walter (later Sir Walter) Buchanan Smith (1879-1944) was appointed Senior Resident. This snapshot is one of the many he took while on tour and shows his assistant Maurice Swabey (b. 1902), who joined the Nigeria Civil Service in 1925.

31 PHOTOGRAPHER UNKNOWN. **Collecting hut tax, Basutoland. c1910.** Taken under British protection in 1868, Basutoland (after a period of administration from the Cape) became one of the High Commission Territories. As in many early African administrations, revenue was raised principally by a tax on huts, which could be paid either in money or labour. The photograph shows men of the Basutoland Mounted Police on a tour of collection.

32 VISCOUNT BLEDISLOE. **Provincial and District Commissioners leaving a 'Boma' (courthouse) in a bushcar, Mongu, Barotseland. 1938.** This is one of a series of snapshots taken by Charles Bathurst, Viscount Bledisloe while Chairman of the 1938 Royal Commission on closer union between Northern and Southern Rhodesia and Nyasaland.

□33 C.W. HATTERSLEY. **Survey team setting out, Uganda. c1906.** With the government's assumption of the Imperial British East Africa Company's responsibilities in Uganda in 1893 and the declaration of a protectorate in Buganda the following year, the delineation of the nature and extent of Britain's new possession became a matter of importance, particularly in regard to the borders with German territory to the south. Before leaving England on his appointment as Special Commissioner in Uganda, Harry Johnston had discussed the need for an accurate survey and made provisions in the estimates for 1900-01 of £2,400 for the setting up of a survey department.

□34 PHOTOGRAPHER UNKNOWN. **Mr Lockhart and Mr Wong fixing the first boundary mark of the New Territorties at Starlet Inlet, Hong Kong. March 17 1899.** Leased from the Chinese for a period of 99 years from July 1 1898, the New Territories were originally required for the colony's defensive purposes. The Colonial Secretary J.H.S. Lockhart (later Administrator of Wei Hai Wei) and Mr Wong Tsun-Shin, the representative of the Viceroy of Canton, fixed disputed portions of the boundary and on April 16 1899 the territories were officially taken over by the British authorities.

F8 MALAYA

35 (JAMES BIRCH). **Birch and Sultan Abdullah at Batak Rabit. April 12 1874.** From late March until early April 1874 Birch, the first British Resident appointed in the Malay states, made a semi-official tour of Selangor and Perak, holding meetings with the various sultans and chiefs. His party arrived at Batak Rabit on April 11 and on the following day 'we all landed... at 8.30 a.m. and had a great interview with a great deal of saluting, and abundance of heat, and crowds of natives. We got one good photograph of the Sultan, Laxamana, Shahbandar and the Sultan's followers.' Frank Swettenham (1850-1946) who accompanied Birch on the tour, stands at his left shoulder. Birch had been appointed Resident at Larut by the terms of the Pangkor Engagement of January 1874 and his murder in 1875 led to the Perak War and affected the spread of British influence over the Malayan Peninsula. Sultan Abdullah was exiled to the Seychelles for his complicity in Birch's murder.

36 J.F.A. MCNAIR. **Frank Swettenham and Tristram Speedy at Kuala Kangsar during the military occupation of Perak. 1876.** Swettenham, who had been sent up-river to deliver proclamations announcing the extension of the British Resident's powers, returned to Pasir Salak to learn of Birch's murder a few days before (November 2 1875). Swettenham recovered and buried his colleague's body, and immediately and unsuccessfully marched against Pasir Salak. The town was taken a week later and following this a large punitive expedition of 1600 men was organized, troops being brought in from Hong Kong and India for the purpose. The military opposition had in fact been greatly over-estimated, and although Perak was occupied until mid-1877 all military action had been completed by the end of 1875. With Swettenham in this photograph is Tristram Speedy (1836-1910), a colourful character who, after periods of service in the Indian Police and in the Abyssinian Campaign of 1867-68, was Assistant Resident at Larut from 1874-76.

□37 PHOTOGRAPHER UNKNOWN. **Officers and NCOs of the Perak Armed Police at Taiping. c1880.** The formation of a police force in Perak was authorised by the Colonial Secretary of the Straits Settlements in 1876, and it became known as the Perak Armed Police from about 1879 when the force consisted of some 600 men under the command of Major Paul Swinburne. At about this time the headquarters were moved from Bandar Bharu to Taiping. In 1884 the First Perak Sikhs were formed from the Armed Police and on Federation in 1896 the Perak Sikhs and the Armed Police from the other Malay states were merged to form the Malay States Guides.

Above: **Cricket match at the Tanglin Barracks, Singapore. 1869-70.** (F6/27)
Below: **H.H. Davies and E.A. Richardson outside the Principal's bungalow, Colvin Taluqdars' School, Lucknow. c1905.** (F7/29)

38 PHOTOGRAPHER UNKNOWN. **The Kuala Lumpur Voluntary Fire Brigade. c1888.** Started in the early 1880s by the Deputy State Engineer, H.F. Bellamy, the Kuala Lumpur Fire Brigade retained its volunteer nature well into the present century. Some of the 18 original members are here seen standing in front of the engine house. In the background are the Police Station (built 1886) at the left, and the Police Barracks (built 1887-88).

39 G.R. LAMBERT & CO. **The Federal Conference at Kuala Lumpur. July 1903.** The year after the federation of the Malay States in 1896 (by which a centralised administration under the authority of a Resident General with headquarters at Kuala Lumpur was set up), Swettenham had held a conference at Kuala Kangsar which he adjudged 'a most unqualified success.' In 1903, shortly before Swettenham's retirement as Governor of the Straits Settlements, a second conference was held, although this did not yield such a whole-hearted expression of appreciation of British rule as its predecessor had done. In particular, the Sultan of Perak complained of the over-centralization of the Federation, the small Malay element in government and the (in practice) absolute control of the Resident General. This latter dissatisfaction was partially solved by Sir John Anderson who in 1909 instituted a Federal Council. On Swettenham's right in this photograph is Rajah Idris of Perak and on his left the Sultans of Negri Sembilan and Pahang.

F9 UGANDA

40 PHOTOGRAPHER UNKNOWN. **Kabaka Mwanga II of Buganda. 1890s.** Mwanga (c1866-1903) reigned as the last independent ruler of the Ganda kingdom in the period of religious strife and civil war leading up to the imposition of British rule. Mwanga inherited from his father Mutesa I in 1884 a country dominated by religious factions – Catholic, Protestant and Muslim – all eager to shape Ganda society according to their own beliefs: Mwanga's attempts to destroy these factions led to a period of exile from 1888. The entry of the Imperial British East Africa Company into Uganda and the establishment of a British protectorate in 1894 heralded a further loss of power for Mwanga and from 1897 until his capture in 1899 he carried on a war against the British. After his capture he was exiled to the Seychelles where he died in 1903.

41 PHOTOGRAPHER UNKNOWN. **Kabaka Daudi Chwa and Regents at Kampala. 1908.** Mwanga was formally deposed by the British in 1897 and replaced as Kabaka by his one year old son Daudi Chwa (1896-1939), who was presided over by four regents until 1914. Of these the most influential was Sir Apolo Kagwa (1865-1927). The leading figure in the Protestant faction, he had been a page at the court of Mutesa I and was Katikiro (Prime Minister) of Buganda from 1889-1926. On Daudi Chwa's left is seated Stanislas Mugwanya (1849-1938), and in the back row Nuhu Mbogo (1835-1921), an uncle of Mwanga, and Zacharia Kisingiri (1858-1917), a Protestant Muganda chief.

Above: **Survey team setting out, Uganda. c1906.** (F7/33)
Below: **Mr. Lockhart and Mr. Wong fixing the first boundary mark of the New Territories at Starlet Inlet, Hong Kong. March 17 1899.** (F7/34)

42 (?) ALFRED LOBO. **Opening of the Kampala Agricultural and Industrial Exhibition. November 9 1908.** Held in an attempt to stimulate agricultural and industrial production in the young protectorate, a variety of crops and Uganda crafts were on display at the exhibition, including examples of the cotton recently introduced into the country. Despite initial mishaps (the fireworks display and the presentation state umbrellas failed to arrive on time and there was a downpour just before the opening) the Governor, Sir Henry Hesketh Bell, was well pleased with the results. The Uganda rulers seen here with Bell are Sir Apolo Kagwa; Kahaya, Kabaka of Ankole; Daudi Chwa; Adereya Bisereko Duhaga II, Kabaka of Bunyoro; and Daudi Kasagama, Kabaka of Toro.

43 (?) ALFRED LOBO. **Wheelwright shop, Public Works Department, Entebbe. c1908.** Wheelwrights are seen at work under the supervision of S. Waite (d. 1944) of the Uganda Public Works Department.

44 ALFRED LOBO. **King's African Rifles outside the guardroom barracks, Bombo, Uganda. c1910.** In West Africa the frontier police of the various territories had been merged in 1901 to form the West African Frontier Force and the same idea was applied to the forces of the Central and East African Protectorates. From January 1902 the men of the Central Africa Regiment, the Uganda Rifles and the East Africa Rifles became the King's African Rifles. The Uganda Rifles formed the 4th Battalion K.A.R., a platoon of which is seen here in the barracks at Bombo (23 miles from Kampala) where their headquarters had been moved in 1907-08. In peacetime men of the K.A.R. also performed civil functions.

45 PHOTOGRAPHER UNKNOWN. **Coronation of Kabaka Mutesa II of Buganda at Budo. 1940.** Kabaka Edward Frederick Mutesa II (King Freddie) was crowned the year after the death of his father Daudi Chwa by the Bishop of Uganda, Cyril Edgar Stuart. King Freddie recalled in his autobiography, *Desecration of my Kingdom* (1967), that although the crown was specially made for the ceremony it was too small for him and in acute danger of falling off throughout the service. Fearing for the position of Buganda in a united Uganda, King Freddie refused to co-operate with British plans and spent the years 1953-55 in exile in England. His second period of exile from 1966 was also spent in England, where he died in 1969.

F10 WEST AFRICA

46 (T.J. ALLDRIDGE). **Her Majesty's Travelling Commissioner for Sierra Leone. 1893.** The terms of the Anglo-French Agreement of 1889 provided for boundary commissioners to fix the frontiers of the two nations' spheres of influence in the hinterland, and Alldridge was one of two travelling commissioners assigned to treaty making with chiefs in what was to become the Protectorate. Behind Alldridge stand bearers holding the Commissioner's canopied hammock, 'the advantages of... (which)... are, that it is a protection from the sun and allows one to jot down topographical observations and to take compass bearings.' With Alldridge stands a member of the Frontier Police, formed in 1890 and merged in 1901 with other forces to form the West African Frontier Force.

47 T.J. ALLDRIDGE. **Colonial cricket, Sherbo, Sierra Leone. January 1899.** 'Cricket... has 'caught on.' I saw the game being played on the main road at Bonthe, about five o'clock one afternoon, and the team kindly stood in position long enough for me to photograph them.' (T.J. Alldridge, *The Sherbo and its hinterland*, 1901).

□48 PHOTOGRAPHER UNKNOWN. **Palaver with Kabba Cham, Chief of North Kommbo, at Sakuta, The Gambia, during Governor's tour. June 1904.** Kabba Cham became headman at Sakuta in 1898 after his predecessor had been deposed, and was described by Francis Bisset Archer as 'very intelligent and understands English fairly well.' It was the King of Kommbo who in 1827 had ceded the island of Saint Mary (the site of the capital, Bathurst) to the British, and the whole of Upper Kommbo was declared British in 1853. Sir George Chardin Denton (1851-1928) was Governor of the Gambia from 1900-11 and made a number of tours (this one in Fogni and Kommbo) through the Colony and Protectorate holding meetings with local chiefs.

□49 LISK-CAREW BROTHERS. **Garden party at Government House, Freetown, Sierra Leone. c1911.** True to the principles of racial segregation introduced in the last years of the 19th century, the Protectorate chiefs are grouped in the foreground while Europeans mingle on the lawn beyond, overlooked by the Tower Hill Barracks.

50 LISK-CAREW BROTHERS. **Departure of Governor Probyn from Freetown, Sierra Leone. November 1910.** Citizens of Freetown present an address to Sir Leslie Probyn (1862-1938) at the end of his term of office as Governor of Sierra Leone (1904-10), while guards of the West India and West Africa Regiments line the pier. Probyn served in the colonial administrations of British Honduras, Grenada, and Southern Nigeria before coming to Sierra Leone, and was subsequently Governor of Barbados (1911-18) and Jamaica (1918-24).

F11

IMPERIAL PORTRAITS

A

Six colonial Governors.

Sir Henry Bartle Edward Frere (1815-1884). Entered Indian Civil Service 1834; Governor of Bombay 1862-67; Governor of Cape Colony 1877-80.

Sir George Grey (1812-1898). Governor of South Australia 1840-45; Governor of New Zealand 1845-53 and 1861-67; Governor of Cape Colony 1854-59; Prime Minister of New Zealand 1877-79.

Frederick John Dealtry Lugard (1st Baron Lugard of Abinger) (1858-1945). Military service in India, the Sudan, Burma, and expeditions to Nyasaland, Uganda, West Africa and the Kalahari on behalf of chartered companies; Governor of Northern Nigeria 1900-07; Governor of Hong Kong 1907-12; Governor of Northern and Southern Nigeria 1912-14; Governor-General of Nigeria 1914-19.

□ **Sir Frederick Aloysius Weld** (1823-1891). Premier of New Zealand 1864-65; Governor of Western Australia 1869-74; Governor of Tasmania 1874-80; Governor of the Straits Settlements 1880-87.

Sir Hugh Charles Clifford (1866-1941). Joined Malay States Civil Service 1883; Governor of British North Borneo 1900-01; Governor of the Gold Coast 1912-19; Governor of Nigeria 1919-25; Governor of Ceylon 1925-27; Governor of the Straits Settlements and High Commissioner for the Malay States 1927-29.

Sir William MacGregor (1847-1919). Medical officer in the Seychelles, Mauritius and Fiji in early 1870s; administrator in the Western Pacific and New Guinea until 1899; Governor of Lagos 1899-1904; Governor of Newfoundland 1904-09; Governor of Queensland 1909-14.

B

Five prominent West Africans.

Dr William Renner (1856-1917). Trained in Liverpool, London and Brussels; Sierra Leone Government Medical Service 1883-1913; acted regularly as head of Medical Department, but debarred by colour from being appointed substantive head; City Councillor and Mayor of Freetown (1916).

James Christopher Ernest Parkes (1861-1899). Studied law in England; joined Aborigines Branch of Colonial Secretary's Office, Sierra Leone 1884; Superintendant 1889-91; Superintendant, Department of Native Affairs 1891-96; Secretary for Native Affairs 1896-99.

□ **John Augustine Ontonba Payne** (1839-1906). Chief Registrar and Taxing Officer, Lagos Supreme Court 1869-99; conducted Lagos census of 1881; compiler of West African almanac issued between 1874 and 1905; murdered by an unknown assailant.

Theophilus Colenso Bishop (1850-1898). Trading agent in the Niger country from 1881 and made treaties on behalf of the Royal Niger Company; in business in Freetown from 1888; member of the Legislative Council of Sierra Leone 1894-98; City Councillor and Mayor of Freetown (1898).

Claudius Ernest Wright (1862-1911). Called to Bar, Gray's Inn 1891; practised at Freetown Bar; City Councillor and Mayor of Freetown (1902, 1903, 1910); member of the Legislative Council of Sierra Leone 1903-11.

C

Consolidators

□ **Sir John Coode** (1816-1892). Civil engineer specialising in harbour works; prepared schemes for harbours in South Africa, Ceylon, Australia and India.

Sir Daniel Morris (1844-1933). Botanist; Assistant Director, Royal Botanical Gardens, Ceylon 1877-79; Director, Botanic Department, Jamaica 1879-86; Assistant Director, Kew Gardens 1886-98; a member of many commissions of investigation into the promotion of economic agriculture in the colonies.

Sir Henry Wickham (1846-1928). Pioneer planter, explorer and colonial administrator; responsible for transporting rubber seeds out of Brazil to Kew.

Alaistair Mackenzie Ferguson (1816-1892). Ceylon tea planting pioneer; on staff of *Ceylon Observer* from 1846 until death; Commissioner for Ceylon at the Melbourne Exhibition of 1880-81.

Sir George Everest (1790-1866). Military engineer and surveyor; entered the East India Company 1806; surveyed Java for Sir Stamford Raffles; Superintendent of the Trigonometrical Survey at Hyderabad 1823-43; Surveyor General of India 1830-43.

Claude Delaval Cobham (1842-1915). Colonial administrator and historian of Cyprus; Commissioner of Larnaca 1879-1907.

Above: **Officers and NCOs of the Perak Armed Police at Taiping. c1880.** (F8/37)
Below: **The Kuala Lumpur Voluntary Fire Brigade. c1888.** (F8/38)

D Three Administrators

□ **James Herman De Ricci** (1847-1900). Barrister, Middle Temple 1872; first Attorney General of Fiji 1875; Advocate General of Mauritius 1876-79; Chief Justice of the Bahamas 1879-80.

William Alexander Pickering (1840-1907). Mercantile Marine Service 1856-62; Chinese Imperial Maritime Customs 1862-66; joined Straits Settlements Civil Service as Chinese interpreter 1872; J.P. and Police Magistrate 1875; Protector of Chinese 1877-90.

John Glasgow Grant (1805-1893). Barrister; member of Barbados House of Assembly 1842; Speaker 1875; Master in Chancery 1854; member of the Legislative Council.

F12 POLICING THE EMPIRE

□51 (?) WILLIAM D. YOUNG. **Convicts at work in Mombasa Prison. c1900.** In all the colonial dependencies convicts were seen as a useful source of cheap labour, whether in the construction of large scale public works such as the Circular Quay at Sydney or the Colombo Breakwater, heavy labouring jobs such as stone-breaking or in smaller projects such as agricultural and craft pursuits.

□52 PHOTOGRAPHER UNKNOWN. **Monthly muster of prisoners, Singapore Convict Gaol. c1871.** An astonishing amount of the work required to transform Singapore from a swampy island to a commercial metropolis was performed by Indian convicts imprisoned on the island. In 1825 the Indian prisoners at Bencoolen were transferred to Singapore and their labour was used in land reclamation, road building, the surveying of the town and other public works. Convict labour built St. Andrew's Cathedral and Government House and even their hunting skills were utilised from 1859 in the eradication of the tigers which infested the island. The main gaol, built by the convicts themselves between Stamford and Brass Basa Roads, was completed in 1860. In 1873 the settlement was closed and the remaining prisoners transferred to the Andaman Islands. The convict system applied at Singapore, with its emphasis on the teaching of crafts and trades and the giving of a measure of responsibility to the prisoners themselves, was widely admired and is described in detail in J.F.A. McNair's *Prisoners their own warders* (1899).

53 PHOTOGRAPHER UNKNOWN. **Prempeh I of Ashanti and dependents in exile in the Seychelles. c1908.** After the British military campaign of 1895 and the occupation of Kumasi in January 1896, Prempeh was removed first to Elmina, then to Freetown and finally to the Seychelles, where he remained with his entourage and dependents from 1900-24. The Seychelles had been used as a secure and isolated place of exile for a number of distinguished opponents of British rule after 1875, including Sultan Abdullah of Perak (1876-95), Mwanga of Buganda (1901-03), Kabarega of Bunyoro (1901-23) and Said Khalid bin Barghash of Zanzibar (1921-22). During Prempeh's period of residence a school was set up especially for Ashanti children and in 1940 John T. Bradley could state that 'the colony is now recognised as the ideal health resort for deposed potentates, political prisoners and all persons of like ilk'.

54 PHOTOGRAPHER UNKNOWN. **Victoria Gaol, Hong Kong. c1890.** A small prison was completed in 1841 soon after the creation of the colony, but with the influx of both Chinese and Europeans larger premises were needed and the more substantial Victoria Gaol was built between 1846 and 1849, with a disbursement a few years later in 1853 for the construction of a treadmill. These buildings in turn soon became inadequate and between 1859 and 1864 a new prison was erected on the site. The average daily number of prisoners in 1890 varied between 500 and 600, and although the annual report for 1889 acknowledged that accommodation in the gaol was 'unquestionably insufficient for the number detained there, and the subject is now receiving the serious consideration of the Colonial Government', it was several years before any significant steps were taken to remedy the situation. This photograph looks north west towards the gaol from the junction of Arbuthnott Road and Chancery Lane.

55 PHOTOGRAPHER UNKNOWN. **The old convict settlement and Emily Bay, Norfolk Island. 1884.** The convict settlement at Norfolk Island, first utilised as such four years after the island's discovery by Captain Cook in 1774, had been abandoned for 28 years by the time of this photograph, taken during the visit of the Governor of New South Wales, Lord Augustus Loftus, in 1884. At this period the island was occupied by Pitcairn Islanders who had arrived in 1856, the year the convicts left, and the pupils and teachers of the Melanesian Mission.

56 PHOTOGRAPHER UNKNOWN. **Police station at Au T'Au, New Territories, Hong Kong. c1900.** Hostility from the Chinese inhabitants of the New territories over the lease to Britain led to sporadic fighting and rioting which was largely quelled by the end of April 1899. A visible police presence was clearly necessary however and by the end of the year 13 stations had been opened, the station at Au T'Au being manned on June 3. By the end of the year a force of 32 Europeans, 86 Indians, 27 Chinese and 7 interpreters were stationed in the New Territories, with an additional 9 Europeans and 41 Chinese patrolling the waters around the leased areas.

Previous left hand page:
Above: **Palaver with Kabba Cham, Chief of North Kommbo, at Sakuta, The Gambia, during Governor's tour. June 1904.** (F10/48)
Below: **Garden party at Government House, Freetown, Sierra Leone. c1911.** (F10/49)

Previous right hand page:
Above left: **Sir Frederick Aloysius Weld (1823-1891).** (F11/A)
Above right: **John Augustine Ontonba Payne (1839-1906).** (F11/B)
Below left: **Sir John Coode (1816-1892).** (F11/C)
Below right: **James Herman De Ricci (1847-1900).** (F11/D)

Above: **Convicts at work in Mombasa Prison. c1900.** (F12/51)
Below: **Monthly muster of prisoners, Singapore Convict Gaol. c1871.** (F12/52)

F13 # PUBLIC WORKS

57 PHOTOGRAPHER UNKNOWN. **Dam construction for St John's, Antigua water supply. 1912.** By the end of 1912 Antigua had suffered three successive years of drought and the water supply to St John's was erratic and occasionally non-existent. In 1910-11 the 'Body Ponds' were partially cleared and new wells sunk, but it was not until a proper dam was constructed in 1912 that an efficient water supply to the capital was assured.

58 PHOTOGRAPHER UNKNOWN. **Building approach walls, New Higginson Bridge, Mauritius. February 22 1910.** The bridge, spanning the Rivière La Chaux outside Mahebourg, was built between 1908 and 1911 at a cost of Rs. 125,000 and named after Sir James Higginson, Governor of Mauritius from 1851-57.

59 PHOTOGRAPHER UNKNOWN. **Road making at Calabar, Southern Nigeria. 1909.** The road shown here under construction and completed in 1909 ran from near the rifle range, along the river front past Duke Town to the Calabar Road near the waterworks.

60 PHOTOGRAPHER UNKNOWN. **Locks under construction on the Johore Causeway. 1923.** The growth in trade and movement of goods down the Malayan Peninsula to Singapore was hampered by the lack of a bridge between Singapore Island and the mainland. By 1903 a railway was in operation between Singapore and Woodlands on the Johore Strait, but goods still had to be transported across to Johore Bahru by ferry. The rapid development of Malaya in the following years led to a survey being carried out in 1917, and two years later the contract for the causeway was given out. The 3465 foot road and railway was officially opened by the Governor of the Straits Settlements, Sir Laurence Guillemard and Sultan Ibrahim of Johore on June 28 1924, although the locks had been open for traffic since the beginning of the year.

F14 # ENGINEERING & IRRIGATION

61 T.G. GLOVER. **The Solani Aqueduct, Mile 18, Ganges Canal. 1867.** Stretching for 300 miles from Hardwar across the *doab*, or tract between the Ganges and the Jumna, the Ganges Canal is a fitting memorial to the perseverance and skill of its designer and chief engineer, Sir Proby Thomas Cautley (1802-1871). The disastrous famines of 1837-38 in northern India had made all too plain the need for a more extensive system of canal irrigation and Cautley, who since 1831 had been in charge of the Jumna Canal, was instructed to survey possible routes. Work began in 1842, but its progress was interrupted not only by the Afghan War but by official misunderstandings and parsimony. The canal was finally opened on April 8 1854, a month after the completion of the massive three mile Solani Aqueduct.

62 T.G. GLOVER. **The Dhunowree Works, Mile 13, Ganges Canal. 1867.** In 1863 Sir Arthur Cotton was requested to inspect the completed work, and his criticisms – relating mainly to the distributory system and the excess of slope on some sections of the canal – led to the extension of the works in the building of the Lower Ganges Canal between 1872 and 1880. These original faults do little to detract from Cautley's achievement which made arable millions of acres of previously barren land. The Dhunowree Works are situated at the intersection between the Ratmoo River and the Canal.

Above: **Road making at Calabar, Southern Nigeria. 1909.** (F13/59)
Below: **Colombo Breakwater: depositing concrete in bags on the sea berm. March 1884.** (F14/64)

63 W.L.H. SKEEN & CO. **Colombo Breakwater, looking landwards. February 1882.** The suggested harbour improvements at Galle had been bedevilled by professional disagreements over the most suitable scheme and in 1870 it was decided that Colombo would be a more favourable location to attract the increase in the steamer trade to the Far East promised by the opening of the Suez Canal. The Colonial Office sent a civil engineer, R. Townshend, to make a preliminary report in 1871 and further studies by the great harbour engineer Sir John Coode the following year led to the adoption of the breakwater project. John Kyle, the Resident Executive Engineer who supervised construction, arrived in 1873 to begin the preparatory work, which included the opening of a quarry at Mahara and the building of a railway from there to the root of the breakwater. Work on the foundations was started in 1874 and on December 8 1875 the Prince of Wales, then visiting Ceylon, laid the foundation stone. Built largely with convict labour, the 4,212 foot breakwater, together with land reclamation and harbour dredging, was completed in April 1885 at a cost of £¾ million. Moored in the harbour in this photograph can be seen H.M.S. *Bacchante* and *Ruby*, in Ceylon from January 25 to February 6 1882 during the visit of the Princes Albert Victor and George.

64 W.L.H. SKEEN & CO. **Colombo Breakwater: depositing concrete in bags on the sea berm. March 1884.** An apron 24 feet broad composed of 10 ton bags of concrete was placed to protect the top of the sea berm from disturbance. This work, performed by the 'Titan' crane, was completed between February 11 and April 2 1884, during which period 712 bags were deposited.

65 F. FIORILLO. **Aswan Dam from west bank looking east. July 7 1905.** The importance of irrigation to Egypt's faltering economy was soon realised after the setting up of the Anglo-French Condominium in 1882 and became a matter of urgency as Egypt's debt mounted. Under Turkish rule the old irrigation canals had become silted up, and when in 1884 William Willcocks repaired the Delta Barrage for an outlay of £25,000 - an investment that yielded an increase in the cotton crop of 3000 tons, worth a little over £1 million - the case for a massive dam to harness the flood waters of the Nile for year round irrigation was amply demonstrated. In succeeding years work was done to create a network of irrigation canals and barrages throughout Egypt and on February 12 1899 the foundation stone of the dam, designed by Sir Benjamin Baker, was laid by the Duke of Connaught. On December 10 1902 his wife placed the final piece of masonry in the dam. In the years that followed the dam was heightened several times and the masonry aprons beneath the sluice gates strengthened (as seen here).

66 F. FIORILLO. **Quarrying granite for the Aswan Dam at Bab el Kebir. April 10 1906.** Supervised by a group of irrigation experts, many of them sent from India for the work, the actual construction of the dam was carried out by an army of fellahin who quarried the rock with pick and shovel, transporting the material in antiquated wooden trolleys.

The arts of peace

The introductions to the earlier sections of this catalogue have been mainly concerned with the photographic aspect of history. This section, reflecting some of the ways in which education, social progress, welfare and culture developed in the Empire, also records some modern examples of the same topics in independent Commonwealth countries, matters which are further illustrated in section K. Cameras became more widely available in the period covered, and three groups exemplify their use for different purposes. A.H. Fisher, already mentioned in Section A, a professional artist specially trained as a photographer, is here seen both as depicting educational activities and providing the material for teaching. Dr J.W.S. Macfie, a skilled amateur (who listed and filed his negatives and prints with meticulous precision) used his photographic skills for his professional reports and records and in showing the way of life of his medical colleagues, as well as the areas in which he worked. The photographs of Commonwealth universities are part of the collection built up by the Inter-University Council and now given to the Royal Commonwealth Society's collection.

Most of the topics illustrated represent a combination of private action, the work of voluntary societies, and the activities of official bodies. The study of tropical diseases, begun by naval surgeons and others in the early days of European travel and settlement in the tropics, owed a great impetus to the work of Sir Patrick Manson (1844-1922) who after experience in China and Hong Kong returned to England and devoted himself to the subject; he was appointed Medical Adviser to the Colonial Office in 1897 and was the founder of the London School of Tropical Medicine. At the same time a similar institution was established in Liverpool, financed by local commercial interests, and this appointed as its professor Sir Ronald Ross (1857-1932), formerly of the Indian Medical Service, whose work, building on Manson's foundations, resulted in the discovery of the cause of malaria. This was followed by other comparable discoveries on the transmission of disease by insects and animals, and a broadening of the subject of tropical medicine from a clinical speciality to a major contribution to public health. Dr Macfie, among the diverse activities of his thirteen years in West Africa, was engaged on an enquiry into one such scourge, sleeping sickness, in Nigeria. Hospitals too have developed through private gifts, through the support of missionary and other societies, and through government initiatives. Health services have been greatly expanded in recent years, but particular problems arise in the case of large populations with inadequate numbers of trained personnel, and in overcoming the obstacles of great distances and poor communications; some contemporary means of tackling these difficulties are illustrated.

Agricultural development has been a major need of many Commonwealth countries, and has been promoted by local schools, agricultural shows and other exhibitions, in the twentieth century by agricultural and forestry research institutions and, from 1921, by the Imperial College of Tropical Agriculture in Trinidad, which provided training and research activities beyond the Caribbean, and is now part of the University of the West Indies. Problems of rural education still exist, and the use of modern communication media for this purpose in India is also shown.

Schools have been established by a variety of bodies, and with diverse objectives, some to provide general education, others directed towards special subjects and needs. The educational value of travel was a concept which gained ground in the inter-war years, and two enterprises which, however limited in objectives and achievements, were pioneers of the widespread developments mentioned in K7, are illustrated.

Higher education made very modest progress in dependent territories before the Second World War. Two major institutions, Fourah Bay College in Sierra Leone and Codrington College in Barbados, were owned by the Church Missionary Society and the Society for the Propagation of the Gospel respectively, and Raffles College, Singapore, was also in part privately financed. Government institutions were on the whole aimed at vocational training, such as the King Edward VII College of Medicine in Singapore, Makerere College in Uganda, the Higher College at Yaba in Nigeria, and the Imperial College of Tropical Agriculture. Of particular interest was Achimota College in the Gold Coast, associated with the remarkable trio of Sir Gordon Guggisberg (unique among colonial governors in having his statue erected in the country he had governed, after it became independent), Dr J.K. Aggrey, and A.G. Fraser. A 'university department' was opened in 1929.

Apart from Malta, with its university dating back to the Knights of St John, the first universities in dependent territories were based on existing medical institutions; the University of Hong Kong, financed in 1911 by private philanthropy, on the College of Medicine founded by Patrick Manson in 1887, and the University of Ceylon (1942) by the combination of the Ceylon Medical College (1870) and Ceylon University College (1921).

When a major step forward was taken by the creation of the Inter-University Council at the end of the Second World War, some universities were developed from such colleges as Fourah Bay and Makerere, others were entirely new foundations, and panel G10 reflects the transition from institutions linked to British universities such as London or Durham for the purpose of conferring degrees, and with largely expatriate staffs, to the vast expansion of higher education in independent Commonwealth countries, with their own high standards of scholarship and research.

Finally the very personal contribution of a necessarily small selection of creative writers, both to their own countries' cultural identity and to the wider understanding of their ways of life and thought, is outlined.

G1 PHOTOGRAPHER UNKNOWN. **Students at the Agrihorticultural College, Aurungabad. c1908.**

G2 TEACHING & TRAVEL

1 PHOTOGRAPHER UNKNOWN. **The Female Industrial School, Macquarie Street, Sydney. c1870.** The Female School was established in 1826 under the patronage of the wife of Governor Darling and educated the daughters of settlers until the age of fourteen. Originally financed by voluntary subscriptions, it later received government subsidies.

2 J.W.H. CAMPION. **Codrington College, Barbados. c1872.** The oldest college in the West Indies, Codrington College was founded through the bequest of Christopher Codrington (Governor General of the Leeward Islands 1699-1704) and opened as a grammar school in 1745. The school was run by the Society for the Propagation of the Gospel, to which Codrington had left two sugar estates for the upkeep of the establishment and for the maintenance of professors and scholars, 'all of them to be under the vows of poverty, chastity, and obedience.' In 1875 the college was affiliated to Durham University as a university college.

3 HERBERT DEVERIL. **Maori school near Auckland. c1875.**

4 PHOTOGRAPHER UNKNOWN. **Bush school at Petrie Creek, North Queensland, c1910.**

5 **School Empire-Tour party in Canada. 1932.** A belief in the educational value of first hand contact through travel led to an exploratory school tour to Australia in 1926 followed by the formation of a permanent Committee in 1927, which organised twenty two tours for schoolboys up to the outbreak of war in 1939. The Honorary Secretary from the beginning was Margaret Best, the Chairman from 1927, Dr. M. J. Rendall, formerly Head Master of Winchester. The death of Margaret Best in 1941 and changing post war circumstances prevented the resumption of these tours but the idea of educational travel, of which they were pioneers has now been widely accepted (see K7). This photograph shows the 1932 party to Canada at the Royal Canadian Mounted Police Barracks, Regina, Saskatchewan.

6 **British School Party in Northern Rhodesia. 1950.** A gift of over £1,000,000 from South Africa to Britain at the end of the second world war was allocated to a variety of socially beneficial causes, about half of it to work for young people. £60,000 of this was used to organise five tours. This photograph was taken at the Kalambo Falls in Northern Rhodesia, the highest in Africa.

G3 & G4 THE VISUAL INSTRUCTION COMMITTEE

A. Hugh Fisher (1867-1945) was employed by the Visual Instruction Committee of the Colonial Office between 1907 and 1910 to travel in the Empire and to take photographs and paint pictures of subjects suitable for making into lantern slides to accompany lectures in schools and elsewhere. In the course of his travels (which included Canada, Australia, New Zealand, India, the Far East, Fiji and the Mediterranean) he took some 4,500 photographs and painted more than 200 scenes in oil and water colour, and in the following years much of the material was utilised in a series of textbooks for schools which accompanied the lectures. Although originally trained as an artist, Fisher, who was taught the use of the camera especially for these tours, was a competent photographer with a good eye for a telling composition. Since his purpose was primarily educational and concerned with showing the young the variety of peoples, trades and scenery of the Empire, Fisher made a point of photographing educational establishments, of which the following prints are a selection. Particularly interesting are his photographs of the Mayo School of Art in Lahore, which was built up almost from nothing by its first principal John Lockwood Kipling (Rudyard Kipling's father) between 1875 and 1893, and did much to foster traditional Indian craftsmanship.

7 **Classroom in the English High School, Nicosia.**

8 **New playground in the English High School, Nicosia.**

9 **Boys' Elementary School, Valletta.**

10 **Sacred Heart Boys' Roman Catholic School, Gibraltar.**

11 **St Mary's Girls' Roman Catholic School, Gibraltar.**

12 **Gymnasium at MacDonald College, Ste Anne de Bellevue, Quebec Province.**

13 **Horticultural class at MacDonald College, Ste Anne de Bellevue, Quebec Province.**

14 **Gymnasts at the Government High School, Peshawar.**

15 **Woodworking class at the Mayo School of Art, Lahore.**

16 **Metalworking class at the Mayo School of Art, Lahore.**

G5 EDUCATION IN WEST AFRICA

17 PHOTOGRAPHER UNKNOWN. **Sir Gordon Guggisberg. c1925.** Sir Frederick Gordon Guggisberg (1869-1930) had served in the Royal Engineers and with the West African Surveys before being appointed Governor of the Gold Coast from 1919-27. A forceful advocate for the expansion of West African educational facilities, he pressed for the establishment of a university in the Gold Coast and was, in partnership with Alexander Fraser, largely responsible for the founding of Achimota College. Achimota was opened in 1924 as a residential college catering for pupils from kindergarten level upwards, and in 1929 the University Department was sanctioned, with students sitting external degrees from London University.

18 PHOTOGRAPHER UNKNOWN. **Dr James Aggrey. c1920.** Dr James Kwegyir Aggrey (1875-1927) was born in West Africa and educated there before leaving for the United States in 1898 to continue his studies. He was a member of two commissions of enquiry into African education in 1920 and 1923, and when Alexander Fraser insisted that the post of his deputy at Achimota be held by an African, Aggrey was appointed to the Vice Principalship in 1924.

19 DOROTHY WILDING. **Revd Alexander Fraser. 1935.** Revd Alexander Garden Fraser (1873-1962) served with the C.M.S. in Uganda (1900-03) and was Principal of Trinity College, Kandy (1904-24) before becoming the first Principal of Achimota College from 1924-35. In later life he was Principal of the Friends' College, Jamaica from 1940-43.

20 PHOTOGRAPHER UNKNOWN. **The Asantehene, Sir Nana Prempeh II, visits Achimota College. 1946.**

21 PHOTOGRAPHER UNKNOWN. **Physical exercises at the Annie Walsh Memorial School, Freetown, Sierra Leone. c1910.** A Female Institution was first established in Freetown by the C.M.S in 1849. In 1865 new buildings for the school, erected with money provided by Revd James Walsh, were opened and in 1877 the school was renamed the Annie Walsh Memorial School.

22 PHOTOGRAPHER UNKNOWN. **Graduation Day at Fourah Bay College, Sierra Leone. March 1911.** Founded by the C.M.S. as a centre for the training of missionaries, teachers and lay workers, Fourah Bay College was affiliated to Durham University as a degree bestowing university college in 1876. Seated in the centre of this group of graduating students is The Right Revd John Walmsley (1867-1922), Bishop of Sierra Leone from 1910-22.

G6 & G7 AGRICULTURAL RESEARCH & DEVELOPMENT

23 PHOTOGRAPHER UNKNOWN. **Early cotton market in Uganda. c1908.** Wild cotton had been reported growing in Uganda by the earliest explorers, but it was not until American seed was imported in 1904 and local varieties destroyed that sufficient quantity and quality was produced for export. In 1907 cotton became for the first time the Uganda Protectorate's most valuable export.

24 PHOTOGRAPHER UNKNOWN. **Sowing para rubber seeds at the Government Plantations, Kampala. 1910.** The photograph shows boys from Mengo High School being instructed in the correct method of sowing rubber seeds.

25 PHOTOGRAPHER UNKNOWN. **Members of the Botanical, Forestry and Science Department, Uganda. 1908.** Seen in this group are, back row (l. to r.): H. Batey (Overseer of Government Plantations); C.G. Gowdey (Entomologist); A.R. Morgan (Cotton Inspector); front row: M.T. Dawe (Officer in Charge); and I.L. Innes-Lillingston (Rubber Expert). Arthur Rea Morgan was Uganda's first appointed cotton inspector and served in that capacity from 1908-30.

26 (?)A.C. GOMES & SON. **The Zanzibar Exhibition. 1905.** Opened by the Sultan of Zanzibar on August 16 1905, the exhibition was visited by the Aga Khan and attracted agricultural, industrial and artistic exhibits from throughout East Africa.

27 **African student at Caribbean experimental farm.** The Imperial College of Tropical Agriculture in Trinidad was founded in 1921 as both a teaching and research institution, and eventually developed post-graduate training for students beyond, as well as within the Caribbean. A West African student is selecting maize seed for trials on the experimental plot of the College farm. I.C.T.A. became the Agricultural faculty of the University of the West Indies in 1960.

28 **Cocoa propagation in Trinidad**
Propagating units at I.C.T.A.

29 **Timber specimens in the Forest Research Institute, Malaya.** The Forest Research Institute included a library of timber specimens.

30 PHOTOGRAPHER UNKNOWN. **In the nursery, the Agrihorticultural School, Aurungabad, The Deccan. c1908.**

31 PHOTOGRAPHER UNKNOWN. **Viticulture students, Agrihorticultural School, Aurungabad, The Deccan. c1908.**

32 PHOTOGRAPHER UNKNOWN. **Stalls at the Ceylon Agrihorticultural Exhibition. 1889.**

33 PHOTOGRAPHER UNKNOWN. **Ceylon Rubber Exhibition buildings, Royal Botanical Gardens, Peradeniya. September 1906.**

34 **Indian Farm Broadcast.** The improvement of rural agriculture in India has been aided by the use of instructional broadcasting.

35 **Satellite Television Education in India. 1975.** A further development in rural education was made by the inauguration in August 1975. of S.I.T.E. (Satellite Instructional Television Experiment) by which government television programmes were relayed by satellite to some 45 million people in six Indian states. The photograph shows the inauguration of the service by Prime Minister Mrs. Gandhi, as seen in a village in Rajasthan.

G8 THE CARE OF THE SICK

36 J.W.H. CAMPION. **The General Hospital, Bridgetown, Barbados. c1872.** Situated at the corner of Bay Street and Martindales Road, the General Hospital was opened in 1844 as a result of an act passed by the Legislature in 1840 which sanctioned the incorporation of 'a Society for the establishment and maintenance of an hospital for the reception and treatment of the sick poor.' The finance for the construction of the buildings was raised by voluntary contributions in Barbados and England.

37 (C.H. EYLES). **Hospital staff, Belize, British Honduras. 1892.** Seated with the Colonial Surgeon Charles Henry Eyles (at right) is Dr P.J. Carpenter, a surgeon and district commissioner in British Honduras from 1892-1899; around the pair are grouped student nurses E. Graham, A. Lindo and P. Pena.

38 PHOTOGRAPHER UNKNOWN. **Opening of the King Edward VII College of Medicine, Singapore. February 1926.** Originally functioning as part of the Government Medical Service, the King Edward VII College of Medicine was amalgamated with Raffles College in 1948 to form the University of Malaya. In the centre of the group stands Sir Laurence Nunns Guillemard (1862-1951), Governor of the Straits Settlements from 1919-27.

39 PHOTOGRAPHER UNKNOWN. **Biochemical laboratories, King Edward VII College of Medicine, Singapore. 1926.**

40 **Indian Midwife 1980.** A traditional midwife in India is presented with a UNICEF midwifery kit on completing her training course.

41 **Fijian Nurses on their rounds.** Owing to difficult travel conditions in the remoter parts of Fiji, nurses travel on horseback to carry out their duties.

G9 MEDICAL SERVICES IN THE FIELD

The West African Medical Service. The following six photographs come from the collection of John William Scott Macfie (1879-1948), who, after studying medicine at Cambridge and Edinburgh, joined the West African Medical Service in 1910. From that date until 1923 he served in Nigeria and the Gold Coast, publishing the results of some of his researches in the report (written with Dr. G.H. Gallagher), *Sleeping sickness in the Eket District of Nigeria* (1914). After his return from Africa he was engaged in teaching and research in tropical medicine and in 1935 joined the British ambulance service in Ethiopia during the Italian invasion (his account of this episode was published as *An Ethiopian diary* in 1936). From 1941-43 he served as a malariologist in the Middle East with the Royal Army Medical Corps. A keen amateur photographer, Macfie's West African photographs picture not only the professional lives of his colleagues but also African trades, crafts, scenery and village life.

42 **On the road from Akuse to Dodowah. December 31 1914.** Alan Chilcott Parsons (b.1873) stops for lunch by the roadside. Parsons served in the W.A.M.S. in Northern Nigeria from 1903-13 and in the Gold Coast from 1914-16.

43 **The doctor on his morning rounds, Ilorin. March 2 1912.** Seated on the railway trolley is Dr George Ryan Twomey, a medical officer in Northern Nigeria from 1903-c15.

44 **Staff at the Medical Research Institute, Yaba, Lagos. August 1913.** John Edward Lionel Johnston (medical officer in Nigeria from 1912-c15) and Sergeant F.G. Phipps are seated on either side of Macfie, with African clerks and workmen grouped around them.

45 **School in the sleeping sickness camp, Ikotobo. November 11 1913.** This open-walled thatched hut served as a school in a camp where most of the patients were children.

46 **The Medical Research Department van at Dodowah. April 17 1922.**

47 **In the laboratory, Medical Research Institute, Yaba, Lagos. August 19 1913.** J.E.L. Johnston and Sergeant Phipps break for tea in the laboratory.

48 **Mobile medical unit in East Africa.** AMREF (the African Medical and Research Foundation) runs mobile units which provide medical services for scattered communities and also training and demonstration for local needs.

22 **Flying Doctor Services in New South Wales.** The Royal Flying Doctor Service of Australia was begun on an experimental basis in 1928 and now attends to some 65,000 patients a year, through flights covering about 3,000,000 miles.

G10 UNIVERSITIES OF THE COMMONWEALTH

50 **Inter-University Council delegates and the Council of Ibadan.** The Inter-University Council for Higher Education in the Colonies was set up in 1946 to restore war-damaged universities in Malta and Hong Kong and to establish new ones in other dependent territories. The Council's work developed far beyond its original purposes, and in a time of rapid political transformation reflected in its change of title to Inter-University Council for Higher Education Overseas, became a body promoting co-operation between universities in independent countries of the Commonwealth and indeed beyond it. University College Ibadan, founded in 1948, was the first of the IUC's completely new creations; it became the University of Ibadan in 1962.

51 **Makerere University.** Founded as a technical college in 1922 and reconstituted as an independent college in 1938, Makerere became a University College in 1949. From 1963 to 1970 it was a college of the University of East Africa, but became a separate university in 1970.

52 **New buildings of the University of Malta.** The University of Malta originated in 1769; in 1964, the year of Malta's independence, the foundation stone of a new complex of buildings two miles outside Valletta was laid.

14 **University of Hong Kong.** Largely on the initiative of Sir Frederick Lugard, Governor of Hong Kong, and with the aid of private philanthropy, the University of Hong Kong was founded in 1911 on the basis of the Hong Kong College of Medicine. Damaged in the Second World War, it has since been greatly developed and expanded.

54 **Faculty of Engineering, University of the West Indies, Trinidad.** The University of the West Indies was set up in 1946 and now has campuses at Cave Hill in Barbados, St Augustine in Trinidad and Mona in Jamaica. The Imperial College of Tropical Agriculture was incorporated in 1960 and Codrington College was affiliated in 1965.

55 **University of Malaya, Kuala Lumpur.** A University of Malaya was created by the amalgamation of Raffles College and King Edward VII College of Medicine in Singapore. Another campus was established at Kuala Lumpur in 1959 and in 1962 separate Universities of Singapore and Malaya were created.

56 **Building the University of Zambia, Lusaka.** The University of Zambia Act 1965 created the University; the first students were admitted the following year.

57 **Library, University of Papua New Guinea.** The University was founded in 1965 during the Australian administration and built at Waigani, seven miles from Port Moresby.

G11 NEW VOICES

One result of overseas settlement was that emigrants during the nineteenth century began to write novels and poems reflecting the new lands they encountered, though on traditional English models. Later in the century a more individual voice was heard from creative writers born in the countries concerned. One of the most remarkable was *The Story of an African Farm* by the young South African Olive Schreiner, published under the pseudonym Ralph Iron in 1883. Diverse aspects of Canada were reflected in its authors. Parker, born in Ontario, wrote many novels on Canadian historical themes, notably *The Seats of the Mighty;* Roberts, from New Brunswick, is particularly remembered for his animal stories but was a prolific writer of fiction, verse and essays. In Australia, Henry Lawson, poet and short story writer, and contributor to the famous literary organ *The Sydney Bulletin,* embodied many of his country's characteristics; *Such is Life,* the massive, rambling masterpiece of Joseph Furphy ('Tom Collins') was described by its author as 'offensively Australian.' It was many years before its qualities were widely recognised, and recognition came late in the life to Henry Handel (Ethel) Richardson, with the publication of her trilogy *The Fortunes of Richard Mahony* in 1929. Katherine Mansfield was born in New Zealand, left it for ever at the age of nineteen, finding it restrictively provincial, but constantly reflected it, directly or indirectly, in many of her works written in Europe. Rudyard Kipling, born in India of British parents, became a gifted journalist there, and on his return to England in 1889 made a sensational impact by his short stories of India, though his masterpiece on the sub-continent, *Kim,* did not appear until 1900. The first major literary voice from India itself was that of Tagore, the publication of whose own translation of his poems *Gitanjali* in 1912 was followed by the award of the Nobel Prize for Literature in 1915. Tagore was a master of diverse literary forms, in English and Bengali, and also a musician, artist, educationalist, and champion of his country's rights.

58 **Olive Schreiner (1855-1920) South African novelist.**

59 **Sir Gilbert Parker (1862-1932) Canadian novelist.**

60 **Sir Charles Roberts (1860-1943) Canadian writer.**

61 **Henry Lawson (1867-1922) Australian writer.**

62 **Joseph Furphy (1867-1912) Australian novelist.**

63 **Henry Handel Richardson (1870-1946) Australian novelist.**

64 **Rudyard Kipling (1865-1936).**

65 **Rabindranath Tagore (1861-1941) Indian writer, artist and educationalist.**

66 **Katherine Mansfield (1888-1923) New Zealand writer.**

Empire to Commonwealth.

The photographs in this section span a period of more than a century, from the consultations which led to the constitution of the Dominion of Canada in 1867, to the patriation of the Canadian Constitution in 1982, but they relate chiefly to events of the first sixty-five years of the twentieth century, a period recorded in extensive detail by the camera, and including the British Empire Exhibition at Wembley in 1924-25, which was the occasion for a vast output of photographic and other postcards, depicting not only the contents of the exhibition, but scenes in the countries represented in it.

Three panels are designed to give a broad perspective of the complex story of the fundamental change from Empire to Commonwealth. The first begins with a gathering of white representatives of the colonies of settlement at a time when Canada was a united Dominion but Australia and South Africa were still composed of separate colonies. By 1911 the title Imperial Conference had been adopted, and Australia, South Africa and New Zealand had achieved what became known as Dominion Status. The 1926 Conference, meeting after the effect of the First World War (see J 52-54) on Imperial relations had become apparent, set up the Committee under Lord Balfour which resulted in the 'Balfour definition' and thence to the Statute of Westminster of 1931, defining the rights of the Dominions. Even greater changes are reflected in the Group with King George VI, containing representatives of the three new Asian members of the Commonwealth, and subsequent photographs indicate the vast expansion during the reign of Queen Elizabeth II, the establishment of the Commonwealth Secretariat, the change of title to 'Commonwealth Heads of Government Meetings,' held in various countries and on a public scale unlike earlier, more informal gatherings. Some other aspects of such meetings are considered in K15.

The second panel concerns the role of the Crown. Royal Tours have been touched in F4. With the exception of King George V's Delhi Durbar, it was not customary for the monarch to travel in the Empire, but to be represented by the heir to the throne or another royal prince. Edward Prince of Wales travelled widely in the inter-war years, but it was his brother who, as King George VI, began the pattern of travel by the monarch, in visits to Canada and South Africa, that has been so assiduously pursued by Queen Elizabeth II. Her many visits have ranged from the informality of 'walkabouts' to attendance at, though not participation in, Heads of Government Meetings, and such special constitutional occasions as the patriation of the Canadian Constitution.

Thirdly, panel H8 shows aspects of diverse legislatures, including contrasting African bodies with all-white and all-African membership, the most ancient elected body outside Britain, the Straits Settlements Council including hereditary rulers, and the growing participation of indigenous peoples shown by the 1954 training session.

The political developments covered in outline by the photographs of successive conferences are treated in more detail; Canada, Australia and New Zealand; South Africa, achieving Union between former combatants of white races, but eventually leaving the Commonwealth owing to the opposition of other members to its racial policy; and India, whose long struggle for independence culminated in the division of the sub-continent into the two nations of India and Pakistan, later to be further divided by the creation of Bangladesh. Three panels give examples of the post-war political changes in other parts of the world – Africa, the Caribbean, South-East Asia, the Mediterranean and the Pacific, including the unsuccessful attempts at federation in the West Indies and Central Africa, the decision of Somaliland, amongst others, not to join the Commonwealth, and the effect of other nations' policies on Commonwealth members such as Cyprus and Belize. The complex story of Rhodesia/Zimbabwe and the Commonwealth involvement in its solution is treated in K12.

Other aspects are also illustrated; conferences on practical issues; endeavours to promote knowledge of the Empire and Commonwealth by exhibitions; the changing nature of population, including the emigration from Britain of earlier years and the immigration to it of the last two decades; and the cultural diversity exhibited in the first Commonwealth Arts Festival in 1965.

Above: **The First Colonial Conference. 1887.** (H2/1)
Below: **Malcolm Fraser opening the Commonwealth Heads of Government Meeting, Melbourne. 1981.** (H2/8)

H1 An episode of major significance in the transition from Empire to Commonwealth was the introduction of internal self government in Kenya on 1 June 1963 with Jomo Kenyatta, who had only recently returned from detention and exile on the grounds of his association with Mau Mau, as Prime Minister. Malcolm MacDonald, one of the most experienced diplomats and administrators in the Commonwealth, and the last Governor of Kenya, is shown greeting Kenyatta at this ceremony.

H2 LEADERS IN CONFERENCE

1 **First Colonial Conference. 1887.** Though the idea of a gathering of representatives of the colonies had been suggested earlier, the first such meeting took place in London in the year of Queen Victoria's Jubilee; it was attended by representatives of Canada, Newfoundland, New Zealand, the Cape of Good Hope, Natal, and the Australian colonies. The main subject was defence.

□ 2 **Imperial Conference. 1911.** Further Colonial Conferences were held, and from 1907 were renamed Imperial Conferences. By 1911 the Commonwealth of Australia and the Union of South Africa had been formed from separate states. The Conference set up a Royal Commission on the Dominions, but by the time of its report in 1917 the impact of war had changed the nature of the Empire to which it related (see J52).

3 **Imperial Conference. 1926: King George V and Prime Ministers.** This is the first photograph to show the monarch with the participants in a conference; the countries represented are Britain, Canada, Australia, New Zealand, South Africa, Newfoundland and the Irish Free State.

4 **King George VI, Head of the Commonwealth, with Prime Ministers. 1948.** The last Imperial Conference was in 1937. In 1944 meetings of Prime Ministers were resumed, but on a less formal basis. The 1948 group includes the representatives of the newly independent Asian countries India, Pakistan, and Ceylon (later Sri Lanka) and is a reminder that the monarch's title "Head of the Commonwealth" was introduced to meet the situation following the desire of India to become a republic but to remain a member of the Commonwealth.

5 **Queen Elizabeth II with Commonwealth Leaders. 1953.** This photograph was taken at the time of the Coronation, and includes heads of government of independent Commonwealth countries and some others (e.g. the Prime Minister of Malta).

6 **Commonwealth Prime Ministers. 1957.** A photograph taken at Downing Street, and including Dr Kwame Nkrumah, leader of the first independent African country in the Commonwealth, Ghana. He was prominent in the opposition which led South Africa to withdraw from the Commonwealth in 1961 (see H29).

7 **Conference in Session. 1965.** The 1965 Conference here seen in session at Marlborough House, made the far-reaching decision to establish a Commonwealth Secretariat and Commonwealth Foundation. The Secretariat then took over the organisation of further gatherings, which in 1971 were renamed Commonwealth Heads of Government Meetings, a recognition of the varied constitutional patterns of the countries concerned. A conference on Rhodesia, the first to take place outside the U.K., was held in Nigeria in 1966, but from 1971 a change of venue for each meeting became customary.

□ 8 **Malcolm Fraser opening Commonwealth Heads of Government Meeting, Melbourne. 1981.** View in Melbourne Town Hall of the Australian Prime Minister opening the conference attended by the representatives of 41 of the 45 Commonwealth countries (most of them Heads of Government). The Independence of Antigua and Barbuda now makes the total 46.

H3 THE CROWN

9 **King George V in India, 1911.** Early tours by members of the royal family were undertaken by two of Queen Victoria's sons, the Prince of Wales and the Duke of Edinburgh. In 1901 the future King George V went to Australia, followed in 1905/6 by a visit to India. He returned there again in 1911 to be acclaimed as Emperor of India at the Delhi Durbar.

10 **Edward Prince of Wales in Borneo. 1922.** The Prince of Wales undertook many lengthy tours of the Empire, beginning with Canada in 1919 and including New Zealand, Australia, the Pacific and the West Indies in 1920, India and other parts of Asia in 1921/22 and West and South Africa in 1925. This photograph shows him in British North Borneo on his way back from India in 1922. Rajah Brooke of Sarawak is seated on the left, the Governor of British North Borneo is fourth from the left and Lord Louis Mountbatten standing second from the left.

11 **King George VI in U.S.A. during his Canadian visit. 1939.** In May-June 1939 H.M. King George VI and H.M. Queen Elizabeth visited Canada, and included a four-day visit to the U.S.A. This photograph, taken after Divine Service at St James Church, Hyde Park, shows Rev. A.R. Smith, Rev. G. Kidd, Queen Elizabeth, King George VI, President Roosevelt, with his eldest son, his mother, and his wife, and Mackenzie King, Prime Minister of Canada, who accompanied the King during his visit to U.S.A.

12 **Queen Elizabeth II in New Zealand. 1954.** Following her Coronation in 1953, H.M. Queen Elizabeth II undertook a Commonwealth tour from November 1953 to May 1954. While visiting New Zealand she was given the flax cloak symbolising Paramount Chieftainship at a Maori gathering at Rotorua.

13 **Queen Elizabeth the Queen Mother in Fiji. 1958.** Many members of the Royal family have visited Commonwealth countries. H.M. Queen Elizabeth the Queen Mother drinks the traditional *yaqona* at welcoming ceremonies at Lautoka, Fiji, in 1958.

14 **Queen Elizabeth II in India. 1961.** Queen Elizabeth II's visit to India and Pakistan in January-March 1961 was the first by a British monarch since the Delhi Durbar nearly fifty years earlier, and under the vastly changed circumstances of the transformation of the sub-continent into two independent republics. Traditional pageantry was however a feature of the visit to Benares.

15 **The Queen in the West Indies. 1966.** H.M. Queen Elizabeth II and H.R.H. the Duke of Edinburgh talk to members of a steel band while visiting Portsmouth, Dominica in February 1966.

16 **Patriation of the Canadian Constitution. 1982.** Though Canada was the first Commonwealth country to achieve responsible government, the British North America Act of 1867 vested the power to amend it in the British Parliament. After extensive discussions in 1980-1981, following the agreement of nine of the ten provinces of Canada the British Parliament acceded to a request for the patriation of the Canadian Constitution. Queen Elizabeth II in her role of Queen of Canada is seen signing the proclamation bringing the Constitution Act into Law on 17 April 1982 in Ottawa.

H4 # THE DOMINIONS

17 **Charlottetown Conference,** leading to Canadian federation. In September 1864 five delegates from each of the three Maritime Provinces met at Charlottetown to discuss political union. Representatives of the Canadian Government also attended and though no agreement was reached at the time this was the effective beginning of Canadian federation, which took place in 1867.

18 **Sir John Alexander MacDonald (1815-1891) first Prime Minister of Canada. 1867.** MacDonald played a leading role in the discussions which led to the creation of the Dominion of Canada by the British North America Act of 1867. He was first Prime Minister of the Dominion and though losing office in 1873 he was again Prime Minister from 1878 to 1885 and won the General Election of 1891, though he died shortly afterwards.

19 **Australian Federal Conference. 1890.** For many years discussions took place aimed at joining the Australian colonies in a federation but the first positive step resulted from the decision of Sir Henry Parkes, Prime Minister of New South Wales, in 1889, to espouse the cause of federation. A conference was held at Melbourne in 1890 attended by the Premiers and leading politicians of New South Wales, Victoria, Queensland, South Australia, Tasmania, Western Australia and New Zealand. Parkes is the white-bearded figure in the centre of the group.

20 **1900. Arrival of the first Governor-General of Australia.** On 17 September 1900 Queen Victoria signed a proclamation whereby the Commonwealth of Australia, composed of the six existing states, would come into being on 1 January 1901. The 7th Earl of Hopetoun (1860-1908) a popular Governor of Victoria from 1889-1895 was appointed first-Governor General of Australia in October, a post he held until 1902.

21 **Inauguration of the Commonwealth of Australia. 1901.** The formal opening of the first Parliament of the Australian Commonwealth took place in the Exhibition Building at Melbourne on 9 May 1901. Queen Victoria had died and King Edward VII was represented by the Duke of Cornwall and York, later King George V.

22 **Proclamation of New Zealand Dominion Status. 1907.** New Zealand declined to join the projected Australian Commonwealth in the 1890s, and on 26 September 1907 Dominion status was proclaimed by the Governor General, Lord Plunket, in the presence of Prime Minister Sir Joseph Ward and a crowd of 10,000.

23 **Parliament House, Wellington, New Zealand.** New Zealand's Parliament House in Wellington was partly destroyed by fire in 1907 and the foundation stone of the main building in this photograph was laid in 1912. On the far right can be seen the corner of the portion which escaped the fire, now the General Assembly Library. The statue is of Richard John Seddon (1845-1906) Prime Minister from 1893 until his death, whose Government introduced votes for women in 1893, the first country to do so.

H5 # SOUTH AFRICA

24 **Peace negotiations after the Boer War 1902.** The Anglo-Boer war began in 1899 and continued, latterly as a guerilla campaign, until 1902. The British and Boer Commanders, Lord Kitchener (3rd from left) and General Botha (second from left) are seen at the meeting which resulted in the Peace of Vereeniging, 31 May 1902.

25 **National Convention. 1908.** The four colonies, two British, two Afrikaner, of South Africa, sent delegates to a National Convention to discuss Union; it met in various centres in 1908-1909. Southern Rhodesia also sent delegates, but without voting rights. As a result of its work the Union of South Africa came into being in 1910.

26 **Jan Christian Smuts.** Smuts' political life covered half a century of South African history; appointed State Attorney of the Transvaal in 1898, he fought through the Boer War and supported Louis Botha in the progress to responsible government and the formation of the Union of South Africa. He commanded South African troops in South West and East Africa in the first World War, subsequently becoming a member of the British War Cabinet and an advocate of greater independence of action for the Dominions. He succeeded Botha as Prime Minister in 1919 but was defeated in 1924. In 1939 he returned to the premiership when Hertzog, who had advocated neutrality, was defeated. In 1948 the Nationalists won the election, and Smuts died two years later at the age of 80.

27 **Africans burning pass books.** The increasing stringency of racial laws following the Nationalist victory in the 1948 election led to protests and demonstrations, and to growing concern in other countries of Africa as more nations achieved independence from European rule.

28 **Harold Macmillan warns of the "Wind of Change." 1960.** In February 1960 British Prime Minister Harold Macmillan addressed a joint meeting of the South African Senate and House of Assembly and spoke of the vast changes taking place in the political aspect of the African continent.

29 **South Africa's Prime Minister at the 1961 Conference when his country left the Commonwealth.** South Africa voted in 1960 to become a Republic the following year. At the Commonwealth Conference in March 1961 Prime Minister H.F. Verwoerd applied to remain in the Commonwealth, but in face of strong opposition to South African racial policy from members of the Conference, he withdrew the application. Dr. Verwoerd is on the right.

H6 # DISPLAYING THE EMPIRE

30 **South Australian Court, Melbourne International Exhibition. 1880.** Many international exhibitions were held in the nineteenth century, the most famous being the Great Exhibition of 1851. These normally included exhibits from the colonies, and this was so in the case of the Melbourne International Exhibition of 1880-81. The majority of the exhibits were samples of products but this corner of the South Australian Court displays aspects of the life of that state.

31 **The Imperial Institute. 1893.** In 1886 a Colonial and Indian exhibition was held on a site adjoining the Albert Hall in Kensington. The success of this gave a new impetus to long-standing ideas for a colonial museum, and part of the ground was assigned by the Commissioners of the 1851 Exhibition for the building of the Imperial Institute, as a commemoration of Queen Victoria's Jubilee in 1887, which was opened by Queen Victoria in 1893.

32 **Aerial view of the British Empire Exhibition Wembley. 1924.** The most ambitious empire exhibition ever held was that at Wembley in 1924 and 1925, visited by twenty-seven million people. This aerial view shows the whole of the site with the stadium, the only building now remaining, on the left.

33 **King George V. and Queen Mary in Maori House, Wembley. 1924.** The Exhibition was opened on St. George's Day by King George V, whose speech was transmitted by wireless, then in its early stages. The King and Queen are seen visiting one of the many pavilions designed to represent a traditional form of architecture.

34 **The East Africa Pavilion at Wembley.**

35 **The Indian Pavilion at Wembley, floodlit.**

H7 THE MOVEMENT OF PEOPLES

36 **Emigrants to Canada. 1908.** A group of emigrants journeying steerage to Canada from Liverpool on the S.S. *Empress of Britain* awaiting disembarkation in the St. Lawrence river 1908. Photograph by A.H. Fisher.

37 **Party of Barnardo children en route for the Fairbridge Farm School Western Australia. 1928.** Barnardo's Homes were among many charitable bodies which organised migration schemes for children. Kingsley Fairbridge (1885-1924) pioneered the idea of farm schools to train emigrants, and his most enduring venture was that at Pinjarra, in Western Australia, which is still in use.

38 **Mennonite Farmers at Rosthern in Saskatchewan. 1908.** In the latter part of the 19th Century many European immigrants of farming stock arrived in the Prairie Provinces of Canada. Rosthern, a major agricultural centre, had many migrant residents, including Mennonites (followers of a religion preaching pacifism and a simple life style) from Russia, Galicians and Hungarians. Photographed by A.H. Fisher.

39 **Fijian Indians.** Migration of Indians to Fiji as indentured labour to work on the sugar plantations began in 1879 and in the ensuing years totalled some 60,000. They now form more than half of the population but retain their traditional costumes and way of life.

40 **Indian Schoolgirls in Britain.** In the 1960s immigration from Asia, Africa and the Caribbean into Britain assumed considerable proportions. The photograph shows Indian schoolgirls in Derby who gained the Duke of Edinburgh's Award.

41 **Brixton Market.** The influx of immigrants to Britain from third world countries of the Commonwealth has brought many changes in the appearance of London and other cities.

H8 A DIVERSITY OF LEGISLATURES

42 **First Legislative Assembly of Southern Rhodesia. 1924.** Rhodesia, administered by the British South Africa Co., from its foundation in 1890, until 1923, was granted a large measure of responsible government by the Constitution of 1 October 1923. A Legislative Assembly of thirty, chosen by an electorate with a high property qualification, was elected in 1924. This group of elected members and officials includes the Prime Minister Sir Charles Coghlan (the fifth from left front row), his successor Sir Godfrey Huggins, fourth from left back row and the first woman member, Mrs. Tawse Jollie.

43 **Meeting of Malay States Federal Council. 1927.** The Council was created in 1909; it included the four Malay rulers and their Residents, nominated unofficial members, and officials. At this meeting of 28 February 1927 the High Commissioner, Sir Laurence Guillemard, is at the head of the table; on his right the Rulers and Residents of Perak, Selangor, and Negri Sembilan, to his left the Chief Secretary and the Legal Adviser.

44 **Opening of Federal Parliament in Canberra. 1927.** The new parliament building in Canberra was opened by H.R.H. the Duke of York (later King George VI) on behalf of his father King George V, 9 May 1927, followed by the first meeting of the Commonwealth Parliament to be held in the new building, the scene shown in this photograph.

45 **H.M. Queen Elizabeth II at the Bermuda House of Assembly. 1953.** The Bermuda House of Assembly originated in 1620 and is the oldest representative body in the Commonwealth outside Britain. Until 1962 it was elected on a very limited franchise.

46 **Parliamentary Course in London. 1954.** Members and Officers of overseas Legislatures, include representatives from Nigeria, Sierra Leone, the Gold Coast, Uganda, Australia, Aden, Singapore, Malaya and the Sudan, at a Parliamentary Course organised by the Commonwealth Parliamentary Association in May, 1954.

47 **Uganda Legislative Council.** In the late 1950s several advances were made in broadening the composition of the Uganda Legislative Council and increasing its elected element. In 1962 Uganda attained internal self-government.

H9 DISCUSSING THE PRACTICAL ISSUES

48 **Imperial Wireless and Cable Conference. 1928.** The conference was called to consider the problem of rivalry between companies involved in beam wireless and the cable service. It began its meetings in January 1928 under the chairmanship of Sir John Gilmour (seated 5th from left) as Chairman and Sir Campbell Stewart of Canada (on his right) as Chairman of the advisory committee. After more than thirty meetings it recommended a union of activities which resulted in the formation of Imperial and International Communications Ltd., which became Cable and Wireless in 1934.

49 **Imperial Press Conference. 1930.** The Imperial Press Union, now the Commonwealth Press Union was founded in 1909 and held a series of conferences at five yearly intervals. The fourth of these was held in London in 1930 and was opened by the Prime Minister, the Right Honorable J. Ramsay MacDonald.

50 **King George VI and participants in the African Conference. 1948.** In September/October 1948 sixty-six delegates from ten African countries attended a conference in London to discuss a wide range of topics including economic policy, local government, information services, agriculture and education. All but ten were unofficial members, elected or nominated, of Legislative Councils, and included some who later played a significant part in independent Africa.

51 **Prime Minister Attlee addressing Commonwealth visitors to the Festival of Britain. 1951.** Ninety distinguished visitors, mainly unofficial members of local Legislative Councils, visited Britain in 1951 as guests of the government. This gathering at Church House is being addressed by the Prime Minister, the Rt. Hon. C.R. Attlee, with the Secretary of State for the Colonies, the Rt. Hon. James Griffiths, on his right.

52 **Commonwealth Economic Conference. 1952.** The conference, attended by the Prime Ministers of Great Britain, Canada, Australia, New Zealand, Pakistan and Ceylon, and the Finance Ministers of India and South Africa, met in December 1952 to consider current economic problems. It recommended measures for increased financial stability and the removal of import restrictions.

53 **Teachers for the Commonwealth Conference. 1960.** A conference was held in Lodon in February 1960 to encourage the recruitment of British teachers for work in Commonwealth countries. Speakers included Alhaji Abdulmaliki, Nigerian High Commissioner and Mrs. V.L. Pandit, Indian High Commissioner, seated in the background.

H10
INDIA

54 **The Indian National Congress. 1885.** The Indian National Congress, with the aim of eventual self-government, was formed in 1885, its first meeting comprising seventy members, mainly lawyers, journalists, and schoolmasters: there were 450 at its second meeting. It steadily grew in political influence.

55 **Mohandas Karamchand Gandhi.** Gandhi (1869-1948) entered Indian political life in 1915, on his return from twenty years in South Africa, during which he had campaigned successfully on behalf of the Indian community. He advocated a simple life-style, and sought to end British rule in India through non-violent means.

56 **The Indian Round Table Conference. 1931.** Gandhi was one of the Indian leaders to attend the Round Table Conference held in London in the summer of 1931, but the discussions ended without resolving the problems of India's political future.

57 **Nehru, first Prime Minister of India and Jinnah, Creator of Pakistan. 1946.** The two other leading figures in Indian politics in the late 1930s were Jawaharlal Nehru, (1889-1964), who had entered Indian politics in 1918 and represented a more westernised approach to India's future than his leader, Gandhi, and Mahomed Ali Jinnah (1876-1948), who as President of the All-India Muslim League campaigned for a separate Muslim state to be called Pakistan as an essential aspect of Indian independence.

58 **The Cabinet Mission in India. 1946.** With the end of the war the new British Labour Government appointed a Cabinet Mission comprising Lord Pethick-Lawrence, A.V. Alexander, and Sir Stafford Cripps (here seen with Jinnah and the Viceroy, F.M. Lord Wavell) which put forward plans for a united India with a federal scheme meeting some of the requirements of the advocates of Pakistan, but the scheme proved unworkable in the face of Hindu-Muslim hostility.

59 **Lord and Lady Mountbatten in Lahore. 1947.** To break the deadlock following the failure of the Cabinet Mission, Attlee appointed Lord Mountbatten Viceroy early in 1947 and set a date of June 1948 for independence. Mountbatten considered that partition was inevitable, and advocated an earlier date for independence; as a result, India and Pakistan came into being on 15 August 1947.

H11
-13
TOWARDS INDEPENDENCE

60 **West Indies federation Conference. 1953.** A conference at Montego Bay in 1947 to consider federation in the West Indies set up a Committee whose proposals were adopted at a further conference in 1953, and the Federation of the West Indian islands (the mainland colonies declined to join) came into being in January 1958. The withdrawal of Jamaica in 1961 led to the dissolution of the Federation. The independence of Jamaica and Trinidad followed and also Barbados in 1966.

61 **Nigerian participants in Local Government Conference. 1955.** Post-war developments in Local Government were a step towards wider political responsibility and thence to independence. A Conference on the Development of Local Government in the Colonies was held under the auspices of the Royal Institute of Public Administration at Cambridge in August 1955.

62 **Motion for the Independence of the Gold Coast.** At this session of the Gold Coast Legislative Assembly, held in July 1953, the Prime Minister Dr. Nkrumah is seen opening the debate on the proposals for independence. The Gold Coast became the first former British Colony in Africa to become independent on 6 March 1957 when it took the name of Ghana.

63 **Malayan Independence Conference. 1957.** In 1948 nine Malay States, with the former Straits Settlements of Malacca and Penang, formed the Federation of Malaya. In May 1957 independence for the Federation was agreed and this photograph shows Tunku Abdul Rahman, first Prime Minister, announcing the agreement.

64 **Malayan Independence Ceremony. 1957.** H.R.H. the Duke of Gloucester speaks at the Independence Ceremony in the Merdeka Stadium, Kuala Lumpur, on 31 August 1957. In the centre is H.M. the Yang di-Pertuan Agong, first elected paramount ruler of the Federation, to his left Tunku Abdul Rahman. Six years later the Federation of Malaysia, including Singapore, Sarawak and British North Borneo (Sabah) was inaugurated, but Singapore became an independent State in 1965.

65 **Cyprus Conference. 1964.** After some years of conflict a Cyprus Constitutional Conference in February 1959, agreed on independence the following year. This photograph of the Conference of January 1964, following further violence the previous year, is a reminder of the involvement of Greece and Turkey in the affairs of Cyprus, culminating in the Turkish occupation of part of the island.

66 **Admission of Nigeria to the United Nations. 1960.** The Federation of Nigeria became independent on 1 October 1960 and its first Prime Minister, Sir Abubakar Tafawa Balewa, is seen addressing the United Nations on 7 October when Nigeria was admitted as its 99th member.

67 **Somaliland Independence, outside the Commonwealth. 1960.** A conference in May 1960 agreed on independence for British Somaliland on the 26 June; the country united with Somalia (formerly Italian Somaliland) to form the Somali Republic and did not seek Commonwealth membership.

68 **Sir Milton Margai welcomed back to Sierra Leone. 1960.** In May 1960 a Constitutional Conference in London agreed that Sierra Leone should become independent on 27 April 1961. Sir Milton Margai, first Prime Minister, is seen informing a crowd on Queen Elizabeth II playing field, Freetown, of the plans for the future.

69 **Tanganyika Independence. 1961.** Julius Nyerere holding a placard "Complete independence 1961" on leaving the Karimjee Hall at the conclusion of the Constitutional Conference. March 1961, which agreed on independence for the following 9 December. Tanganyika became a Republic the following year with Nyerere as its first President and in 1964 Tanganyika and Zanzibar became the United Republic of Tanzania.

70 **Jamaican Independence Conference.** Jamaican independence was agreed at a conference held in February 1962. By the date of independence, 6 August, the Prime Minister Norman Manley (left) had lost the election to opposition leader Alexander Bustamante (signing the agreement).

71 **Demonstration against Federation in Northern Rhodesia. 1962.** Federation of the Rhodesias and Nyasaland was established in 1953. There was considerable objection in Northern Rhodesia and Nyasaland and when Mr. R.A. Butler, recently appointed to take charge of the Central African Office, visited Northern Rhodesia in May 1962, he was met by placards hostile to the Federation. It was dissolved at the end of 1963 and Northern Rhodesia became independent as Zambia in October 1964.

72 **R. A. Butler and Dr. Banda, first Prime Minister of Malawi. 1962.** A new constitution for Nyasaland was agreed at a conference in London in November 1962, leading to internal self-government with Dr. Banda as the first Prime Minister. Following the dissolution of the Federation, Nyasaland became independent as Malawi on the 6 July 1964 with Dr. Banda as Prime Minister and later President.

73 **Kenya Independence. 1963.** On 12 December Kenya proceeded to full independence and in this photograph Malcolm MacDonald is second from the left, the remaining figures in the front row being H.R.H. The Duke of Edinburgh, Jomo Kenyatta and Mrs. MacDonald.

74 **Basutoland/Lesotho Constitutional Conference. 1964.** At the conference held in London in April 1964 a new constitution with an undertaking of eventual independence, was agreed. The delegates seen here include, on the left, Chief Leabua Jonathan, first Prime Minister when the country became independent as Lesotho on 4 October 1966.

75 **King Sobhuza of Swaziland. 1967.** On 25 April 1967 the former High Commission territory of Swaziland became a protected State under a new constitution signed the previous day by the King and the Queen's Commissioner. Swaziland became independent on 6 September 1968, with King Sobhuza as Head of State.

76 **Coronation of the King of Tonga. 1967.** H.M. King Taufa'ahau Tupou IV became King on the death of his mother Queen Salote in 1967. In 1970 it was agreed that the U.K. government should cease its responsibility for the external relations of the Kingdom of Tonga which had existed since 1900, and Tonga became a full member of the Commonwealth.

77 **Fiji Independence Agreement. 1970.** Lord Shepherd, Minister of State, Foreign and Commonwealth Office, shaking hands with Ratu Sir Kamisese Mara on the conclusion of the Fiji Constitutional Conference 6 May 1970. Sir Robert Foster, Governor of Fiji, is in the background and S. Koya, Leader of Fiji's Opposition, on the right. Fiji became independent on 10 October with Ratu Mara as Prime Minister.

78 **The Prince of Wales in Papua New Guinea for Independence celebrations. 1975.** Papua New Guinea became independent on 16 September 1975; the Prince of Wales represented the Queen, and is greeted by Girl Guides on his arrival at Port Moresby.

79 **Independence Day in Belize City. 1981.** Belize, formerly British Honduras, became independent on 21 September 1981, after negotiations protracted by the territorial claims of neighbouring Guatemala on Belize and the necessity to secure adequate guarantees of its future security.

H14 COMMONWEALTH ARTS FESTIVAL. 1965.

The first Commonwealth Arts Festival was held in Britain in 1965 after some nine years of discussion. It lasted seventeen days, with events in London, Cardiff, Glasgow and Liverpool. Its diverse activities included music and dance, particularly in the great Dance Gala with 300 participants from nine countries, drama, art, poetry, films and discussions. In addition to the more formal gatherings, some performances were given in the streets.

80 **Ravi Shankar.** Ravi Shankar is an outstanding exponent of the Sitar, the major melodic instrument of India, a plucked string instrument with twenty movable frets, six main strings and 19 sympathetic strings.

81 **Maori Singers in Trafalgar Square.** Singers from Wellington Anglican Maori Club of New Zealand were among the participants in the festival and performed at lunch time in Trafalgar Square, helping to bring the festival to the man in the street as well as in the theatre.

82 **Ugandan Drummer.** Ugandan drummers were part of the Drum Company 'Heart Beat of Africa' which participated in the Dance Gala held in the Royal Albert Hall and other centres.

83 **Nigerian Folk Opera in St. John's Market, Liverpool.** The Duro National Theatre Oshogbo from Western Nigeria appeared in all four centres, and is seen performing 'Oba Koso' (The King does not Die) in St. John's Market in Liverpool.

84 **Kandyan Dancers. Sri Lanka.** The traditional Kandyan dance emanates from the temple and is ritualistic, based on highly sophisticated rhythms.

85 **Theatre du Nouveau Monde of Montreal in 'Klondyke'.** The TNM, as it is known, as founded in 1951 and performed entirely in French. *Klondyke* was a dramatic musical play alternating tragedy and comedy, based on the Gold Rush of 1896.

86 **Australian Ballet.** The Australian Ballet Company was formed in 1962. This photograph shows Barry Kitcher in the Lyrebird costume worn in Robert Helpmann's Ballet *The Display.*

87 **Jamaica National Dance Company.** The National Dance Theatre Company of Jamaica was formed from a number of dance groups specialising in modern and in interpretative dancing based on the folk idiom.

88 **Sierra Leone National Dance Troupe.** The Sierra Leone National Dance Troupe was made up of sixty dancers selected from more than 20,800 auditioned throughout the country. The dances are drawn from ritual and ceremony and include a devil figure.

The Impact of War

Though for many years the main brunt of military operations in the Colonies was borne by British troops, there was a steady rise of local militia and other units, going back in the case of Canada to the 18th century. The main non-British force was the Indian Army, founded in the 1740s, and from the middle of that century employed in operations in many parts of the world including Ceylon, Mauritius, Egypt and Aden. The Abyssinian expeditionary force of 1868 was entirely composed of Indian Troops, and is the first of their campaigns to be photographically recorded. Ten years later Indian units were sent to Malta, and towards the end of the century they also served in Egypt and the Sudan, East Africa and China.

Moral support for Britain in wartime was expressed in Canada as far back as the Napoleonic Wars, when funds were raised in Quebec and Montreal. A large memorial in Halifax, Nova Scotia, commemorates two officers from the Colony who fell in the Crimean War. The first significant involvement of Empire personnel was, however, in the operations at the time of the fall of Khartoum in 1885, when Canadian boatmen served (though in an unofficial capacity) with Wolseley's expedition up the Nile, and troops from New South Wales joined British and Indian units at Suakim. In the Boer War, large scale volunteering from the Empire brought units from Canada, Australia and New Zealand to join the conflict.

In the early years of the twentieth century there was an expansion and reorganisation of local units in the colonies and a growing involvement of the Dominions in national defence, for example the creation of the Australian navy. The War of 1914-1918 involved the Empire on an unprecedented scale, and with far-reaching effects on its future nature. The exploits of the Australian and New Zealand Army Corps in the ill-fated Gallipoli campaign made ANZAC Day an occasion for the assertion of national identity. South African forces fought in South-West and East Africa and in France; Canada sent troops to Europe and was also reminded of the cost of war nearer home by the explosion of a munition ship in Halifax Harbour; and India provided both combatant and labour units. Small colonies raised units for service overseas as well as for local defence, as witnessed by many scattered war memorials.

One aspect of co-operation to emerge from the war was the Imperial, later Commonwealth, War Graves Commission, which with meticulous and sensitive care marked the graves of those killed in the conflict, and erected memorials to the missing on the battlefields, a task it was to repeat a generation later.

The outbreak of war in 1939 found a Commonwealth whose members had developed considerable independence in foreign policy, but they aligned themselves with Britain, though not before a crucial vote in the South African Parliament had rejected the policy of neutrality advocated by some members of the Government.

The diversity of involvement of small colonies as well as major Dominions is reflected in these panels, including the role of islands as remote from each other as Malta and the Solomons; there were also other aspects which portended post-war change. The fall of the apparently impregnable fortress of Singapore to the Japanese was a great blow to the reputation of British rule in Asia; the opposition of India's political leaders to a war in whose initiation and conduct they had no responsible share created far-reaching problems; and the use of troops from some colonies in battles on the other side of the world widened horizons and ensured that there would be a broader outlook, and a call for greater self-government, in the years following the peace.

For the Commonwealth, the world wars were not merely chapters in national military history but had more fundamental results for each country and for the Commonwealth itself. 'The comradeship of wartime was balanced by the national pride that was flowering in the dominions' and this found expression in the views of the Imperial War Conference of 1917 and the Dominions role at the Peace Conference. Differing views on strategy and long-term aims as well as measures to achieve victory, had their part in the top-level conferences of the Second World War. In both conflicts the British War Cabinet had a member from overseas – General Smuts from South Africa in the first, and R.G. Casey of Australia in the second. Post-war Commonwealth co-operation in defence matters is also reflected in this section.

Early war photographers were handicapped by the cumbersome nature of photographic apparatus and the difficulty of making an adequate record of moving peoples and objects. By the First World War the situation had changed considerably, and that conflict is recorded by official photographers, as well as by pressmen and by amateurs among the combatants. An even greater output in these categories resulted from the Second World War, and the massive collections in the Imperial War Museum and in national archives form an important resource for the study of these events. The Commonwealth War Graves Commission has made photography an important aspect of its work and has built up an impressive graphic record of its cemeteries and memorials.

J1 **Canadians entering Cambrai. 1918.** Canadian troops were involved in the heavy fighting in front of Cambrai in the autumn of 1918. The final attack was launched in the morning of the 9 October and by 8.30 in the morning the ruined city had been occupied. Photograph by William Rider-Rider.

J2 IMPERIAL CO-OPERATION IN WAR AND DEFENCE

1 **Indian Unit in Abyssinian War. 1868.** Indian troops were engaged in numerous military enterprises outside their own country; this is the earliest photograph known of such units and shows a Baluch Regiment. Some 13,000 troops from India were engaged in the campaign of 1868 to release the Europeans held captive by King Theodore of Abyssinia.
In 1878 Indian troops were brought into Europe for the first time when 7,000 were sent to Malta and later Cyprus as an emergency force at the time of the Russo-Turkish war. In a parliamentary debate on this episode W.E. Forster commented, 'If India is to help us in carrying out our foreign policy, we shall have to consult Indian feeling in framing that policy: and, in my opinion, we should have to treat India rather as an ally than as a dependency.'

2 **Canadian Steamboat Pilots in the Sudan campaign. 1884.** When Lord Wolseley was appointed to command the Gordon Relief Expedition in 1884, he recalled his experiences in the Red River expedition and obtained some 400 seasoned Canadian boatmen to assist in the journey up the Nile. The photograph shows four from Manitoba; Captains William Robinson, R.A. Russell, John S. Segers and Jerry Webber.

3 **Departure of Australian troops for the Boer War. 1899.** Troops from New South Wales were the first Australians to serve overseas when a contingent of 800 was sent to Suakim to join British troops following the fall of Khartoum. The first major involvement was in the South African War, in which more than 16,000 Australian troops served, as well as 6,000 from New Zealand and 7,300 from Canada. This photograph shows men of A. Battery of the New South Wales Artillery leaving Port Jackson on 30 December 1899 on S.S. *Warrigal.*

4 **Somaliland Troops.** African units were raised in Central and East Africa in the 1890s and a combined force, the King's African Rifles, created in 1901. A sixth battalion was raised in Somaliland in 1904.

5 **Royal Canadian Regiment. 1908.** Machine gun detachment of the Royal Canadian Regiment (founded 1883, and the senior Canadian regular infantry regiment) parading at Halifax, Nova Scotia, in 1908. Photograph by A.H. Fisher.

6 **Lord Roberts inspecting South African troops. 1911.** Many contingents from the Empire took part in the Coronation Procession of King George V in June 1911 and this photograph shows representatives of various South African units being inspected by Field Marshal Earl Roberts at the Duke of York's School, London.

7 **Indian Mountain Artillery. 1908.** The unit shown is the 32nd Mountain Battery, raised at Dehra Dun in 1907, armed with six ten-pounder guns carried on mules, its personnel half Jat Sikhs and half Punjabi Muslims.

8 **Esquimalt Harbour British Columbia. 1867-70.** Esquimalt was a British Naval Base on the West Coast of Canada and this photograph by Frederick Dally shows part of the British Pacific fleet at anchor. British troops were withdrawn from Canada in 1871 apart from the Naval Bases at Esquimalt and Halifax, Nova Scotia, whose defence was not taken over by Canada until 1906.

9 **Grand Harbour, Malta from Corradino.** Malta was seized from the Knights of St. John by Napoleon in 1798, taken by Britain in 1800, and its possession confirmed in 1814. The fine anchorage of Grand Harbour and the adjoining creeks made it an important naval base.

J3 WORLD WAR I: THE DOMINIONS AND INDIA

10 **Recruiting in Sydney.** On the outbreak of war in 1914 the Australian forces included an army for home service, but the day before the actual declaration of war the Australian Cabinet offered the British Government to raise an expeditionary force of 20,000 to serve where required and the offer was accepted. An entirely new army called the Australian Imperial Force was, therefore, recruited.

11 **Anzacs at Gallipoli, 1915.** The first units of the Australian Imperial Force were sent overseas in October and a combined Australian and New Zealand Army Corps created in Egypt. It led the landing on the Gallipoli Peninsula on 25 April 1915 in what became known as Anzac Cove. The achievements and sacrifices of the Corps in the campaign against the Turks did much to strengthen the sense of national identity of the countries concerned.

12 **General Chauvel and the Australian Light Horse.** General Sir Harry Chauvel (1865-1945) was a Cavalry Officer who was appointed to command the First Australian Light Horse Brigade. He took it dismounted to Gallipoli and later was a successful Cavalry Commander in the operations in Egypt and Palestine which included the capture of Damascus and Aleppo. He was the first Australian to reach the rank of Lieutenant-General. General Chauvel is seen leading the Light Horse into Damascus.

13 **H.M.A.S. Sydney.** Launched in 1913, this was one of the light cruisers escorting the Australian Imperial Force across the Indian ocean. On the 9 November 1914 she sank the German raider *Emden,* the first action in which the Australian Navy was engaged.

14 **King George V and New Zealand Troops. Western Front, 1918.** After the abandonment of the Gallipoli campaign Australian and New Zealand forces were transferred to France and divided, the New Zealand government expanding its Infantry Brigade into an Infantry Division.

15 **20th Deccan Horse in India. 1916.** Indian troops served in France, the Middle East and East Africa and 64,000 were killed or died on active service. Some Cavalry units were posted to the Western Front and in general were unable to operate effectively though the Deccan Horse had the opportunity of a successful charge against the Germans in no-man's-land in the summer of 1917.

16 **South African Troops in Windhoek. 1915.** On the declaration of war in 1914 the Government of the Union of South Africa offered to occupy the German colony of South West Africa, and this was carried out. Windhoek, the capital, fell on 12 May. The photograph, showing the scene after the raising of the Union Jack, was taken by S.A.M. Pritchard, the Director of Native Labour in the Union, who became first Administrator for Native Affairs in the newly-occupied territory.

17 **Newfoundlanders in France. 1917.** The Newfoundland Regiment was composed almost entirely of those born in the island. It served at Gallipoli and later in France; in all nearly 5,000 men were sent overseas from the island of whom 1,250 were killed or missing. The photograph shows transport of the Newfoundland Regiment at Berneville, 9 May. 1917.

18 **Explosion Damage at Halifax Nova Scotia. 1917.** On the morning of 6 December 1917 a French munitions ship collided with a Norwegian vessel, was abandoned, drifted towards the shore and exploded. At least 2,000 lives were lost and large parts of Halifax and of Dartmouth on the other side of the harbour were devastated.

J4 WORLD WAR 1: THE COLONIES

19 **Nigeria Regiment on the march, East Africa. 1917.** Nigerian Troops served in the campaign against the Germans in East Africa. Walter Buchanan-Smith, the photographer, Assistant Commissioner of Lands in Lagos, was attached to the Nigeria Regiment and went to East Africa in November 1916. This photograph shows the 3rd Nigeria Regiment on the march near Nyengedi August/September 1917.

20 **Hong Kong Volunteers.** Before 1914 there was a small volunteer force in Hong Kong; on its outbreak so many men volunteered that it was not possible to train them all and some were utilised as special constables releasing other police for military duties.

21 **Bahamians leaving Nassau.** Recruitment in the Bahamas began in 1915 and in all some 700 went on active service.

22 **West Indian Troops in France. 1916.** In 1915 a British West Indies Regiment, drawn from the islands of the Caribbean, from British Guiana and British Honduras was created and eventually more than 15,000 men served in it. Members served in the Jordan Valley, in France and in East Africa.

23 **Armistice Day at the North Borneo memorial.** Many members of the North Borneo administration joined the forces and volunteers from the Railway Department served in Mesopotamia. The memorial shown here is typical of many erected in the colonial Empire.

24 **Mombasa Memorial. 1914-1918.** This memorial shows four types of African involvement in the East African campaign of the first world war. They are, from left to right, an Arab rifleman, a King's African rifleman, an Askari Scout, and a porter. It is estimated that 200,000 porters from Kenya 'the feet and hands of the army' were engaged in the campaign, of whom 40,000 died, and large numbers also served in Uganda.

J5 WORLD WAR II: A GLOBAL CONFLICT

25 **Australian Troops in New Guinea.** By the end of the second world war the strength of the Australian army was 358,000 men and 22,700 women. They had fought in the Middle East, Greece, and Crete and Malaya, but were particularly concerned in the fight back against Japan in the Pacific and the long struggle in New Guinea. The photograph was taken north of the Ramu Valley.

26 **Canadians in Italy: 1943.** The first units of the Canadian army to fight in the second world war were involved in the unsuccessful raid on Dieppe in August 1942. The following year Canadian forces landed in Sicily and on September 3 crossed to Italy. The photograph shows troops of the Royal 22nd Regiment making a night advance to Mount Gildone South of Campobasso on 11 October 1943.

27 **Gurkhas in the Pacific War.** Gurkha units were extensively used in the war against Japan and are shown training for jungle warfare.

28 **South African troops in Abyssinia. 1941.** South African units played a prominent part in the defeat of the Italians in Abyssinia and prisoners are seen marching past the South Africans after the surrender of Fort Toselli.

29 **New Zealand Troops at Monte Cassino. 1944.** New Zealand forces served in Egypt and later in Italy. They were particularly involved in the attacks on the German stronghold in the Abbey of Monte Cassino and the 19th Armoured Regiment entered Cassino on 18 May. The fighting in this area alone cost 460 New Zealand lives and 1,800 wounded.

30 **Australian Coast Watchers and Solomon Islanders.** Coast watchers of the Royal Australian Navy played an important part in observing Japanese movements. In this photograph, Solomon Islanders are indicating the whereabouts of Japanese patrols in New Georgia.

31 **Convoy Reaching Malta, August. 1942.** Malta suffered its first air raid when Italy entered the war on 10 June 1940. The island suffered severely from aerial attack and from the cutting off of supplies, particularly when the North African coast was in German hands. Throughout the war materials could only reach the island by convoys operating at a heavy cost. The arrival of the remains of a convoy, including the tanker *Ohio,* in August 1942 staved off defeat until the victory of El Alamein cleared the African coast of enemy forces. In this photograph *Brisbane Star* is entering Grand Harbour on 22 August. King George VI awarded the George Cross to Malta on 15 April 1942.

32 **Gibraltar Evacuees in Jamaica.** After the fall of France in 1940 it was decided to evacuate from Gibraltar all under 17, all women, men over 60 and all over 45 on non-essential work. Some went to Madeira, some to England and about 1500 to Jamaica where a camp was set up in which a community life developed.

33 **Training Air Crews, Southern Rhodesia.** Extensive training of air crews was carried out beyond the zone of hostilities in Canada and in Southern Rhodesia.

34 **Caribbean Troops in the Middle East. 1945.** Men of the First Caribbean Regiment training with carriers.

35 **Cyprus Mule Corps, Lebanon.** Mules were used for transport in mountain regions; this group is carrying supplies for defence work.

36 **No. 218. Gold Coast Bomber Squadron. 1945.** A number of R.A.F. Squadrons were named after Colonies which had either 'adopted' that unit or had raised local funds for the war effort. The Gold Coast 'Spitfire Fund' reached £100,000 in its first two years and in 1941 218 Bomber Squadron had the title 'Gold Coast' conferred on it. The photograph shows a visit to the Squadron at R.A.F. Chedburgh in July 1945 by Sir Alan Burns, Governor of the Gold Coast, and Lady Burns.

J7 THE PRICE OF VICTORY

37 **Canadian Memorial, Vimy Ridge, France.** The memorial, unveiled by King Edward V111 in 1936, was designed by the Canadian sculptor, W.S. Allward, and bears the names of 11,180 Canadian dead and missing. It also honours all the 65,000 Canadians who died in the 1914-1918 War.

38 **Thiepval Memorial, Somme, France.** 82,000 soldiers of the Commonwealth fell in this area between July 1915 and March 1918 and those that have no known grave are commemorated on the memorial, other than those from Canada, Australia, New Zealand and India, who are commemorated on their own national memorials. Over 72,000 names are inscribed on its panels, more than on any other memorial in the Commission's care. The memorial, designed by Sir Edwin Lutyens, was unveiled by the Prince of Wales in 1932.

39 **South African National Memorial, Delville Wood, Longueval, France.** The memorial (designed by Sir Herbert Baker) honours all South African Servicemen killed in the First World War. The names of South African missing are commemorated elsewhere.

40 **The Neuve-Chapelle Indian Memorial, France.** On the site of this memorial designed by Sir Herbert Baker, the Indian Corps fought its first great action in March 1915. On panels within the memorials are engraved the names of 5,000 officers and men of the Indian Army, recruited from all parts of what is now India, Pakistan and Bangladesh, who were killed in France and Belgium in 1914-1918 and have no known grave.

41 **The Commonwealth Air Forces Memorial, Malta.** 2,300 men of the Commonwealth Air Forces who lost their lives in raids and sorties over Malta, Gibraltar, the Mediterranean, Adriatic, Tunisia, Sicily, Italy, Yugoslavia and Austria in World War II and who have no known grave are commemorated on the Malta Memorial. It was designed by Sir Hubert Worthington and unveiled by Her Majesty Queen Elizabeth II in May 1954.

42 **Australian Memorial, Villers-Bretonneux, Fouilloy, France.** The memorial, designed by Sir Edwin Lutyens and unveiled by King George VI in 1938, commemorates by name the Australian soldiers who fell in battlefields of the Somme, Arras and the Hundred Days and is also dedicated to all other Australians who fought in France and Belgium in the 1914-1918 War and have no known grave.

43 **Beaumont-Hamel (Newfoundland) Memorial, France.** This memorial, designed by R. H. K. Cochius and surmounted by a giant Caribou, stands in a memorial park planted with trees from Newfoundland and the trenches and dug-outs of 1916 have been preserved. It serves a dual purpose of a a battle memorial and a record of 820 men of Newfoundland whose graves are unknown.

44 **Hill 60 (New Zealand) Memorial, Anzac, Gallipoli.** The names of 182 New Zealanders who fell in the Hill 60 actions in August and September 1915, and who have no known grave, are inscribed on the panels built into the base of the memorial which is an obelisk 22 feet high with a cross in relief on each side. The memorial was designed by Hurst Seager.

J8 WORLD WAR II: THE SEEDS OF CHANGE

45 **Japanese Troops entering Hong Kong, 1941.** On 7 December 1941 the Japanese carried out an air raid on the U.S. base at Pearl Harbour and on the following day attacked Hong Kong. The heavily outnumbered garrison surrendered on 25 December.

46 **The surrender of Singapore. 1942.** On the outbreak of hostilities Japanese forces moved with unexpected rapidity down the Malay Peninsula and British forces retired into Singapore. The anticipated strength of the island proved illusory and General Percival, here seen approaching the Japanese lines, surrendered on 15 February 1942.

47 **The Emir of Kano with West African troops.** The troops for the West African colonies were organised in the Royal West African Frontier Force. This was substantially expanded, and additional units raised during the war in the course of which West African units fought in East Africa and the Burma campaign.

48 **West African Troops in Burma.** At the beginning of 1943 it was decided that West African troops should be sent to Burma and for more than two years they were widely engaged in operations there. These photographs show West Africans entering a transport plane.

49 **1/1 King's African Rifles parading in Madagascar.** East African units fought in Abyssinia and Burma, and also carried out the campaign against the French in Madagascar in 1942. Lt. Genl. Sir William Platt is seen taking the salute at a victory parade in Tananarive on 3 October 1942. Photographed by Sgt. J. D. Morris.

50 **Maori Soldiers with captured gun. 1941.** In the first world war a Maori Pioneer Battalion was raised but in the period leading up to the second world war Maori leaders advocated the formation of a military unit recruited from their race. The 28th (Maori) Battalion was formed in October 1939, went to Britain in 1940, served in Greece and Crete, and battles in the Western Desert, and at the end of the war was in Italy. The photograph shows an anti-tank gun captured south of Gazala in the Western Desert in December 1941.

51 **Trinidad Sergeant in Middle East. 1945.** In 1943 it was decided to raise a West Indian force for service overseas, and the 1st Battalion, Caribbean Regiment, of 1,000 men from all parts of the West Indies was formed.

J9 CO-OPERATION IN WAR AND PEACE

52 **Imperial War Cabinet. 1917.** In 1917 two bodies met in parallel in London, the Imperial War Cabinet and the Imperial War Conference. On 16 March 1917 the Conference approved a resolution drafted by General Smuts which envisaged a post war relationship 'based upon full recognition of the Dominions as autonomous nations of an imperial Commonwealth and of India as an important portion of the same,' and should recognise their rights of an adequate voice in foreign policy.

53 **Canadian troops with Prime Minister Sir Robert Borden. 1918.** In July 1918 Canada's control of her overseas forces was improved through the formation of a Canadian section of the General Headquarters of the British armies in France. The Canadian Prime Minister visited troops on the Western Front at the time of this agreement.

54 **The British Empire delegation at the Paris Peace Conference. 1919.** Towards the end of the war empire leaders, particularly Smuts, Hughes and Borden, urged that the Dominions should be separately represented at the Peace Conference. This was eventually accepted and the treaty was signed by two representatives each of Canada, Australia, South Africa and India and one for New Zealand. This photograph taken in Lloyd George's flat shows leading participants such as Botha and Smuts (South Africa), Hughes and Ward, (Australia,) Foster and Doherty, (Canada), Ward and Massey (New Zealand) and E.S. Montagu (Secretary of State for India).

55 **R. G. Casey in the Middle East, 1943.** In 1942 the Australian R.G. Casey (1890-1976) was appointed Minister of State resident in the Middle East and a member of the British War Cabinet. This photograph was taken in Cairo with British war leaders in 1943. He was subsequently appointed Governor of Bengal and ended his public career as Governor-General of Australia.

56 **Commonwealth Prime Ministers on the Eve of the Invasion of Europe. 1944.** Winston Churchill with Mackenzie King, Peter Fraser, General Eisenhower, Sir Godfrey Huggins, General Smuts on a railway station 'somewhere in England.'

57 **Quebec Conference. 1944.** Several transatlantic meetings were held to discuss the strategy of the war. In this view of a conference held in Quebec in September 1944 British representatives are seen on the left and Canadians on the right. Malcolm MacDonald is the second from the left and beyond Winston Churchill, are Field Marshal Sir Alan Brooke, Admiral Cunningham, Air Marshal Portal and General Sir John Dill. Canadian Prime Minister Mackenzie King is sitting opposite Churchill.

58 **Transfer of Frigate from Britain to Bangladesh. 1976.** The former HMS. Llandaff became the B.N.S. Umar Farooq on her transfer from the Royal Navy to the Bangladesh Navy. Her old and new Commanders are shown on board.

59 **Signature of Military Training Agreement for Uganda. 1981.** Following a request at the Melbourne Heads of Government Meeting a thirty-six man Commonwealth Military Training team, supported in funds or personally by twelve Commonwealth countries., was sent to assist in training the Uganda Army. This photograph shows the signing of the agreement by the Secretary General of the Commonwealth and the Uganda High Commissioner in London.

The Commonwealth today

1965 was of major significance for the Commonwealth, for in that year the Commonwealth Secretariat and Commonwealth Foundation were set up and, though housed for convenience in London, financed, staffed, and operated as instruments of the whole Commonwealth. The Secretariat runs Conferences not only for Heads of Government but for those engaged in a variety of tasks throughout the Commonwealth, including health, work with youth, economic progress, law, and in many other fields. Specialised programmes in which the skills of Commonwealth countries contribute to each others' progress have been developed through the Commonwealth Fund for Technical Co-operation, and supervisory and investigating teams sent to countries such as Uganda.

The major political problem confronting the Commonwealth during this time was that of Rhodesia, and the role played by the Commonwealth Heads of Government Meeting of 1979 in making a break-through, and of Commonwealth Observers at the subsequent election, is depicted.

Commonwealth countries not only operate within the Commonwealth framework, but play their part in other international groupings; they have made significant contributions to the work of the United Nations, and have played a major part in peace-keeping forces under its auspices.

The Commonwealth Foundation is primarily concerned with financial support for professional bodies working in the Commonwealth as a whole, and also by the creation of local professional centres to make maximum use of limited resources. There still remain many voluntary bodies, operating in professional, welfare, and other fields, and increasing knowledge of the Commonwealth. These are represented in this section, but in spite of the vast output of photographs which is a feature of contemporary life, many valuable aspects of Commonwealth co-operation do not readily lend themselves to significant visual illustration – a photograph of a conference group or even a session can give little idea of its purpose or achievements.

Recreation and culture have their place – sport, which can divide as well as unite, the stimulating growth of Commonwealth literature, and the impact of varied traditions of Commonwealth peoples in festivals. The role of the Commonwealth Institute in diverse educational activities is also illustrated.

A reminder that the Commonwealth concerns people and not merely political and administrative structures is given by panel 15, where the less formal side of Commonwealth Conferences is indicated, including the interest shown by students in staging their own version of such a gathering, the visible expression of the Commonwealth of which they form a part.

K1 **Commonwealth Heads of Government at the opening of their 1981 meeting.**

K2 THE COMMONWEALTH SECRETARIAT

1 **Marlborough House, Headquarters of the Commonwealth Secretariat and Commonwealth Foundation.** Built by Wren in 1709-10 for the Duke of Marlborough, and much altered since, Marlborough House became a royal palace. In 1959 H.M. Queen Elizabeth II offered it for use as a Commonwealth Centre; it was first used for that purpose in 1962 and since the creation of the Secretariat and the Foundation has been used for part of their activities, and for conferences.

2 **Arnold Smith, First Commonwealth Secretary-General.** The Canadian diplomat Arnold Smith was chosen as the first Secretary-General of the Commonwealth Secretariat in 1965 and held office for the first, formative, ten years of the new organisation.

3 **Shridath Ramphal, Second Commonwealth Secretary-General.** Shridath S. Ramphal, then Foreign Minister of Guyana, was chosen at the Commonwealth Heads of Government Meeting in 1975 to succeed Arnold Smith, and was reappointed for a second five-year term from 1980.

4 **Visit of H.M. Queen Elizabeth II to Marlborough House.** H.M. Queen Elizabeth II, as Head of the Commonwealth, visits Marlborough House annually on Commonwealth Day. On this 1972 visit she is talking to the wives of High Commissioners.

5 **Commonwealth Group of Economic Experts. 1976.** The 1975 Heads of Government Meeting set up a group of economic experts, chaired by Alister McIntyre, Secretary-General of the Caribbean Community, to consider practical measures to reduce the gap between rich and poor nations. Three meetings, each producing a report, were held between 1975 and 1977; that shown was in London, 1976; Mr McIntyre is flanked by Arthur Hazlewood, Secretary of the Group, and the Commonwealth Secretary-General.

6 **Commonwealth Observers for Uganda. 1980.** The Commonwealth Secretary-General with the members of the team sent, at the request of the Uganda Government, to observe and report on the conduct of the elections held in December 1980.

K3 COMMONWEALTH FUND FOR TECHNICAL CO-OPERATION

7 **Indian Fisheries Adviser in the Caribbean.** The Commonwealth Fund for Technical Co-operation (C.F.T.C.) was established in 1971 to provide technical assistance to developing countries on a multilateral basis, 'bringing Commonwealth skills to Commonwealth needs.' A major aspect is the supply of experts; here A.I. George from India is seen advising Caribbean fishermen.

8 **Sri Lankan Structural Engineer in Barbados.** Mr. Gilbert Munasinghe of Sri Lanka in Barbados as an expert Structural Engineeer.

9 **C.F.T.C. Expert in Montserrat.** Greg Luke in Montserrat in 1979.

10 **Ship Building Adviser in Malta Docks.** Dilip Sheth, ship-building adviser to Malta dry docks.

11 **Crop Expert in Western Samoa.** Dr. Edwin Dharmaraju, C.F.T.C. crop production expert in Western Samoa coconut plantation.

12 **Pacific Islanders in Broadcast course, Malaysia.** C.F.T.C. also undertakes training courses; a woman from Tuvalu and a man from the Cook Islands are seen interviewing a Malaysian farmer as part of a course on broadcasting, attended by nineteen participants from Asia and the Pacific.

13 **Zimbabweans learning engineering in Malta.** Before the independence of Zimbabwe more than 4,000 Zimbabweans were training outside their country under a special Commonwealth programme, launched in 1966 and co-ordinated by C.F.T.C.

14 **Namibians travelling to Jamaica.** Since 1975 nearly 250 Namibians have received C.F.T.C. awards at seventy institutions in ten Commonwealth developing countries.

K4 THE COMMONWEALTH IN THE WORLD

15 **Nehru addressing the United Nations. 1960.** Prime Minister Nehru speaking at the United Nations General Assembly on 5 October 1960 on the resolution submitted by five countries, including India, calling for renewed contacts between the U.S.A. and Russia.

16 **Kenya's President at Economic Commission for Africa meeting. 1965.** President Jomo Kenyatta opening the 7th Session of the Economic Commission for Africa held in Nairobi from 9-23 February 1965.

17 **United Nations Women's Conference. 1980.** Delegates signing the Convention at the United Nations Women's Conference in Copenhagen in July 1980. On the left is Lucille Mair from Jamaica, Conference Secretary-General.

18 **Canadian Peacekeeping Force, Gaza Strip. 1956.** A United Nations force was set up following the hostilities at the time of the Suez crisis of 1956. Members of the 8th Canadian Hussars are renting camels to help them in patrol duties.

19 **Indian Troops in the Congo. 1961.** United Nations Forces were engaged in the Congo from 1960 to 1964 during the Civil war. Indian troops formed one third of the force of nearly 100,000 men in a particularly dangerous and difficult undertaking.

20 **Canadians in Cyprus. 1965.** Inter-communal strife between Greeks and Turks in Cyprus erupted late in 1963, and a U.N. Force early in the following year included Canadians. Ferret scout cars of Lord Strathcona's Horse are shown in a village near Nicosia.

K5 THE COMMONWEALTH FOUNDATION

21 **Commonwealth Foundation Seminar, Jamaica. 1975.** A gathering of Dr. Amiel, Past President, Professional Centre of Jamaica; Sir Hugh Springer, KCMG, CBE, Chairman, Commonwealth Foundation; H.E. Florizel Glasspole, Governor General of Jamaica; John Chadwick, first Director, Commonwealth Foundation and Miss E. Tullock, Secretary, Professional Centre, Jamaica.

22 **Director of the Commonwealth Foundation in Malawi. 1981.** Ric Throssell (Director of the Commonwealth Foundation since 1980) in discussion with Dr. Donton S.J. Mkandawire, Education Authority in Malawi, April 1981.

23 **Fiji's Professional Centre, Suva.** The Commonwealth Foundation has established Professional Centres in many Commonwealth countries. Their aim is to break the isolation sometimes felt by professional people, to link different professions within the communities in which they work, and to provide common services for their members, thus keeping administrative costs low.

24 **Caribbean and Pacific delegates at the Barbados Professional Centre. 1982.** Delegates from Western Samoa, Fiji, Tonga, Barbados and Guyana, with the Director of the Commonwealth Foundation in the Barbados Professional Centre during a seminar on 'The Development of appropriate skills and qualifications required to serve the community in small island states.'

25 **Regional Deaf Teacher Training School, Montford, Malawi.** Largely financed 1968-77 by Commonwealth Foundation grants.

K6 THE COMMONWEALTH PEN.

While the older Commonwealth countries have continued to produce outstanding writers, including one Nobel Prize winner, Patrick White, an important feature of the last thirty years has been the emergence of creative writers of a high order from newer Commonwealth countries remarkably alike for their presentation of the outlook and way of life of their countries and for their abilities in solely literary terms, not least in their sometimes complex and adventurous use of English.

26 **Chinua Achebe (b.1930). Nigerian Novelist and Poet.**

27 **Wole Soyinka (b.1934). Nigerian dramatist.**

28 **Ngugi wa Thiong'o (b.1936). Kenyan novelist.**

29 **Bessie Head. Novelist and short story writer in Botswana.**

30 **R.K. Narayan (b.1907). Indian novelist and essayist.**

31 **V.S. Naipaul (b.1932). Trinidadian novelist.**

32 **Derek Walcott (b.1930). St. Lucian poet.**

33 **Frank Sargeson (1903-82). New Zealand writer.**

34 **Patrick White (b.1912). Australian novelist and Nobel Prize winner.**

35 **Hugh MacLennan (b.1907). Canadian novelist.**

36 **Mordecai Richler (b.1931). Canadian novelist.**

37 **Margaret Atwood. Canadian novelist and critic.**

K7 YOUTH AND EDUCATIONAL TRAVEL

38 **First Winners of Commonwealth Youth Awards. 1976.** The Commonwealth Youth Programme was set up in 1973 and made its first awards in 1976, the winners being groups from Canada and Malaysia; the latter, here seen with the Commonwealth Secretary General, initiated production and training schemes in farming in Kelantan.

39 **Developing the Youth Programme in St. Lucia.** David Ursell from Wales was sent to St. Lucia under the Commonwealth Youth Programme, to promote the training of youth workers in St. Lucia, where he had twenty-eight participants.

40 **C.I.S.G.O. in India. 1980.** Mrs. Gandhi, Prime Minister of India, welcomes the fifteenth Commonwealth Interchange Study Group (C.I.S.G.O.) in Delhi in 1980. This scheme is organised by the Royal Commonwealth Society to give groups of young business and professional people the opportunity of an intensive study tour of other Commonwealth countries.

41 **C.Y.E.C. Exchange for the Young Disabled. 1981.** The Commonwealth Youth Exchange Council, which exists to promote contacts between Commonwealth young people, organised a visit for ten handicapped and ten able-bodied young Britons to the Bahamas, in conjunction with the Bahamas Association for the Physically Handicapped. A reciprocal visit is planned for 1983.

42 **COMEX member entertaining an Indian audience.** COMEX (Commonwealth Expedition) was founded by Lionel Gregory to organise international tours of students and young professional people travelling by road to other parts of the Commonwealth and emphasizing contacts at personal level.

43 **Commonwealth Participants in Scout/Guide Folk Music Festival. 1981.** The Scout and Guide Associations, which originated in 1908 and 1910 respectively spread rapidly through the world and are active in most countries including those of the Commonwealth. This photograph shows members from Trinidad, Bangladesh and Malaysia in London for 'Folk Fest X' 1981.

K8 PRACTICAL CO-OPERATION

44 **Commonwealth Magistrates' Association. 1970.** The Association was formed in July 1970; delegates attending the inaugural meetings were presented to H.M. Queen Elizabeth the Queen Mother at a garden party of the Magistrates Association of England and Wales held at Blenheim; in this picture are seen Tom Skyrme, first President, and representatives of Uganda, Australia, and India.

45 **Employer and Trade Union representatives at Labour Conference.** Indian and Nigerian delegates, representing employers' and trade union organisations at a session of the International Labour Conference.

46 **Commonwealth Parliamentary Association Conference. 1973.** The Commonwealth Parliamentary Association was formed in 1911 and was a pioneer in inter-Commonwealth co-operation. Its 19th Conference, attended by 200 members of Commonwealth legislatures, was opened in Westminster Hall by H.M. Queen Elizabeth II on 12 September 1973; in this photograph the representative of Sri Lanka is addressing the Conference.

47 **Commonwealth in Books Exhibition.** In 1964 a Commonwealth Book Exhibition was held at Marlborough House and thereafter exhibitions were regularly held, often with a special emphasis on Commonwealth literature, run by the National Book League and the Commonwealth Institute in co-operation with the Foreign & Commonwealth Office and with support from other appropriate bodies but have not been held since 1979.

48 **Commonwealth Pharmaceutical Association Conference in Bombay.** The Association was formed in 1969 and its second conference, with accompanying Trade Exhibition, was held in a specially designed auditorium, with an exhibition area made to resemble an Indian village.

49 **Health Ministers' Conference, Mauritius. 1981.** A meeting of health ministers for east, central, and southern Africa was held in Mauritius in November 1981.

K9 MEETING NEEDS

50 **New Zealand Volunteer in Malaysia.** Dick Pardy from Auckland, who with his wife Chris, a teacher went to Malaysia under the auspices of Voluntary Service Abroad.

51 **V.S.O. Agriculturalist at school for the Mentally Handicapped, Kenya.** Voluntary Service Overseas was founded in 1950. Carol Williams is working as an agricultural therapist providing practical experience for handicapped children at Karatina School in Kenya.

52 **Royal Commonwealth Society for the Blind in India.** The Royal Commonwealth Society for the Blind is concerned with blindness and its prevention in the developing countries of the Commonwealth. Many of its activities are carried out on the spot through eye camps and travelling specialists.

53 **Leprosy Expert in Malawi.** LEPRA began as the British Empire Leprosy Relief Association in 1924. It raises funds to finance its own direct work in Malawi and to support the work of other bodies active in the field.

54 **Save the Children Fund polio Campaign in Swaziland.** Save the Children Fund is a child welfare organisation working in Britain and the developing world. In 1979, the year of its Diamond Jubilee, it launched a Stop Polio Campaign to extend the use of immunisation vaccine, here seen being administered at an open-air session in rural Swaziland.

K10 PROMOTING UNDERSTANDING

55 **African Student in the Royal Commonwealth Society Library.** The Royal Commonwealth Society, founded in 1868, is the oldest of the voluntary bodies concerned with the Commonwealth and its members, and now has branches, some of them autonomous, and affiliated bodies throughout the Commonwealth. It pursues a varied educational programme, has extensive club facilities, and is widely known for the Library, estimated to contain over 400,000 items and forming a major research collection.

56 **R.C.S. Essay Competition winner.** Kavita Ramdas, the winner of Class A of the 1978/79 Essay Competition organised each year since 1913 by the Royal Commonwealth Society to encourage Commonwealth studies in schools throughout the world. She is pictured enjoying her prize of a trip to Britain and is accompanied by Sanjay Kalra, also from Springdales School in Delhi.

57 **Julius Nyerere addressing the Royal Commonwealth Society.** From its earliest days the Society has provided a forum for speakers with first-hand knowledge of their subjects. In recent years the leaders of independent nations of the Commonwealth have welcomed the opportunity of speaking to informed but unofficial audiences under its auspices. The Chairman of this meeting was Malcolm MacDonald, President of the Society from 1971 to 1981.

58 **The Royal Overseas League Musical Competition.** Among its varied activities for Commonwealth understanding, the League (founded in 1910) pays particular attention to music, and organises an annual festival for music students.

59-64 **Commonwealth Day Multi-faith Observance. 1982.** The Commonwealth Arts Festival of 1965 included an observance attended by representatives of the major faiths of the Commonwealth. This idea was adopted as a regular form of celebration of Commonwealth Day, the first occasion being in 1966 at St. Martins in the Fields. Since 1972 the observance, which is organised by the Joint Commonwealth Societies' Council, has been held in Westminster Abbey, and frequently attended by H.M. Queen Elizabeth II, Head of the Commonwealth. The photographs include the Queen's arrival, the religious representatives and the flags of Commonwealth countries.

K11 SPORT

Many sports have been enthusiastically adopted in lands far beyond their countries of origin and sporting contacts have often fostered understanding between peoples. However, racial issues have also emerged, creating tensions between Commonwealth members, and in order to face these the Commonwealth Heads of Government approved the Gleneagles Agreement on sporting contacts with South Africa in 1977.

65 **Cricket in Fiji. 1956.** Cricket has a long tradition in Fijian sport; this match was played by a local team of Europeans, Fijians and Indians against the visiting West Indies.

66 **Hockey Players at Chandigarh.** Hockey players from India and the South Pacific are seen in the course of a visit to the National Institute of Sport at Chandigarh during a Training Conference.

67 **Tanzanian Victor in Marathon. 1978.** Gidemas Shihanga won the gold medal for the Marathon at the 11th Commonwealth Games held at Edmonton in August 1978.

68 **Relaxation at Heads of Government Meeting. 1981.** Participants in the C.H.O.G.M. of 1981 on the Government House tennis court in Canberra.

K12 RHODESIA TO ZIMBABWE

69 **Commonwealth meeting at Lagos to discuss Rhodesia. 1966.** Meeting of Commonwealth Heads of Government in Lagos (the first time it was held outside London) in January 1966 to discuss the situation created by Rhodesia's Unilateral Declaration of Independence on 11 November 1965, by its Prime Minister, Ian Smith.

70 **Rhodesian Guerrillas.** During the ensuing years various discussions took place in a vain endeavour to arrive at an acceptable constitution for an independent Rhodesia. In 1972 fighting began between African guerrillas of the Patriotic Front (ZAPU and ZANU), seen here in a training camp, and Government forces, and continued despite an internal settlement reached between Ian Smith and Bishop Abel Muzorewa in 1978.

71 **Commonwealth Discussions on Rhodesia at Lusaka. 1979.** Lee Kuan Yew of Singapore, President Kaunda of Zambia, Lord Carrington, British Foreign Secretary, and Mrs. Thatcher, British Prime Minister, in conversation between sessions of the Commonwealth Heads of Government Meeting at Lusaka, 1979, during which plans for a Constitutional Conference on Rhodesia were agreed.

72 **Rhodesian Cease-Fire Agreement. 1979.** Signing the cease-fire agreement for Rhodesia at the end of the fifteen week Conference which began at Lancaster House, London, in September. Seated are S. Mundawarara, Bishop Muzorewa, Lord Carrington, Sir Ian Gilmour (Lord Privy Seal), Joshua Nkomo (ZAPU), Robert Mugabe (ZANU).

73 **Commonwealth Troops for Rhodesia. 1979.** British members of the Commonwealth force sent to monitor the Rhodesian Ceasefire embarking at RAF Brize Norton, 22 December 1979.

74 **The Commonwealth Election Observers Rhodesia. 1980.** Mr. Justice Nurul Islam of Bangladesh, one of the team of Commonwealth Observers sent to Rhodesia for the elections on 27-29 February 1980, examining a ballot box before the polls opened. The result declared on 4 March was a victory for Robert Mugabe's ZANU party, and on 17 April Rhodesia became independent as Zimbabwe.

K13 THE COMMONWEALTH INSTITUTE

The Commonwealth Institute in London was constituted in 1958, replacing the former Imperial Institute, and its new building in Kensington High St. was opened in 1962. Its purpose is to promote a better understanding of the modern Commonwealth and it is financed by grants from British and other Commonwealth governments. In addition to its extensive exhibition galleries, with Art Gallery and Theatre, it works with visiting school groups and teachers, providing talks, conferences and courses. Its library and resource centre includes a special collection on Commonwealth Literature and provides a loan service of books and audio-visual materials.

75 **Ugandan Guide with Children at the Uganda Exhibition.**

76 **Institute Guides helping children to make a mask at the Masks Exhibition. 1980.**

77 **Activity Session at the Permanent Indian Exhibition.**

78 **Notting Hill Carnival Reception in Main Galleries of the Institute.**

79 **Steel Band Players at Annual Trinidad Carnival.**

80 **Library & Resource Centre.**

81 **A Corner of the Malta Exhibition.**

K14 THE ARTISTIC DIVERSITY OF THE COMMONWEALTH

82-93 **Commonwealth Carnival Edmonton. 1978.** As a result of an Arts Festival in Malta in 1975 a Commonwealth Arts Association was set up with John McKenzie as Manager: it was asked to organise the Commonwealth Carnival which was a feature of the cultural Festival 78 held at the time of the 1978 Commonwealth Games at Edmonton. A particular feature of this colourful event, with 400 participants from twenty-four countries, was the great extent to which performances took place in shopping centres and other venues in the middle of the life of the city.

94-98 **Indian Ocean Arts Festival. 1979.** Perth, Western Australia was the focus of performances from many countries bordering the Indian Ocean for a fortnight in September-October 1979. Music, dance, mime, drama, exhibitions of visual arts, lectures and demonstrations covered a wide field.

K15 HEADS OF GOVERNMENT MEETINGS: THE INFORMAL ASPECT

99 **Commonwealth Conference. 1965.** D.K. Jawara, Prime Minister of The Gambia, which had become independent the previous February, is seen talking to L.B. Shastri, Prime Minister of India.

100 **Informal group at 1966 Prime Minister's meeting.** Front row, left to right: Dr. Obote (Uganda), Lester Pearson (Canada), Dr. Banda (Malawi), Tunku Adbul Rahman (Malaysia), Lee Kuan Yew (Singapore), Sardar Swaran Singh (Minister for External Affairs, India). Patrick Solomon (Deputy P.M., Trinidad), Keith Holyaoke (New Zealand) and Harold Holt (Australia) are prominent in the second row.

101 **Chairman Trudeau in action. 1973.** Canadian Prime Minister Pierre Trudeau presiding over the Ottawa Conference of 1973.

102 **A lighter moment at the 1975 CHOGM.** Mrs. Gandhi (India) speaking at the 1975 meeting in Jamaica. To her left, Michael Manley (Jamaica); to her right, Arnold Smith (Commonwealth S-G) and Abp. Makarios (Cyprus).

103 **Entertainment during a Retreat. CHOGM 1981.** As a counter to the pressures of the large formal sessions of Heads of Government meetings it is customary to give opportunities for more relaxed personal contacts and thought at 'Retreat' attended by Heads of Government but not their delegations away from publicity. Such occasions have oten been successful in resolving controversial issues. A local youth choir seen entertaining delegates at 'The Lodge' in Canberra.

104 **Students' CHOGM, Ottawa. 1981.** In 1973 the Ottawa Branch of the Royal Commonwealth Society pioneered the idea of a gathering of students who would discuss topics of Commonwealth interest with each participant adopting the role of a head of government. This has continued annually in Canada and in 1979 was taken up in Australia.

Faces & places

1-5 A selection of Lord Snowdon's photographs of Australia, South East Asia, the Far East and Hong Kong.

1 **Street scene, Nigeria.**

2 **Carpets for sale, Singapore.**

3-5 **Nigerian portraits.**

6 **Dyak Girl.**

7 **Schoolgirl, Brunei.**

8 **Hong Kong woman.**

9 **Fish seller, Hong Kong.**

10 **Boatman, Hong Kong.**

1-12 **Australian portraits.**

13 **Rubber tapper, Malaysia.**

14 **Girl and child, Singapore.**

15 **Girl with batik cloth, Malaysia.**

16 **Stonemason, Hong Kong.**

17 **Craftswoman with bamboo, Brunei.**

18 **Brunei landscape.**

19 **Australian landscape.**

Index of Photographers

The following index provides brief biographical details of photographers up to 1914 whose work is featured in the exhibition. In many cases these men left little or no information concerning themselves and documentary evidence of their professional activities is limited to the brief entries in the commercial sections of the yearly almanacs published in most territories. The growing interest in historical photographs from all parts of the world has led in recent years to the publication of numerous photographically orientated pictorial books and these have been freely drawn on in the compilation of these entries. Of those dealing specifically with the history of photography, the following books give a fuller picture of its growth in various parts of the Commonwealth, together with more detailed accounts of the careers of some of the more celebrated figures whose names are found below: Jack Cato, *The story of the camera in Australia* (Melbourne, 1955), Marjorie Bull and Joseph Denfield, *Secure the shadow. The story of Cape photography from its beginnings to the end of 1870* (Cape Town, 1970), Hardwicke Knight, *Photography in New Zealand* (Dunedin, 1971), Ray Desmond, *Photography in India during the nineteenth century* (pp 5-36 of India Office Library and Records report for the year 1974), Ralph Greenhill and Andrew Birrell, *Canadian photography 1939-1920* (Toronto, 1979). Commercial photographers working in England are not included in the index.

AFONG. Commercial, Hong Kong. Business established c1860; photographs by Afong are described by John Thomson (qv) as 'being extremely well executed, (and) are remarkable for their artistic choice of position'; business continued into present century by son.

ALLDRIDGE, Thomas Joshua (1874-1916). Amateur, Sierra Leone. Arrived in Sierra Leone 1871, employed for several years as Randall and Fisher's agent on York Island; Travelling commissioner, Sherbro hinterland 1889-94; accompanied Governor Cardew on his first tour of the hinterland 1894; District Commissioner, Sherbro 1894-1905 and witnessed much of the fighting during the Hut Tax War of 1898; author: *The Sherbro and its hinterland* (1901), *A transformed colony: Sierra Leone as it was and as it is* (1910).

ANJO, Jose. Commercial, St John's, Antigua c1900-c20; also photographed in Dominica and St Kitts.

ARMSTRONG, BEERE & HIME. Commercial, Canada. Firm of Armstrong, Beere and Hime, photographers, civil engineers and draughtsmen founded c1856; Humphrey Lloyd Hime (1833-1903) arrived in Canada 1854; accompanied Red River Expedition of 1858 as photographer; left firm to become a stockbroker c1860 and was President of the Toronto Stock Exchange in 1868 and 1888; William Armstrong (1822-1919) came to Toronto in 1851 and was a water-colourist of note and a civil engineer; abandoned photography in the 1860s; Daniel Beere, a relative of Armstrong, returned to Dublin c1866.

AVERY, William F. Commercial, British Honduras. Studio in Belize 1890s-c1930.

BEATO, Felix Antonio. Commercial. Naturalised British citizen of Venetian origin; in partnership with James Robertson, Chief Engraver at the Imperial Mint in Constantinople, and photographed with him in Malta and the Middle East c1853-c56; photographed with Robertson the aftermath of the Indian Mutiny 1858; studio in Calcutta 1858-59; photographed China War 1860; photographer and general trader, Japan c1864-84; photographed Korean War 1871 and the Wolseley Nile Expedition of 1884-85; photographer and general trader, Mandalay and Rangoon c1886-c1908; published *Native types* and *Views of Japan* c1868.

BEATTIE, W. Commercial, New Zealand. Photographer with *New Zealand Herald* 1898.

BEERE, Daniel. See: ARMSTRONG, BEERE & HIME.

BIRCH, James Wheeler Woodford (1826-1875). Amateur, Ceylon and Malaya. After brief service in Royal Navy joined Ceylon Civil Service 1846-70; Colonial Secretary, Straits Settlements 1870-74; British Resident in Perak 1874-75; took photographs of the ruins of Polonnaruwa in Ceylon, later marketed by W.L.H. Skeen (qv); sent a series of photographs of his tour in Selangor and Perak in 1874 to the Colonial Office; two photographs by Birch are pasted into some copies of *Memoranda, etc. on the Malayan Peninsula and Perak . . .* (Calcutta, 1875).

BOURNE, Samuel (1834-1912). Commercial, India. Employed by Moore and Robinson's Bank, Nottingham until 1862; in India 1863-70; made three long photographic journeys of exploration in Kashmir and the Himalayas (1863, 1864, and 1866) described in a series of letters to *The British Journal of Photography* (1863-70); joined firm of Howard and Shepherd, Allahabad c1864; business of Howard, Bourne and Shepherd in Simla c1865-70; Kenneth Murray a partner in Simla c1869-72; Howard left 1870 and firm became Bourne and Shepherd, still trading to present day; Charles Shepherd left India c1885; on return to England, Bourne founded cotton doubling firm, and turned his attention away from photography to water-colour painting.

BRAGGE, James (1833-1908). Commercial, South Africa and New Zealand. Apprenticed to a cabinet maker; emigrated to South Africa early 1860s and started practice as a commercial photographer; arrived New Zealand mid 1860s, in Wellington by 1866; to Auckland 1871; returned to Wellington by 1873; album of 50 views, *Wellington to the Wairarapa,* issued 1876; 2nd trip to Wairarapa 1878; left for Auckland 1888; returned to Wellington by 1891.

BRITTAIN, Revd Arthur. Amateur, Pacific. Member of the Melanesian Mission. Accompanied Bishop Montgomery on Melanesian tour 1892.

BRUTON, James Edward (1838-1918). Commercial, South Africa. Born at Port Elizabeth of 1820 settler parents; opened first photographic studio opposite Lyceum, Port Elizabeth 1858; moved to Jetty Street 1859-74; to Cape Town 1874; left South Africa for Douglas, Isle of Man 1890s.

BURKE, John. Commercial, India 1860s-c1907; studios at Rawalpindi, Murree and Lahore; commissioned by government to photograph 2nd Afghan War; photographs by Burke appear in Henry Hardy Cole, *Illustrations of ancient buildings in Kashmir* (1869).

BURTON BROTHERS, Walter John (c1836-1880) and Alfred Henry (1834-1914). Commercial, New Zealand. Business founded 1867; photographic tour of Pacific islands 1884; business taken over by Muir and Moody 1898.

CAIRE, John Nicholas (1837-1918). Commercial, Australia. Arrived in Adelaide c1860 and learnt photography from Townsend Duryea; made photographic tour of Gippsland 1865; opened studio in Adelaide 1867; moved to Talbot, Victoria 1870; in Bendigo c1874-76; to Melbourne 1876; produced a number of albums with letterpress captions: *Views of Bendigo* (1875), *Views of Victoria* (1877-1879), *Victorian scenery* (c1883), *Views of Sydney Harbour and New South Wales* (c1877), *Gippsland scenery* (c1886).

CAMPION, John William Henry. Commercial, Bridgetown, Barbados 1870s-80s.

CLIFFORD, Samuel. Commercial, Tasmania. Active 1860s and 1870s; received a bronze medal at Sydney Exhibition of 1870.

COONLEY, J.F. Commercial, Bahamas. Worked as a photographer for the Union side with Brady and Gardiner during the American Civil War; studio in Masonic Hall, Bay Street, Nassau 1880s-90s.

CROMBIE, John Nicol (c1831-1879). Commercial, New Zealand. Originally an engineer, emigrated to Melbourne 1852 and became assistant to Melbourne photographers, Meade Brothers; to New Zealand c1854, opened photographic business in Nelson, moved to Auckland 1855; photographic tour of southern provinces 1856-59; to England 1862; died at Melbourne while returning to New Zealand.

DALLY, Frederick (b.c1840). Commercial, British Columbia. Arrived in British Columbia 1862; opened studio in Victoria 1866; visited the Cariboo goldfields 1867; opened studio in Barkerville in 1868 which was destroyed in the fire of September 1868; sold stock to Green Brothers and left colony 1870; received diploma in dentistry from Philadelphia College 1872.

DAVIS, J. (d.1893). Commercial, Samoa. Photographic studio in Apia 1880s; business taken over at death by A.J. Tattersall (qv.).

DEEN DIYAL, Lala (1844-1910). Commercial, India. Attended Thomason College at Roorkee; took up photography 1874; photographed Prince of Wales' visit to Indore 1875-76; appointed court photographer to Nizam of Hyderabad 1884; work commissioned by the Archaeological Survey of India and 89 collotypes from Deen Diyal's photographs used in Sir Lepel Griffin, *Famous monuments in Central India* (London, 1886); business carried on by descendants to present day.

DEVERIL, Herbert. Commercial, New Zealand. Arrived in Wellington from Melbourne (where he had also worked as a photographer) in 1873 to take over photolithographic department of Government Printing Office; active as a photographer until mid 1880s; commissioned by New Zealand government to take a series of photographs for the 1876 Philadelphia Exhibition.

DEVINE, H.T. Commercial, British Columbia 1890s.

DUPERLY, Adolphe & Sons. Commercial, Kingston, Jamaica. Originally an engraver and printer, Duperly produced I.M. Belisario's *Sketches of character in illustration . . . of the negro population of Jamaica* (1837); published *Dageurian (sic) excursions* (Paris, ?1844) containing 24 lithographs from his own daguerreotype views of Jamaica; Adolphe died 1865 and business continued by his son Armond and in turn by his son Théophile; original premises destroyed in fire in which Théophile lost his right hand; business continued into 1920s.

EYLES, Charles Henry. Amateur, British Honduras. Assistant Colonial Surgeon, Gold Coast 1883-87; Colonial Surgeon, British Honduras 1888-1906.

FIEBIG, Frederick. (?)Amateur, India. Originally a lithographer, published *A panorama of Calcutta in six parts* in 1847; in 1856 wrote to the Directors of the East India Company offering for sale 437 salt prints (plain or hand coloured) of the 'principal buildings and other places of interest at Calcutta, Madras, the Coromandel Coast, Ceylon, Mauritius, and the Cape of Good Hope'.

FIORILLO, F. Commercial, Egypt, fl.1900s. Took progress photographs of Aswan Dam construction.

FIORILLO, L. Commercial, Egypt. Studio in Place Mehemet Ali, Alexandria 1870s-80s; *cartes de visite* praised in *Murray's Handbook for Egypt* (1875).

FISHER, A. Hugh (1867-1945). Artist, writer and photographer. Abandoned work in city office to study art; exhibitor at Royal Academy, Paris Salon, New English Art Club; artist and photographer to the Colonial Office Visual Instruction Committee, and commissioned for three years to travel about the British Empire 1907-10; author: *Through India and Burmah with pen and brush* (1911), *Poems* (1913), *The marriage of Ilario* (1919), etc.

FLOYD, William Pryor. Commercial, Hong Kong c1865-74.

FRY, William Ellerton (1846-1930). Amateur, Rhodesia. Arrived in South Africa 1872 and variously a farmer, trader and prospector; secretary and computer at Royal Observatory, Cape Town 1872-90, rising to position of Assistant Astronomer Royal; official photographer, assistant to Selous, intelligence officer and meteorologist in Mashonaland Pioneer Column 1890; later worked on the Salisbury-Tete telegraph and travelled in Australia and New Zealand.

GEDGE, Ernest (1862-1935). Amateur, East Africa. Manager of tea estate in Assam 1879-88; IBEACo. employee 1888-91; *Times* correspondent in Uganda 1892-93 and Mashonaland 1893; prospecting and investigating mineral resources in Yukon 1898-99, Rhodesia 1900, East Africa 1902-05, Malaya, Borneo and Java 1911-12; extensive travelling elsewhere.

GLOVER, Thomas George (d.1881). Amateur, India. Joined Royal Engineers 1844; retired as Colonel 1870; served Punjab 1848-49 and Mutiny 1857-58; produced a series of portraits of officers, mainly Mutiny veterans from the Bengal and Bombay Engineers c1862; died at Neuenaher, Prussia; author: *The Ganges Canal illustrated by photographs taken by T.G. Glover* (Roorkee, 1867).

GOMES, A.C. & SON. Commercial, Zanzibar. Firm reputedly founded c1868; premises in Main Street, Zanzibar; briefly in partnership with J.B. Coutinho in mid 1890s; business continued by P.F. Gomes (d.1932); Dar es Salaam branch in 1930s.

GRANT, James Augustus (1827-1892). Amateur, East Africa. Soldier and explorer: served Bengal Army 1846-68; accompanied Speke Expedition of 1860-63; took photographs at Zanzibar in 1860 but abandoned photography in favour of sketching; served as intelligence officer with Abyssinian Expedition of 1867-68; author: *A walk across Africa* (1864), etc.

GRAY BROTHERS. Commercial, Kimberley 1872-?.

GREGSON, Francis. Amateur, Sudan. War correspondent during Sudan Campaign 1898.

GROS, H.F. Commercial, Transvaal. Of Swiss origin, arrived in South Africa c1869; studios at Bloemfontein and Kimberley early 1870s; visited Pilgrim's Rest goldfields 1874-75; studio in Pretoria 1876-?95; made a photographic tour of the Transvaal after the 1st Boer War, published as *Picturesque aspects of the Transvaal* (dated 1888, although some of the photographs are later); returned to Europe 1895.

HALL, 'Professor' Robert (c1821-1866). Commercial, Australia. Purchased daguerreotype camera from S.T. Gill; set up studio in Currie Street, Adelaide 1846; took the first portraits in Perth in November 1846.

HARRIS, Robert. Commercial, South Africa. Studio in Port Elizabeth c1880-c94; produced several photographically illustrated books: *Photographic views of Port Elizabeth and neighbourhood* (c1876), *Southampton to South Africa* (by Charles Cowen, photographs by Harris, 1882), *Photographic album of South African scenery* (1880s), *South Africa illustrated* ((1888).

HARVIE & SUTCLIFFE. Commercial, Melbourne 1890s-1900s.

HATTERSLEY, Charles William (1866-1934). Amateur, Uganda. C.M.S. missionary in Uganda from 1897; author: *Uganda by the pen and camera* (1906), *The Baganda at home* (1908), *Erastus, slave and prince* (1910).

HAWES, Albert George Sidney (d. August 6 1897). Amateur, Nyasaland. Royal Marines 1859-69; Japanese Service 1871-84; 'Consul for the territories of the African Kings and Chiefs in the districts adjacent to Lake Nyasa' 1885-87; special duty, Zanzibar 1888-89; Consul for Society Islands 1889, promoted Commissioner and Consul General, Sandwich Islands and Dependencies 1894; died at Hito; author: (with Sir Ernest Satow), *A handbook for travellers in Central and Northern Japan.*

HIME, Humphrey Lloyd. See: ARMSTRONG, BEERE & HIME.

HOLM, N. Walwin (b.1865). Commercial, West Africa. Business started in Accra c1882; moved to Lagos 1896; enrolled as member of Royal Photographic Society 1897; to England to study law 1910; called to Bar 1917 and returned to Lagos to practise as a barrister; his son J.A.C. Holm (b.1888) joined firm c1906 and ran business while his father was in England; Accra branch re-opened 1919.

HOSE, Charles (1863-1929). Amateur, Sarawak, Entered service of Rajah of Sarawak 1884; member of the Supreme Council and Judge of the Supreme Court of Sarawak 1904; retired 1907; author: *The pagan tribes of Borneo* (1912), *Natural man: a record from Borneo* (1926), *Fifty years of romance and research, or a jungle-wallah at large* (1928).

JOHNSON, William. Commercial, Bombay. Uncovenanted civil servant, Bombay c1848-c61; daguerreotype studio, Grant's Road, Bombay c1852-c54; photographer c1854-c60; founder member of Bombay Photographic Society (1854) and editor of journal; produced, with William Henderson with whom he was briefly in partnership, *The Indian amateur's photographic album* (24 issues, December 1856-October 1858); author: *The oriental races and tribes, residents and visitors of Bombay* (2 vols., London, 1863 and 1866).

JOHNSTON (P.A.) & HOFFMANN (Theodore J.). Commercial, India. Studios at Calcutta and Darjeeling; business founded c1882 and continued under various managements (European and Indian) into 1950s.

LAMBERT, G.R. & CO. Commercial, Singapore. Business founded 1875 by G.R. Lambert of Dresden; taken over in 1885 by Alexander Koch; run from 1905-? by H.T. Jensen from Reutlinger's of Paris; head office at Gresham House, Battery Road, Singapore with branches at Orchard Road, Singapore and Kuala Lumpur.

LEOMY, Dionysius. Commercial, Freetown, Sierra Leone 1890s.

LINDT, John William (1845-1926). Commercial, Australia. Born at Frankfurt, ran away to sea and deserted at Brisbane; joined business of the photographer Wagner in Grafton, New South Wales and bought him out in 1868; moved to Melbourne 1876; official photographer to Sir Peter Scratchley's New Guinea expedition of 1885; photographed Chaffey brothers' irrigation works on the River Murray; toured New Hebrides 1890; visited Fiji and photographed fire-walking ceremony 1892; closed Melbourne studio 1894; author: *Picturesque New Guinea* (1887).

LISK-CAREW BROTHERS, Alphonso and Arthur. Commercial, Sierra Leone. Photographic and fancy goods premises at East Brook Lane, Freetown 1905-?20s.

LLOYD, James. Commercial, South Africa. Studio in Smith Street, Durban c1875-c88.

LOBO, Alfred. Commercial, Uganda. Studio at Entebbe 1900s-20s; possibly previously employed in Locomotive Department of Uganda Railway.

MARTIN, Josiah (1843-1916). Commercial, New Zealand. Specialised in ethnographical subjects; editor of *Sharland's New Zealand Photographer* for several years at turn of the century.

McNAIR, John Frederick Adolphus (1828-1910). Amateur, Malaya. Entered Madras Artillery 1845; Private Secretary to Governor of Straits Settlements 1857; Comptroller of Indian convicts in the Straits 1857-73; as Colonial Engineer built Government House, Singapore; officiated as Lieutenant Governor of Penang 1880-84; author: *Perak and the Malays: Sarong and Kris* (1878), *Prisoners their own warders* (1899).

MEE, J.R. Commercial, South Africa. Studios in Durban 1880, Cathcart 1884, Kimberley 1889-91, Wynberg 1891.

MEE CHEEUNG. Commercial, Hong Kong 1890s-c1925.

MELUISH, William (1823-1888). Commercial, New Zealand. Opened photographic studio at corner of Dowling and Princes Streets, Dunedin 1856; business sold to D. Mundy (qv) 1864, but Meluish continued photography for some years; died in England.

MERLIN, Henry Beaufroy (1830-1873). Commercial, Australia. Arrived Australia c1849; established in Victoria as a travelling photographer by 1866; trained Charles Baylis as his assistant; working in country areas of New South Wales 1870-71; official photographer to the Victoria and New South Wales Eclipse Expedition of 1871; photographed Hill End and Gulgong for Bernard Holtermann's Great International Travelling Exposition 1872.

MIDDLEBROOK, J.E. Commercial, South Africa. Operating from the Premier Studio, Du Toits Pan Road, Kimberley 1888-94 and 396 West Street, Durban 1898-99.

MITCHELL, Thomas. Amateur, Paymaster on H.M.S. *Discovery* during Arctic Expedition of 1875-76; instructed in photography by Royal Engineers at Chatham.

MOORE, C.H. Commercial, Queensland. Studio in Wharf Street, Maryborough 1870 (possibly earlier); based in Mount Perry 1871-72; (?) returned to Maryborough by 1875.

MUNDY, Daniel Louis. Commercial, New Zealand. Made photographic tour of Southern Alps 1858; probably took over William Meluish's (qv) business in 1864; in partnership with La Mert in Christchurch 1865; lectured to Photographic Society in London 1873; 16 collotypes from Mundy's photographs included in D.L. Mundy and Ferdinand von Hochstetter, *Rotomahana; and the boiling springs of New Zealand* (1875).

NETTLETON, Charles (d.1902). Commercial, Victoria, Australia. Arrived in Melbourne from England 1854; employed by photographers Duryea and McDonald; took official progress photographs showing the growth of the city of Melbourne and was also the police photographer; opened his own studio 1858; retired from photography 1890.

NICHOLAS, John P. Commercial, India. Business operating from Mount Road, Madras c1858-c1905, although Nicholas left Madras c1895; in partnership as Nicholas and Curths c1869-73; branches at Bangalore c1872-73, and Ootacamund c1868-75.

NORTON BROTHERS. Commercial, British Guiana. Studio at Murray Street, Georgetown c1876-c78, and Church Street, Georgetown c1879-c87; possibly moved to St Vincent 1890s.

NOTMAN, William (1826-1891). Commercial, Canada. To Canada from Scotland 1856; opened studio in Bleury Street, Montreal 1856; *Notman's photographic selections* published 1863 (1st series) and 1865 (2nd series); in late 1860s branches opened in Ottawa, Toronto and Halifax and later in the United States; Montreal firm became Notman and Sandham in 1876 and William Notman and Son in 1880.

PARSONS, Simeon H. (1844-1908). Commercial, Newfoundland. Business established 1871; studio and fine art emporium at 310 Water Street, St John's; business continued by sons after death; awarded silver medal and certificate of honour at Barcelona Exhibition 1888.

PAUL, Alfred Wallace (1847-1912). Amateur, India. Indian Civil Service 1870-95. Political Officer on Macaulay mission to Sikkim 1884. Deputy Commissioner of Darjeeling.

PENN, A.T.W. Commercial, Ootacamund, India 1875-1913; (?) in Europe 1902-04, 1910, 1912; also managing the Reliance Auction and Commission Agency, Ootacamund 1905-09 and the Farington Hotel, Ootacamund 1913.

PORTMAN, Maurice Vidal (1861-1935). Amateur, India. Appointed to Andaman Islands 1879; on sick leave 1880-83; Assistant Superintendent, Port Blair 1883-99; presented a large collection of Andaman artefacts to the British Museum; author: *Notes on the languages of the South Andaman group of tribes* (Calcutta, 1898), *History of our relations with the Andamanese* (2 vols., Calcutta, 1899).

ROBERTSON & BEATO. See BEATO, Felix Antonio.

ROWLAND, Dr. John William C.M.G. (1852-1925). Amateur, Lagos. Served in India 1877-78; Assistant Colonial Surgeon, Lagos Colony 1880-83; Colonial Surgeon 1887-97; compiled an album of Lagos views 1885; accompanied Sir Gilbert Carter's Lagos Interior Expedition of 1893 as botanist.

ROYAL ENGINEERS. Photographic section formed as part of the Telegraph School at Chatham 1856; separate School of Photography and Chemistry formed in 1874 and retained independent status until merged with Survey School in 1904; engineers connected with running of photographic section included Major General Henry Schaw (1828-1895), Colour Sargeant James McDonald, Captain Sir Willliam de Wiveleslie Abney (1834-1921), Sergeant John Harrold; important photographic work carried out in connection with the British North American Boundary Commissions of 1858-62 and 1872-76, surveys of Jerusalem (1864) and Sinai (1868), the Abyssinian Campaign of 1867-68, the Suakin Campaign of 1885.

SCOWEN, Charles T. Commercial, Ceylon. Arrived in Ceylon early 1870s; first employed by R. Edley, Commission Agent, Kandy; operating a photographic studio in Trincomalee Street, Kandy by 1876, later with branch in Colombo; M. Scowen working for firm in 1880s; stock probably sold to Colombo Apothecaries Company in mid or late 1890s; M. Scowen remained in Ceylon as proprietary planter.

SHEPHERD (Charles) & ROBERTSON (Arthur). Commercial, India. Business in Agra c1862-63, Simla 1864; many of their pictures are included in John Forbes Watson and John William Kaye's *The People of India* (8 vols, 1868-75); Charles Shepherd later in partnership with Samuel Bourne (qv).

SIMPSON, Sir Benjamin (1831-1923). Amateur, India. Joined Indian Army as Assistant Surgeon 1853, rising to Surgeon General of the Indian Medical Service 1885-90; surgeon with Sir Ashley Eden's mission to Bhutan 1863-64; in Burma 1889 to advise on medical establishments for military police; exhibited a large collection of Indian portraits at London International Exhibition of 1862; lithographs of photographs by Simpson used in Edward Dalton, *Descriptive ethnology of Bengal* (1872).

SIZA, Julio Augusto. Commercial, British Guiana. Operated The Lusitana Photographic Gallery, Water Street, Georgetown c1885-c96; stock probably acquired by Jardine.

SKEEN, William Louis Henry & Co. Commercial, Ceylon. William Skeen appointed first Government Printer of Ceylon in 1849 and purchased the photographic business of J. Parting for his son in 1860; business known as S. Slinn & Co. during 1860s (after S. Slinn Skeen); W.L.H. Skeen arrived in Ceylon c1862 and worked in partnership with John Edward Wilshaw; F.A.E. Skeen joined business 1878 and opened Rangoon branch with H.W. Watts c1888; returned to Ceylon on death of W.L.H. Skeen in 1903 and continued business until (?)1920s, when stock was acquired by Platé and Co.

TATTERSALL, A.J. (b.1861). Commercial, Samoa. Born in Auckland and arrived in Apia in 1886; employed as assistant to J. Davis (qv) whose business he took over in 1893; still operating in 1907.

TAYLOR, A. Sylvester. Commercial, Barbados. Stereophotographer in New York 1850s-60s and Costa Rica 1860s; photographer, Barbados 1870s-80s; cabinet portraits state on reverse 'from Boston'.

THOMSON, John (1837-1921). Commercial, Far East and Cyprus, and instructor in photography to the Royal Geographical Society. Short visit to Far East in early 1860s cut short by illness; studio in Singapore 1865; returned to England 1866; studio in Hong Kong 1868-72 and travelled extensively in China; pioneer of the photographically illustrated travel book; author: *The antiquities of Cambodia* (1867), contributed illustrations and articles to *The China Magazine* (1868), *Illustrations of China and its people* (4 folio vols, 1873-74), *The Straits of Malacca, Indo-China and China* (1875), *Street life in London* (1877), *Through Cyprus with the camera in the autumn of 1878* (1879), etc.

TURTON, W.S. Amateur, Lagos. Messanger, Public Works Department, Lagos Colony 1891-94; accompanied Sir Gilbert Carter's Lagos Interior Expedition of 1893 as photographer.

VALLÉE, Louis Prudent (1837-1905). Commercial, Canada. Born in Quebec, learned photography in New York and returned to Quebec to practise in 1867; in partnership with F.X. Labelle for a short period; studio at 10 St John Street, Quebec, moved to number 16 shortly before death.

WATSON, J. Commercial, Queensland. Studio in Queen Street, Brisbane c1866-c75; operating a photographic warehouse c1874-c77; published *Watson's Queensland album of photographic scenery* (1st and 2nd series, 1873).

WELCHMAN, Revd. Dr. Henry. Amateur, Pacific. Member of the Melanesian Mission. Accompanied Bishop Montgomery on Melanesian tour 1892.

WHITE, George. Amateur, Arctic. Assistant Engineer on H.M.S. *Alert* during Arctic Expedition of 1875-76; instructed in photography by Royal Engineers at Chatham.

WILSON, J.C. Commercial, St Vincent. Active 1890s-c1920.

WOOLLEY, Charles A. (1834-1922). Commercial, Tasmania. Photographs commissioned for the Tasmanian display at the Melbourne Intercolonial exhibition of 1866.

YOUNG, William D. Commercial, India and East Africa. Came to Africa late 1890s after working as a railways photographer in eastern India; freelance photographer during construction of Uganda Railway; studio in Macdonald Terrace, Mombasa c1899-1904; studio at Victoria Street, Nairobi 1905-07; 'Dempster Studio', Nairobi 1908-c19; later manager of the Swift Press, Nairobi until late 1920s.

ZANGAKI. Commercial, Egypt. fl.1880s.

ACKNOWLEDGEMENTS

The photographs in this exhibition come primarily from the collection of the Royal Commonwealth Society, who wish to thank the British Library for financing the cataloguing of the collection. In preparing so extensive an exhibition, the organisers have necessarily had to draw on the resources of the many other institutions, libraries and archives whose contributions are listed below. The assistance of all these bodies in making material available for exhibition and in giving copyright permission is gratefully acknowledged, and special thanks must also be given to the Central Office of Information, the Commonwealth Foundation, the Commonwealth Institute, the Commonwealth Secretariat, the Commonwealth War Graves Commission, the Royal Engineers Institution and the Imperial War Museum for their particular efforts in seeking out relevant material. The largest single source of material apart from the Royal Commonwealth Society was the photograph collection of the Foreign and Commonwealth Office Library, London, whose Librarian Harry Hannam and his staff were unfailingly helpful and co-operative in granting access to the collection and in providing facilities for re-photographing. None of the custodians of material used in the exhibition is in any way responsible for the use made of their photographs or the catalogue entries relating to them. Whilst every effort has been made to acknowledge all contributions to the exhibition, the organisers apologise for any inadvertent omissions in the following list.

African Medical and Research Foundation: G48.
Alexander Turnbull Library, Wellington: C57; D3; H22 (Christchurch Press Collection).
Associated Press H28.
Australian Information Service: D27-28; G49; H8, 19, 21; K34, 68, 103.
Canadian High Commission: H16; K35-37.
Central Office of Information: H6-7, 15, 29, 40-41, 46, 51-53, 60-61, 67, 70, 72, 74, 77, 79, 81; J58; K1, 4-5, 47, 69, 72, 99-100.
Church Missionary Society: C9(C-D); F40.
City of Toronto Archives, James Collection: J18.
Commonwealth Broadcasting Association: G34.
Commonwealth Foundation: K21-25.
Commonwealth Institute: H31; K75-81.
Commonwealth Nurses Federation: G40-41.
Commonwealth Pharmaceutical Association: K48.
Commonwealth Secretariat: J59; K3, 6-14, 39, 49, 58, 66, 67, 71, 94-98.
Commonwealth War Graves Commission: J24, 37-44.
Commonwealth Youth Exchange Council: K4, 41.
The Fairbridge Society/Weidenfeld & Nicolson: H37.
Foreign and Commonwealth Office Library: B3-6, 10, 15, 20; C9(F); C44-46, 48-51; D5, 19-21, 30-31, 35, 42, 56-57, 61-62, 69-71, 72-74, 77; E8, 11, 14, 17-18, 22-24, 28(A)-29, 44-45, 49; F5, 9-11, 16, 25, 27, 34-35, 37-38, 48, 51-60; G1, 2, 36-39; H2, 20; J10, 23, 32.
Grange Museum of Local History: H32-33, 35.
The Guide Association: K43.
Heinemann Educational Books: K26-29.
Imperial War Museum: J1, 11-15, 17, 20-22, 25-29, 31, 33-35, 45-51, 52-56.
India Office Library: B41; E2; H56-58.
LEPRA: K53.
John McKenzie: K82-93.
Mitchell Library, Sydney: D1, 12.
Museum of Mankind: B19.
National Army Museum: H24.
National Museum of New Zealand, Wellington: D18; E28.
National Portrait Gallery: F11C(5).
Provincial Archives of British Columbia: D4, 24; J8.
Public Archives of Canada: H17; J (title panel), J2; K 18, 20.
Royal Commonwealth Society for the Blind: K52.
Royal Engineers Institution: B1, 2; C41-43, 47; F61-62.
Royal Geographical Society: B39; C6(C).
Royal Society of Arts: C30-32.
Save the Children Fund: K54.
Ian Straker: C6(B).
Trades Union Congress: K45.
Voluntary Service Overseas: K51.
Sir Duncan Watson: H50, 71.

THE BRITISH EMPIRE 1900

This map shows the extent of the Empire, including protected states and other territories in special relationships to Britain.

Canada
Newfoundland
Bermuda
Bahamas
Turks and Caicos Islands
Jamaica
Leeward Islands
Barbados
British Honduras
Windward Islands
Trinidad
British Guiana
Christmas Is.
Gilbert and Ellice Is.
Fiji
New Hebrides
Tonga
Pitcairn Is.
Norfolk Is.
Falkland Is.
Graham Land

THE COMMONWEALTH 1982

This map shows the forty-six sovereign nations comprising the Commonwealth. It does not show dependent territories or countries whose external affairs are the responsibility of Commonwealth members. There are twenty-six of these, among the better-known being Bermuda, Hong Kong, the Falkland Islands, Gibraltar, Pitcairn Island, Norfolk Island and Niue.

Canada
Bahamas
Antigua and Barbuda
Dominica
St. Lucia
Barbados
St. Vincent
Belize
Jamaica
Grenada
Trinidad and Tobago
Guyana
Kiribati
Nauru
Tuvalu
n Islands
Western Samoa
Fiji
uatu
Tonga
w Zealand

The Exhibition was sponsored by the Australia Council and arranged by the International Cultural Corporation of Australia Limited with assistance from the Royal Commonwealth Society, London (Stephen Kemp, Secretary General); the Australian High Commission, London; the Department of Foreign Affairs; Department of Home Affairs and Environment and the Queensland Art Gallery.

WARANA AND COMMONWEALTH FESTIVAL

Patron in chief: The Right Honourable
Sir Zelman Cowen, AK, GCMG, GCVO, K.St.J., QC.
Patron: His Excellency Sir James Ramsay, KCMG, CBE, DSC, Governor of Queensland.
President: The Honourable J. Bjelke-Petersen, MLA, Premier of Queensland.
Vice Presidents: The Honourable J. A. Elliot, MLA (Minister for Tourism, National Parks, Sport and the Arts).
E. D. Casey, MLA (Leader of the Opposition)
The Right Honourable The Lord Mayor (Alderman W. C. R. Harvey)
A. J. Campbell, AM, OBE, OMRI.

FESTIVAL '82 COMMITTEE:

Chairman: Lester Padman
Deputy Chairman: Kevin Siddell
Peter Dent, Robert Edwards, Mike Evans, Tony Gould, Raoul Mellish, Robert Minnikin, Peter Botsman, Brian Sweeney.
Executive Director: Norman Llewelyn.

FUND RAISING COMMITTEE:

Chairman: V. B. (Barry) Paul.

INTERNATIONAL CULTURAL CORPORATION OF AUSTRALIA LIMITED:

Chairman: James Leslie
Deputy Chairman: Norman Baker
Jean Battersby, Franco Belgiorno-Nettis, Ivor Bowden, Edmund Capon, Michael Darling, Ann Lewis, John Lockhart, David Thomas.
Executive Director: Robert Edwards
Project Manager: Graham Richards

THE EXHIBITION:

Project Co-ordinator: Prunella Scarlett
Research: John Falconer
Design: Robin Wade Design Associates Australia Pty. Ltd.
David McCabe
Robin Wade

LENDING INSTITUTIONS:

Science Museum of Victoria
Museum of Applied Arts and Sciences, New South Wales
MacLeay Museum, The Sydney University

EXHIBITION CONTRACTOR:

Hutchison, Brunhuber, Rozario Display Industries Pty. Ltd.
Robin Hutchison

CATALOGUE:

Text: Donald Simpson, Peter Lyon
Design: Robin Wade Design Associates (U.K.)
Robin Johnson
Photo reprographic: Brook Tella
Production: Clemenger Harvie Pty. Ltd. Melbourne

Printed by: Wilke and Company Limited
37-49 Browns Road, Clayton, Victoria, Aust.

A National Tour of the Exhibition "Commonwealth in Focus" has been made possible by the generous Sponsorship of